Radical
Business Model
Transformation

Radical Business Model Transformation

Gaining the competitive edge in a disruptive world

Carsten Linz
Günter Müller-Stewens
Alexander Zimmermann

Kogan Page

Publisher's note
Every possible effort has been made to ensure that the information contained in this book is accurate at the time of going to press, and the publishers and authors cannot accept responsibility for any errors or omissions, however caused. No responsibility for loss or damage occasioned to any person acting, or refraining from action, as a result of the material in this publication can be accepted by the editor, the publisher or the author.

First published in Great Britain and the United States in 2017 by Kogan Page Limited

2nd Floor, 45 Gee Street	c/o Martin P Hill Consulting	4737/23 Ansari Road
London	122 W 27th St, 10th Floor	Daryaganj
EC1V 3RS	New York, NY 10001	New Delhi 110002
United Kingdom	USA	India

www.koganpage.com

© Carsten Linz, Günter Müller-Stewens and Alexander Zimmermann, 2017

The right of Carsten Linz, Günter Müller-Stewens and Alexander Zimmermann to be identified as the authors of this work has been asserted by them in accordance with the Copyright, Designs and Patents Act 1988.

ISBN   978 0 7494 8045 5
E-ISBN 978 0 7494 8046 2

British Library Cataloguing-in-Publication Data

A CIP record for this book is available from the British Library.

Library of Congress Cataloging-in-Publication Control Number

2016046148

Typeset by SPi Global
Print production managed by Jellyfish
Printed and bound by CPI Group (UK) Ltd, Croydon CR0 4YY

References to websites (URLs) were accurate at the time of writing. Neither the author(s) nor Kogan Page is responsible for URLs that may have expired or changed since the manuscript was prepared.

CONTENTS

ABOUT THE AUTHORS

Carsten Linz is an entrepreneurial leader and expert on innovation-led business transformation. He has successfully built-up several €100 million businesses and led company-wide transformation programmes affecting more than 60,000 employees. For SAP, he leads the Center for Digital Leadership, a renowned C-suite think tank showcasing next-generation innovation and transformation approaches. He is an active business angel, serves on the investment committee of Europe's largest seed stage fund and holds various advisory board seats. Dr Linz is an adjunct faculty member and teaches in executive programmes at Mannheim Business School, the University of St Gallen, the Karlsruhe Institute of Technology and Stanford Graduate School. He is a sought-after keynote speaker and acts as adviser to CxOs around the world. His blog is carstenlinz.com.

Günter Müller-Stewens is professor of strategic management and director of the Institute of Management at the University of St Gallen. He has authored multiple books, articles and case studies in academic- and practitioner-oriented journals. His most recent main research interest is corporate strategy, as well as the competences and contributions of strategists in organizations. He has acted as dean of the business school at the University of St Gallen and served as the academic director of several master's programmes. Furthermore, he founded the journal *M&A Review* and acts as a member of multiple editorial boards. He is a member of the advisory board of several firms, consultant and trainer to international companies, and invited speaker at many conferences and meetings.

Alexander Zimmermann is an assistant professor of organization and strategic management and the project manager for the Center for Organizational Excellence (CORE) at the University of St Gallen. He has authored several practitioner-oriented and academic articles, case studies and book chapters on sustainable growth and organization design. His main research interest is how firms can reconcile trade-offs such as change versus stability, innovation versus efficiency, and economic versus social value creation through strategy, organization and leadership. He teaches at the master's and executive education level and acts as a moderator and coach to assist companies' strategic and organizational transformation processes.

CONTRIBUTORS

The three authors have been driven by the question of how to transform a company's business model into the next one.

From the start of this project, we were clear that we wanted to discuss our ideas extensively with other business leaders and academic experts. In the early days, this took place through ad hoc personal conversations with individuals. As the project progressed, the approach became more structured, including the form of an online community in which we discussed our ideas.

At the same time, we started to apply our framework in executive education courses at the universities and business schools where we are active as senior lecturers – the University of St Gallen, Stanford Graduate School, Mannheim Business School and Karlsruhe Institute of Technology – and also in several in-house training settings. This proved to be an important asset for us. The interactions with business leaders from all sorts of industries and company sizes, often over a course duration of several days, allowed us to discuss our concepts in quite some detail with more than 500 executives to date.

During this time, the idea emerged to further develop and refine our conceptual framework by involving leaders who have themselves experienced a transformation journey. We therefore selected exciting cases from different industries and for different transformation types and invited the relevant executives to write about their stories. Nine months and a large number of conference calls later, we have 11 in-depth case studies, ranging from exponential-growth companies like Netflix to global players like Xerox, SAP and Daimler and mid-sized hidden champions like Knorr-Bremse and Kaba–LEGIC. The unifying element is that all these companies went through or are in the process of completing a major business model transformation. The cases also illustrate in detail what the leaders did to successfully manage the radical shift.

The case authors are as follows:

Guido Baltes is full professor and director of the IST Institute for Strategic Innovation at Konstanz University of Applied Sciences (HTWG). His research focus is on entrepreneurship and corporate entrepreneurship.

Matthias Barth is global solution director for the professional services industry at SAP. He is global solution owner for SAP Hybris Billing (SSB) and SAP Flexible Solution Billing.

Silke Bucher is a senior coach for organizational development at a global consulting firm based in Costa Rica.

Christoph Färber is head of Strategic Future Projects for Mercedes-Benz Cars in Stuttgart. He was the long-time head of finance of the car2go/ Mobility organization commercializing Mobility at Daimler.

Jacqueline Fechner is a managing director at Xerox, heading all business activities in Germany. She leads operations and technology sales for large enterprise companies in the DACH region.

Markus Frank is the executive director of the Executive School at the University of St Gallen. He heads the Custom Programmes business and represents the school in international learning communities.

Ulrich Frei is the executive president of FUNDES International, Costa Rica. He uses his for-profit experience to unleash the full power of business and wealth generation in service of human dignity.

Rolf Haerdi is a member of the executive board of Knorr-Bremse Systeme für Schienenfahrzeuge. He is responsible for various European countries as well as engineering globally.

Urs Jäger is an associate professor and director of the Latin American Center for Entrepreneurs at the INCAE Business School, Costa Rica, with focus on social enterprises.

Klaus U Klosa is a board member of Touchless Biometric Systems and Motcom Communication. He was CEO of LEGIC Identsystems and responsible for its business model transformation.

Bertram Langhanki is a board member at Knorr-Bremse PowerTech. He is responsible for global sales of power converters to international train builders.

Ronnie Leten is the president and CEO of Atlas Copco and chairman of the board of directors of Electrolux.

Andreas Löhmer is director of corporate programmes at the Executive School of Management, Technology and Law at the University of St Gallen. He is author of articles on executive education.

Ivanka Visnjic is an assistant professor of innovation at ESADE Business School in Barcelona and a visiting scholar at Haas School of Business, UC Berkeley. She focuses on how established companies use service and open business model innovation to resist disruption.

As the book took shape and word about it began to spread through our teaching and case authors, we were approached by top executives to assist and guide them through their transformation journeys. Based on the tools we developed for these projects, we decided to develop the step-by-step business model transformation manual, which you will find in Chapter 11 of this book.

Our approach to leveraging the wisdom of our crowd paid off tremendously. The feedback and input of so many talented people were instrumental in reaching the framework's maturity level. It also helped us to separate the useful from the superfluous, and thus to distil the core of our thinking. Many of the company examples in this book come from our crowd contributors and help to illustrate and make the content digestible.

Thank you very much for your support!

PREFACE

One key challenge of writing about business model transformation is that the subject is a moving target. Every day there is new information; new articles are published, you hear about new trends and interesting cases, and so on. But one day you must decide to end the writing process, because a pattern has emerged in your mind that covers what you read, see and hear. This took place in June 2016.

Despite the fact that business models attract much interest, some key questions remain unanswered. A particularly important open question is how to systematically change and transform a business model – from today's model into tomorrow's model – to (re)gain competitive advantage. Most companies already act within a given business model and rarely can start completely greenfield again.

In 2013, we decided that we wanted to learn more about how established firms could successfully and dynamically change their business models, and to turn this into a book on business model transformation. We have subsequently studied more than 380 companies or lines of business so as to better understand whether businesses changed their business models, which businesses opted for what kind of model, and how they have adjusted it. We conducted many interviews about companies' choices of business model and their adaptation processes to a changing business environment. The more we deepened our research, the more we discovered that many companies we observed had to master more than simply an incremental change process if they wished to stay ahead of the competition – they had to master deep fundamental change and bring about a radical shift. Thus, in this book, we decided to focus on the challenges of leading such radical business model transformation processes.

Our book addresses the needs of executive-level managers as well as academics with an interest in the subject. The book provides answers to some key questions today's leaders face: What business model choices are there? Where does our firm stand now? Is our current business model sustainable, or do we need to change it? If we need to change, how can we transform our business model? Which options do we have, and what are the specific challenges and requirements of each path? What were the experiences of other firms and leaders on their radical transformation journeys?

By answering these questions, the book delivers three key benefits. First, it helps to provide a systematic and more integrated understanding of the often fuzzy topic of business models and their transformation. Second, it presents practical insights, recommendations and experiences of how to radically shift a business model. In-depth case studies of business leaders who have successfully led such a business model transformation journey help to illustrate the *how*. Third, it provides a proven framework and shared language to involve others in discussing and developing business model transformations.

Writing such a book over several years has been intellectually enriching and fun, as well as highly time-intensive and energy-intensive. Thus, first, we thank our families, specifically our spouses, Yvonne, Isabelle and Sina, for their unconditional support.

We thank our contributing crowd, especially our case study (co-)authors. They helped us to develop and refine our framework, and to fill it with life, through their exciting cases of radical transformation. By sharing their rich practical experience, they have provided us with much detailed knowledge and best practices. We also thank all our colleagues, friends and professional partners for their critical feedback, reflections, comments and suggestions to improve our book.

Our sincere thanks to our publishers, the team at Kogan Page, for their commitment and professional guidance in getting our book to you today.

Carsten Linz
Günter Müller-Stewens
Alexander Zimmermann

PART ONE
Why business models need to radically shift

One secret to maintaining a thriving business is recognizing when it needs a fundamental change.

MARK W JOHNSON, CLAYTON M CHRISTENSEN
AND HENNING KAGERMANN[1]

Most established companies understand their business model from the inside out. They have continuously fine-tuned their established business model to stay aligned with changes in the environment, but they have not questioned their type of business model. Today, however, sporadic changes and megatrends coming from outside the business, such as digitization and servitization, are putting more and more established business models under pressure. Incremental fine-tuning of the current business model will not suffice. Innovation competition has shifted from technological and process innovation to business model innovation, because start-ups, niche players and small and medium-sized businesses today have the means to challenge established players with relatively limited investment.

For example, it is doubtful whether automotive companies can survive just by producing and selling cars. Some of them fear they will be demoted to being low-margin metal-bashers if they are unable to take advantage of the entertainment and e-commerce services that could be offered on screens inside the car of the future. These 'smart services' are often far removed from the principal use of the product,[2] requiring an account ID to participate in their monetization and hence would mean a radical shift of an automotive company's business model, including a deep cultural change. Many media companies have already had to undergo reformation. Print and online advertising revenues continue to fall. Content is still king but the new delivery formats are many-fold and journal- and newspaper-based subscription has limited reader acceptance. Media companies are challenged to monetize content consumption across media formats and per usage; block chain technology can be a game changer. Radical transformation is required, fine-tuning existing business models is not enough.

While business model research has flourished over the past decade,[3] most of it is focused on the value proposition or structure of a business model. For example, we have learned much about what the components of a business model, the actors and their interactions should look like. Of course, this information is helpful if you are a start-up company with all the flexibility to design your business model from scratch, or if you are a company that is looking for completely new business models outside its existing one, but for many existing companies this is not the case. In many established firms and even some industries, including private banks, energy providers, telecom providers, bookstores and many more, the dominant business model is under fire. They have to think about options to adapt and transform their business models and about ways in which to manage change and evolution. Managers are facing a number of challenging questions: How do we adapt our front end and our products and services to satisfy the needs of our targeted customers? What are the implications for the back end to make these products and services possible? What is the best monetization mechanism to create sustainable value for the company and its stakeholders?

The core question for many established firms is whether they can operate in the long run by just focusing on and defending their current business model, or whether they have to make a fundamental change in the way they create and appropriate value. It is our observation that more and more companies are discovering the painful truth that an incremental fine-tuning of the current business model is not enough to stay competitive in the future. The only way forward is a radical shift.

But transforming to a new business model is often easier said than done, as in many cases it means changing the very DNA that has made a firm successful over time. Additionally, the 'Googles' of this world are of little help as future blueprints for established firms, because they have never undergone a business model transformation. However, established firms also have strong advantages over new entrants, because they know the existing products and customers in the market and often have important competences and resources at their disposal. The expertise of the incumbents may be hard to replicate, and they often control access to decisive resources like data or knowledge.

The objective of this book is to guide leaders in established firms through the process of radical business model transformation. 'Radical' means they have to change the type of business model, at least for major parts of the company. That often also includes a shift in a firm's mission and value proposition. There are several reasons why we have recently seen an increasing number of cases where minor adjustments to the business model – for example, adding an online sales channel – are not sufficient, and more fundamental changes are needed. One cause might be the rise in new technologies, which has changed the strategic context profoundly, or new entrants, which might come from another competitive arena and have a completely new business model. For example, Google discovered manufacturing as a new growth sector. Benefiting from its Google Maps data, it entered the automotive market with its own self-driving concept car and is about to become a mobility competitor for the established car producers – not to be underestimated because Google has a different mental model understanding of what a car represents. The new strategic alliances of BMW with Chinese search giant Baidu, chipmaker Intel and supplier Mobileye show their commitment to produce fully autonomous cars by 2021 in preparation for the transformation of their classical business model.

Using many practical examples, we show in this book how firms can respond to similar challenges by turning their heritage from an impediment to change into a competitive advantage to successfully establish an entirely new way of doing business. Of course, such a radical transformation is very challenging and often has a high risk, but in many cases there are no other options available to a company that wants to remain successful in the long term. For example, many think they can survive by selling solutions instead of products, but we notice that only a few are really capable of managing such a fundamental transformation. Asian Paints, India's largest paint company, was a traditional paint supplier. They transformed themselves into a solution provider as a 'hassle-free premium home painting service' with a one-year guarantee delivered by trained painters from their network of more than 10,000 painters. Their end-to-end offering includes prefabricated painting themes, an interior decorator advice service, the brokerage of academy trained local painters, final inspection and warranty.

In Part One of this book, we explain in Chapter 1 why so many existing business models are under fire and why a radical shift of at least parts of a company's business model seems to be the only option. In Chapter 2, we introduce a typology of business models that helps us to show the options there are when choosing or applying a new business model. Chapter 3 gives a short overview of the discussion of business models and shows the shortcomings on which this book is focused.

Endnotes

1　M W Johnson, C M Christensen and H Kagermann (2008) Reinventing your business model, *Harvard Business Review*, **86** (12), pp 53–63.

2 The Economist (2013) Does Deutschland do digital? Europe's biggest economy is rightly worried that digitisation is a threat to its industrial leadership, *The Economist*, 21 November, p 59.

3 B W Wirtz, A Pistoia, S Ullrich and V Göttel (2016) Business models: Origin, developments and future research perspectives, *Long Range Planning*, 49, pp 1–19; C C Markides (2015) Research on business models: Challenges and opportunities, *Advances in Strategic Management*, 33, pp 133–47.

Taking consequences from digitization and servitization

Two megatrends – digitization and service orientation ('servitization') – make business model transformation a key strategic priority for many leaders. While *digitization* influences the technical opportunities for firms to develop, produce and deliver their offerings and to manage their customer interactions at scale, *servitization* represents a fundamental shift in the customer value proposition towards co-creation and offering individualization. Innovative new services are often generated out of the data coming from a digitized business model. It is very challenging to respond to these trends, as both may have different implications for a firm's business model, and there is the risk of getting caught in the extremes. To avoid this, digitization requires a balance between digital and physical assets ('phygital'), while servitization calls for a balance between service and product orientation ('hybrid') (see Figure 1.1). New and better physical offerings can be developed out of the knowledge taken from digitized business models ('physication'); innovative standardized products can be developed out of the experiences taken from extremely customized business models ('productization').

'Phygital': Torn between digital and physical orientation

The digital revolution is far more significant than the invention of writing or even of printing.

DOUGLAS ENGELBART[1]

Over the past few years, exponential progress in information technology has brought the digital revolution to nearly everybody in the business world. Digitization is rewriting the rules of competition, and incumbent firms are

Figure 1.1 Balancing digital and physical assets as well as service and product orientation

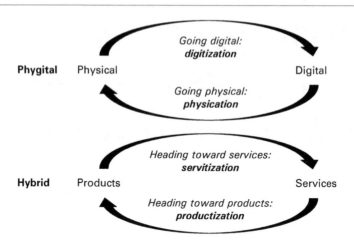

most at risk. Attackers are growing at an incredible speed worldwide, because digitization knows no borders and redefines the distribution of the profit pool. Companies that dominated the national market for decades are suddenly confronted with new competitors that are redefining entire industries and hence restricting the incumbents' strategic freedom to shape their future. For example, we see national telecom providers being curtailed and becoming pure infrastructure providers because of companies like Google, Netflix and Facebook. New leaders emerge out of nowhere. The automotive industry has started to be disrupted by Tesla, Google and Apple, as software is taking over hardware in connected and self-driving cars. According to a CNBC prognosis, 40 per cent of the S&P 500 companies will no longer exist in 10 years' time if they do not keep up with the trends in technology.[2] In the digital age, industry boundaries are blurring.

Digitization is not a new phenomenon. Defined as the transformation of analogue into discrete values with the goal of storing or processing them, digitization started back in the 1980s, with the first digital products being digital watches, CD players and internet routers. This was followed in the 1990s by the rise of digital services such as search portals, e-commerce sites and marketplaces. Around the turn of the century – after the dot-com bubble – the focus shifted to digital distribution and relations, then coined Web 2.0, with social media business and e-commerce for content. Around 2010 the age of digital orchestration and anything-as-a-service models started and promoted platforms with their business networks and ecosystems. Digitization has evolved from a purely technical into a holistic phenomenon and impacts nearly every company function as business processes become increasingly digitized.

At the beginning, the impact of the digitization trends was more visible in the B2C (business to consumer) world at companies like Amazon and eBay – both founded before the dot-com bubble burst in 2000. In the meantime, it also reached the more physical industrial B2B (business to business) world. The 'Internet of Things', in which previously dumb objects like robots or spare parts are connected and communicate with each other ('smart factory'), is becoming a reality on factory floors.[3] For example, the German government launched an initiative called Industrie 4.0 to push its industrial companies faster into the digital age. Digitization can help manufacturers to get closer to their customers and build up customer loyalty more easily. For example, Sonos is producing 'smart speakers' that 'listen' to the place where they are located. The music system measures the acoustics in any room by itself, analysing size, layout and furnishings, among other things. Consequently, it fine-tunes the speakers, which are controlled by a single app. Another example is John Deere, which produces agricultural equipment like tractors and harvesters for farms. These machines can now all be connected to each other, and they can be centrally steered based on data like weather or soil conditions to optimize sowing and harvesting.

Today, it is obvious that the physical and digital worlds have converged and must work hand in hand. This integrative perspective stands in sharp contrast to the either-or view from back in the dot-com years, when e-businesses competed with bricks-and-mortar businesses. The two were seen as incompatible approaches. For business success in the digital age, an intelligent combination of physical and digital assets is needed, which led to the creation of the term 'phygital' (physical *and* digital).

Going digital: Toward digital customer insights and virtual stickiness

In the digital economy, we have seen a fundamental shift in how firms compete against each other. The key criterion for differentiation in the market is no longer better quality or lower prices but a superior business model. This puts particular strain on established firms that have followed the same recipe for success for many decades. Research shows that, in 2013, 90 per cent of chief executive officers (CEOs) said the digital economy would have a major impact on their industry by disrupting their business models.[4] This makes business model transformation their number one priority. However, only 25 per cent of the CEOs actually have a digital transformation plan in place, and less than 15 per cent of them are currently funding and executing the plan.

Take Sony as an example, a firm that was once the world's leading micro-electronics company. Its decline was not caused by a loss of its trademark innovation ability but by the fact that its business model was no longer competitive. Under Steve Jobs, Sony's competitor Apple put substantial strain on all those companies that only produce single products or services. Through its integrated and comprehensive offering, which consists of hardware, software, content and a multisided platform, Apple has won and locked in its customers and made it incredibly hard for others to compete in each of these individual markets alone. Thanks to its superior business model, Apple did not necessarily need to be cheaper or technologically more advanced to dominate the competition, as the value proposition stemmed from the platform that seamlessly brings everything together thanks to its superior integration functionality.[5] When incumbent firms like Sony started to strike back, they actually attacked Apple in the 'wrong' business model, as they still perceived it as a product company. For the moment, only Samsung has been able to catch up with Apple; however, it is strongly dependent on partners such as Google's mobile operating system Android to reach a similarly comprehensive offering.

It is easy to recognize that the capabilities needed to compete successfully in the digital world are changing. Companies have to rethink their core competencies. If these capabilities are not available in time, established firms may soon find themselves outmatched by the new digital players. Business model innovation does not require large R&D budgets and can start on the back of an envelope. Today, start-ups with little capital can innovate on top of platforms and by leveraging highly scalable IT cloud infrastructures, which increases the pressure on incumbents' business models. Most established companies therefore have to seek these capabilities on the labour market or through acquisitions, because they are not available in-house.

As always when new knowledge begins to replace established competences, these moves into uncharted terrain raise fear and resistance within established organizations. Cultural clashes can occur. For example, companies will need to recruit many more IT experts for data management, but how will they fit into a culture dominated by mechanical and electrical engineers? Specifically, many digitization initiatives struggle because there is a fear that new digital endeavours will cannibalize existing businesses. Or think about all the concerns about privacy and cybersecurity. However, neglecting the digitization trend is not really an option, because a new entrant or established competitor could use the new opportunities and put the entire company at risk. Specifically in industries with low entry barriers, incumbents should take action before new digital rivals enter their markets.

The digital revolution can lead to completely new client value propositions, different client relationships, innovative revenue models, new market access, more efficient processes and so on. One of the most important effects of digitization is that tangible products are replaced by or extended with intangible, digital information that can be offered as services and transferred and shared at no cost. Three examples from the music, retail and entertainment industry illustrate how digitization has already changed the rules of the game. Music labels used to have contracts with artists, record their music, produce CDs and ship them to wholesalers and retailers, which then sold the music through their stores to the customer. Digitization has made many of these roles obsolete, as it allows musicians to record their songs themselves, and sell them through digital stores such as iTunes or streaming services like Spotify. However, the artists are left with minor margins and hence predominantly focus on live concerts to make their money. In the retail industry, Amazon allows even niche third-party vendors to sell at scale on Amazon Marketplace and to directly interact with their customers. By hitting the buy button, the customer can instantly order intangible offerings like e-books or physical products like coffee makers, which get shipped to the customer's doorstep. Digitization allows Amazon to sell a seemingly infinite number of products and services on its platform, which by far exceeds the capacity of traditional stores that are limited by shelf space, investments in stock and so on. Finally, in the entertainment industry, digital platforms take the idea of the analogue shopping centre or multiplex cinema to the next level by integrating and presenting an offering portfolio – which can contain both physical and digital assets – in a comparable way on a single platform.

Digital platforms foster recurring business transactions with the same buyer. This is comparable to the 'razor-and-blade' approach in the physical product system world, where the system architecture secures the technical fit of the next purchase. The digital equivalent creates technical lock-ins like registration procedures or provides premium services like free-of-charge delivery for a monthly subscription fee (eg Amazon Prime). Digitization also helps to create better customer insights by facilitating effective two-way communications between firms and their customers and end-users. Chat forums and communities as first-level support are examples that allow new levels of mutual company–customer interaction at scale. Consequently, in order to improve the quality of portfolio decisions, it is simpler to get to know the customers and their concrete needs, even in global markets. For example, Netflix, the leading provider of on-demand internet streaming media, provides sophisticated and personalized recommendations generated out of the data of the millions of interactions its users have every day. Interestingly enough, the company also uses these data for portfolio decisions when it invests in the development of its own content (eg new series such as *House of Cards*). We see that, with an increasing number of transactions, the platform company learns about its customers' preferences and can provide recommendations to complement the actual purchase, optimize its offering portfolio and even generate new cash streams by selling these transaction data to third parties. Going digital can create new business opportunities; however, not every digital initiative equals a transformation of the business model. For example, when ARRI – the largest manufacturer of professional motion picture equipment in the world – transformed themselves from analogue to digital cameras, they stuck to their product business model.

Going physical: Toward asset- or human-based and discrete business

Despite the shift toward digital assets, it goes without saying that the physical world will never completely disappear. For example, retailers want to offer the same brand experience at every customer touch point, whether as a physical store or an online channel, to realize an omnichannel or multichannel strategy. We also see that pure online retailers are now opening physical stores to boost their business (eg Amazon, Warby Parker, Bonobos, Zalando, Cyberport).[6] The same applies to digital platforms that orchestrate and aggregate physical assets from many suppliers into an integrative offering for their customers. For example, Uber, the world's largest taxi company, does not own any vehicles, but its business model would not be feasible without any physical cars. Similarly, Airbnb, the world's largest accommodation provider, could not offer its peer-to-peer exchange of private rooms if there were no bricks-and-mortar houses. Airbnb – like many other internet platforms – acts as a trader of physical assets: an agent between supply and demand.

There is a difference between industries, as digitization makes faster advances in content-heavy, asset-light businesses such as music and film. At the same time, the profit pool is re-allocated along the value chain or network. A key question regarding digitization's impact on business models is how the digital and the analogue (asset- and human-based) parts of value creation will be distributed across companies and individuals. Who supplies whom with what kind of offering (analogue products, digital services, phygital hybrids)? Connected to this is the question of which player has the most power and can thus appropriate the biggest share of the profit pool, and which companies will become more or less dependent suppliers. We can expect that some companies will focus specifically on the physical part of the business, provided that they find ways to keep direct customer interaction. This could be in the area of project-based facility, infrastructure or construction businesses as well as product-centric businesses that supply success-critical modules or components for larger systems or platforms (eg high-end displays for smartphones or precision tools for industrial robots). Such asset- and human-based businesses can be very lucrative.

Conclusion: Creating a new synthesis between digital and physical orientation

Having looked more closely at what going digital versus going physical means, we can conclude that digitization drives the following key business model trends:

- Digitization allows for more comprehensive transactions, as it facilitates the integration of a large scale and scope of digital products and services that could not be physically offered out of one location.

- Conversely, digitization provides the data that can inform the development and improvement of physical products or services that can be sold in stand-alone transactions, either directly to the customer or as a key component of a larger value network.

- Independently of these two trends, digitization provides the communication channels that enable new levels of bi-directional company–customer interaction, facilitating the customization of an offering to individual needs.

- At the same time, digitization may drive the standardization (or productization) of what were formerly individual offerings, as it provides the data to identify the most dominant customer demands and the means to turn individual human-based services into standardized software-based products.

We see that the business model trends may act in opposite directions along two dimensions (comprehensive versus stand-alone transactions and individualized versus standardized offerings). The tension between these poles sets the scene for leaders to define their individual strategic path, balancing digital and physical.

'Hybrids': Torn between service and product orientation

And what the customer buys and considers value is never a product. It is always utility, that is, what a product or service does for him.

PETER F DRUCKER[7]

With products being commoditized ever faster owing to accelerated innovation cycles and the rising outcome economy, the importance of service businesses has been growing for years. This trend is referred to as 'servitization', in other words the development of an organization's capabilities and processes to shift from selling products to selling integrated products and services that deliver value in use.[8] On average, it shifts companies' offerings toward higher service portions and drives the transformation of business models. Companies are changing gear from 'services around products' to 'products around a service core', with the goal of potentially achieving higher margins, at least relative to their existing business. Servitization mainly refers to product-centric companies that engage in complementary service activities to create more value for themselves and their customers, often after their products have started to become commodities. They try to differentiate themselves by offering supplementary services. Some of these services are even provided free to keep the customer close to the firms' core product businesses, which essentially drive their profits.

Heading toward services: Toward co-creation and individualization

Servitization takes the customer problem as a starting point. The first level of servitization is about complementing a firm's products with services to make the offering more comprehensive. These can range from classical maintenance services that allow the functioning of a product to be secured (eg software updates for a machine) to value-added services that allow customers to make better use of their products (eg training or real-time traffic data services provided by car manufacturers). All these services are highly standardized and inherently bound to the products a firm sells. Thus they not only represent additional opportunities to generate business from customers but also bind these customers more closely to them through regular interactions.

The second level of servitization refers to services that adapt an offering specifically to each customer's individual needs instead of being standardized. Therefore, customers are strongly involved in the value (co-)creation process, and the last mile is completed through an implementation project for individualization on-site.[9] The next level is reached when the service provider operates a holistic and tailored solution on behalf of the customer, for example the aircraft engine manufacturer Rolls-Royce through its Total Care offering. The company realized that its airline customers do not want to purchase engine products, pay maintenance fees and invest in infrastructure. Hence they introduced a 'power-by-the-hour' solution to provide a highly reliable and safe full service for aeroplanes with minimal turnaround times. In other words, the service becomes the core of the offering, while the product becomes the means to deliver it. In such cases, the vendor becomes more dependent on its customer because of its customer-specific pre-investments, which for the most part cannot be reused for other customers. These full service or total solution cases, where products are consumed as a service typically following a service level agreement (SLA), can be categorized as the most comprehensive and sophisticated service offerings.

Though, many companies struggle to turn their new services into a sufficiently profit-making business. Often they underestimate the back-office capabilities needed for offering complex services, or they are not able to leverage the newly developed practices across cases because of the highly customized client requirements. Additional challenges lie at the front end, where salespeople think that selling services is the same as selling products with basic service contracts; they fail to realize that servitization means switching focus to the nature of the customer's problem. The outcome economy requires a deep change in the business model, new organizational capabilities and new business process capabilities. It also requires a quite different approach to product design and cost management across the life cycle.

Heading toward products: Toward standardization and automation for scale

There are good reasons why venture capitalists avoid investing in businesses with a high proportion of human-based services. The primary disadvantage of driving individualization and co-creation with the help of services is that servitization works against scale effects, as business and employee growth are tightly linked. Its countermeasure is called 'productization', a strategy that develops repeatable (ie standardized) services to enable scalability – despite a certain level of customized outcomes. Practically, you can think of a consulting project in which the project team captures key learnings and procedures in the form of reusable templates, a standard methodology or even a software tool. Another example is technical services that can be standardized and scaled. As productization automates services, it requires less involvement by a human workforce and therefore allows non-linear growth.

University education is a good example of the impact of the productization trend. The industry faces the intermittent threat of companies like

Coursera or edX, offering massive open online courses (MOOCs), in which software takes over the role of the professor.[10] The idea behind MOOCs is to standardize (or productize) teaching content, which is then shared as a digital lecture by the best professors in the world. These digital lectures can be accessed by anybody, at any time, everywhere in the world ('pull' approach). While this comes at the expense of the distinctive aspects that individual lecturers bring to the topic, as well as the personal interaction with and among students, MOOCs can substantially reduce costs for universities, increase accessibility for students and still provide very high-quality teaching. Similarly, in the software industry, productization refers to a shift from unique customer projects where new software is developed and customized for each client to standardized software offerings and packed implementation content that cover most of the needs of average customers around the globe.[11]

Conclusion: Crafting a strategic path between service and product orientation

Following the comparison between the strategies (heading toward services versus heading toward products), we can conclude that servitization and productization drive several business model trends:

- Through the first level of servitization, a firm's tangible product offering is complemented by intangible, value-adding services that make the overall transactions more comprehensive, while they remain standardized and can easily be scaled across customers.

- The second level of servitization adopts the offering to the customers' individual needs. The firm therefore invests in customer-specific capabilities and involves customers through the co-creation of single offerings or holistic and tailored solutions.

- Conversely, productization refers to standardizing what was formerly an individual offering to appeal to many different customers. This trend strongly overlaps with the digitization trend described previously.

The last two trends act in opposite directions, as servitization through co-creation and offering individualization drives economies of scope and economies of customer integration, whereas productization aims to standardize a previously customized offering via automation and packaging to make it repeatable and more broadly available and hence augments economies of scale. But, as we saw, each new development in one direction has to be seen in the light of developments in the other direction. There is no one-size-fits-all: every leader needs to define an individual strategic path by balancing between heading toward services and heading toward products to find the appropriate synthesis.

Endnotes

1 Douglas Engelbart.

2 L Ioannou (2014) A decade to mass extinction event in S&P 500, *CNBC*, 5 June, http://www.cnbc.com/2014/06/04/15-years-to-extinction-sp-500-companies.html.

3 E Fleisch, M Weinberger and F Wortmann (2015) Geschäftsmodelle im Internet der Dinge, *Schmalenbachs Zeitschrift für betriebswirtschaftliche Forschung*, **67**, pp 444–64.

4 M Fitzgerald, N Kruschwitz, D Bonnet and M Welch (2013) Embracing digital technology, Study by *MIT Sloan Management Review* and Capgemini, 7 October, http://sloanreview.mit.edu/projects/embracing-digital-technology.

5 W Isaacson (2011) *Steve Jobs: The exclusive biography*, Simon & Schuster, New York.

6 See http://www.cnbc.com/2014/04/11/online-retailers-betting-on-physical-stores.html; http://www.sueddeutsche.de/wirtschaft/online-handel-laden-als-labor-1.2283358; http://www.heise.de/newsticker/meldung/Onlinehaendler-Cyberport-eroeffnet-Ladengeschaeft-in-Oesterreich-1383937.html.

7 P F Drucker (1974) *Management*, Routledge, London, p 57.

8 T S Baines, H W Lightfoot, O Benedettini and J M Kay (2009) The servitization of manufacturing: A review of literature and reflection on future challenges, *Journal of Manufacturing Technology Management*, **20** (5), pp 547–67; S Vandermerwe and J Rada (1988) Servitization of business: Adding value by adding services, *European Management Journal*, **6** (4), pp 314–24.

9 Increasingly customers are even willing to take over part of the provider's value chain in order to achieve the last mile of the solution individually, what is termed 'prosumerism' by Alvin Toffler; see A Toffler (1980) *The Third Wave: The classic study of tomorrow*, Bantam, New York.

10 R Lyons (2015) Haas dean confidently predicts demise of business schools, Interview by Della Bradshaw, *Financial Times*, 10 April.

11 K Alajoutsijärvi, K Mannermaa and H Tikkanen (2000) Customer relationships and the small software firm: A framework for understanding challenges faced in marketing, *Information and Management*, **37**, pp 153–59.

Assessing your current business model 02

Defining a strategic path for a business model (BM) transformation requires clarity regarding the starting and target positions. By comparing the overlapping effects of the megatrends discussed in Chapter 1 with each other, we have seen that they drive business model decisions along two dimensions: 'inclusiveness of transaction' and 'customization of offering'. They help us to derive a generic typology of business models, where each type can be a firm's starting position, and another type can be its intended target position. They help us to assess our current business model and put it in the context of possible alternatives. This means there are strategic choices when it comes to shaping the future business model of the company. Some fit the strengths and weaknesses of the company better, while others fit them less well.

Types of business models

Each of the two dimensions opens up a range of strategic options between their respective demarcation points:

- 'Inclusiveness of transaction' dimension: *From* stand-alone, often physical offerings with vastly independent transactions *to* comprehensive and interconnected offerings with recurring transactions.

- 'Customization of offering' dimension: *From* standardized, packaged and automated offerings *to* individualized offerings that are co-created by company and customer.

The degree of *inclusiveness of transactions* refers to two complementing factors. First, it indicates to what extent a transaction is *comprehensive* in the sense that it includes a broad scope of products and services regarding the needs of the customer. Additionally, it reflects to what extent the transaction is *integrative* in the sense that the products and services share a common architecture linking them together – often operated on a powerful platform.

The combination of comprehensiveness and integration is not limited to a single transaction but binds the customer into a series of related transactions over time. In many cases, the first transaction creates a kind of stickiness.[1] If the level of stickiness is high, the customer can no longer make fully independent buying decisions and is forced into a series of related business transactions with the same vendor.

Apple's business model is an example of very high inclusiveness: a very comprehensive offering (iPhone, Watch, iPad, iPod, iCloud, MacBook, Apple Music, Apple TV, etc) with deeply integrated components leads to a strong lock-in or stickiness for the firm's customers. This represents the upper end of the inclusiveness dimension: these are highly comprehensive and integrated transactions that are continuously consumed in a long-term customer relationship. As an example, 'phygital' is what Apple has been offering since 2015: in-house developers can use the Swift programming language to connect external hardware like a medical device to a platform in order to take measurements with the HealthKit iPhone app, which creates physical stickiness. If these customers want to keep consistent health records, they have little other choice than to stick with the Apple world of devices and software. On the lower end of the inclusiveness dimension, we find discrete stand-alone transactions of single products or services that are independent from one another. This was Sony's dominant business model: selling very successful electronic products that were, however, focused on a single functionality, were not integrated through a common architecture and were not suitable to bind in the customers in the long run.

The second dimension is the *customization of offerings*. It ranges from fully *standardized* products and services that are not adapted at all to the individual customer and are often sold via mass channels to fully *customer-individual* and customer-centric products and services that are only developed once for a single customer. The more customized an offering, the stronger the vendor dependency, as the individualization effort requires a certain customer-specific, upfront investment from the vendor. Most of these investments cannot be used for other customers.

Many business models score either high or low on these two dimensions. However, there are examples of business models that have developed in between the extremes. One example is mass customization: customers can choose from a sometimes broad variety of components to create their individual product or service. Car manufacturers are a very good example, as they allow their customers to come up with thousands of different configurations of colours, interiors, technical gadgets and so on. However, each of these components is fully standardized (often even across vehicle models and brands) and can be applied without causing extra customer-specific investments by the manufacturers. Another example of such a hybrid is the blended learning approach used in many executive education programmes, in which customers first learn the standardized basic knowledge through an e-learning tool. Subsequently, during participants' time on campus, this knowledge is developed and applied according to highly individual use cases and needs.

The two dimensions introduced above allow us to distinguish four generic types of business models between which transformation may occur (see Figure 2.1): the product BM (low degree of inclusiveness and customization), the platform BM (high degree of inclusiveness and low degree of customization), the project BM (low degree of inclusiveness and high degree of customization) and the solution BM (high degree of inclusiveness and customization).

Figure 2.1 Business model typology

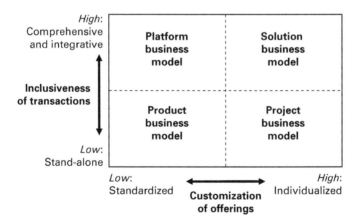

The goal of this typology is to bring clarity and structure to the discussion about the business model type that a company or its business unit applies and where it is heading. This clarity will enable us to analyse the current strategic position ('Where do I come from?') and to identify – given the specific company and market situation – a promising target position ('Where do I want to be?'). Just as with travelling, a business model transformation requires a good understanding of the start and end points of the journey. On this basis, we can think about how radical the transformation needs to be, what steps have already been taken and what additional changes are needed to successfully transform the business model. It is important to note that none of these business model types is generally superior, but each type has its specific strengths, weaknesses and challenges.

As suggested before, such a typology implies a certain level of simplification and should therefore not be regarded as a black-versus-white categorization scheme. Even radical business model transformations are not always one-time shifts from one business model type to another but can start with gradual changes into the hybrid areas between the generic business model types before the full transformation is completed. We will see this in many of the case studies in this book.

In the following we describe the characteristics, the pros and the cons of the four business model types, including recommendations regarding which type fits the best given particular internal and external factors.

Product business model

A product BM is characterized by standard products or services offered on a large scale and sold to many (often anonymous) customers in a standalone transaction. It follows the logic of 'build a great product and win'. Standardized after-sales services like guarantee, inspection and maintenance services often complement the physical products. As products become increasingly digitized, software-enabled features and services play a more important role to differentiate the core product. For example, Tesla's car facelifts happen in the form of software updates.

In the lower parts of the product BM box in Figure 2.1, a transaction ends immediately after the purchase of a product or service. Hence, vendors develop all kinds of strategies in order to make their offerings the customer's favourite choice in the next transaction as well, for example by offering multiple categories under the same strong brand, which serves as a buying compass (eg luxury goods producers like Hermès), or by providing customers with benefits for future transactions (eg customer retention programmes such as Singapore Airlines KrisFlyer).

Dyson: Engineering-driven products that challenge the status quo

The British company Dyson had a turnover of £1.74 billion and a profit of £448 million in 2015, employed more than 4,500 people and sold products in over 65 countries around the world.

The Dyson story began back in 1978, when James Dyson became frustrated with his vacuum cleaner's diminishing performance, as the bag was clogging with dust, which caused suction to drop. He built an industrial cyclone tower for his factory that separated paint particles from the air using centrifugal force. To apply the same bagless principle on a smaller scale in a vacuum cleaner, it took him five years and 5,127 prototypes. His G-Force vacuum cleaner design was first licensed by a Japanese manufacturing company and sold in Japan. It quickly became a status symbol, selling for $2,000. In 1993, with the royalties from G-Force sales, James Dyson was able to set up his own company, Dyson Ltd, with a research centre and factory in Wiltshire, in the UK.

Many innovative products followed, at first centred on new vacuum cleaners with his Cyclone technology, which was constantly improved. By 2009, Dyson had begun extending beyond vacuum cleaners with the creation of other air-powered technologies like the AirBlade hand drier, the Air Multiplier bladeless fan and the Dyson Hot bladeless fan heater.

Dyson's enthusiasm for the engineering approach puts the product at the centre of all his firm's activities: 'Like everyone, we get frustrated by products that don't work properly. As design engineers, we do something about it. We're all about invention and improvement.' To spread this idea, since 2002 the James Dyson Foundation has sought to inspire young people to study engineering and become engineers.

In order to increase inclusiveness while still following the logic of a product BM (upper half of the box in Figure 2.1), some vendors develop offerings with a built-in system logic (eg interlocking Lego[2] bricks and the Original Gardena garden hose connection system). Such product systems apply a modular approach in which a certain logic in each building block ensures overall integrity; hence every module with its specific function fits and works together with the others to perform the overall task. This allows the typical scale effects for a product offering, but one whose level of flexibility is based on the modules. *Razor-and-blade*[3] is a special 'sticky' form of this product system strategy: the central building block is often sold at a low price, or even given away free,[4] while it can then only be used with complementing non-durable products or services that create a continuous consumption stream (eg Hewlett-Packard's inkjet printers and ink cartridges, communication providers with (subsidized) mobile devices and service contracts, and the Nespresso coffee machines and capsules).

A product BM is a good choice if it is possible to create a standardized offering that applies to the mass market and if the product itself offers a clear and unique value proposition. Competitive advantages can be achieved by means of technological breakthroughs, cost advantages, unique processes, user experiences and design. The advantages of a product BM are that its complexity is relatively low and that it allows economies of scale if it can be applied like a 'well-oiled machine'. The disadvantages are that it requires substantial marketing investments to capture a significant mind and market share, and that the company remains relatively distant from the end customer if it does not have its own sales channels. For example, it is often the case for household products that companies such as AMC, Tupperware and Vorwerk have proprietary direct sales channels.

Platform business model

Standardization and large scale also characterize a platform BM. In contrast to the product system, where different components can be seamlessly connected to each other, a platform additionally serves as a foundation that architecturally integrates a comprehensive set of products and services, defines the rules and conditions for interactions – for example governance, workflows and processes – and enables the users by offering shared functions and tools.[5]

Platforms are an enabling tool. They can organize market interactions in different, technology-based ways. Markets have existed for centuries, linking consumers and merchants, but what's changed is that information and communication technology has heavily reduced the need to own physical infrastructure and assets. Today platforms come in many varieties, but they all have an ecosystem with the same four types of actors:[6]

1 *The owners:* They control their intellectual property and the governance of the platform by deciding who may participate and in what ways. For example, Daimler owns the mobility platform moovel.

2 *The providers:* They offer the interface of the platform with the consumers. For example, smartphones are such kind of providers on moovel.

3 *The complementors:* These are strategic partners that create and produce the different offerings of the platform, for example the mytaxi app on moovel. The interaction between such a complementor and the users happens in this case by smartphone (as provider). Complementors are often driven by heterogeneous sources of motivation. Sometimes they are even unpaid and work outside of a price system.[7]

4 *The users:* They are the consumers of the offering, and can be vendors or buyers.

Such a market intermediary platform can only exist if all parties are able to achieve gains from trade at least in the long run when they participate in the platform.[8] These gains can be unevenly distributed, but initially all participants must be better off.

We will now differentiate between three types of platform BMs and also describe the evolution of this type of business model. Platforms that facilitate interactions between two or more distinct but interdependent types of users – and provide each other with network benefits – are called *multisided*; hence the term 'multisided networks' is also used.[9] These platforms have different groups of customers or partners that businesses have to get and keep on-board in order to succeed. These businesses range from dating platforms (men and women) to gaming platforms (game developers and users).[10]

The more users join the platform, and the more apps and other offerings they generate, the higher the value for each of them, as the number of interactions – for example between producers and consumers, suppliers and demanders or senders and receivers – is potentially increasing. Facebook's exponential growth attracted even more customers, as the users could expect their friends to use the platform as well; the same logic drove their $22 billion acquisition of WhatsApp with its 600 million users in 2014. In consumer markets, by exploiting this network effect, new entrants can become dominant in a very short amount of time; however, there is evidence that it takes more time to establish a dominant industry platform, as the expertise of incumbent industry players is harder to replicate, and – more importantly – in many cases they control access to the data their products generate.[11] Besides network benefits, the breadth and depth of the integrated portfolio of products and services, premium services (eg personalized recommendations, free-of-charge shipping) and subscription-based monetization models can increase the probability that the customer will continue the relationship with the platform provider and can often lead to a chain of transactions.

Multisided platforms can be either a *shop*, which means customers buy from a vendor-defined assortment (eg online stores for own goods such as

H&M at hm.com, Amazon in the early years, or aggregators like Booking.com), or *marketplaces*, where the users' interactions shape the offering portfolio, and the platform provider facilitates the interactions and runs the process (eg Amazon Marketplace, Wikipedia, Uber, Airbnb). If a platform BM is open for third parties, providers can use the data they get from the sales of the marketplace partners to offer their best-selling products themselves.

In order to drive standardization and inclusiveness even further, a new, third type of platform BM has been introduced over the past decade. It provides a platform on which other platforms can be developed or, in other words, 'an evolving system made of interdependent pieces that can be innovated upon'.[12] In this case, the platform provider offers a foundation for others to innovate and develop on top of and often builds an *ecosystem of providers* that offers complementary offerings, for example from customers, other firms and/or partners.[13] These *meta-platforms* do not provide given functionalities (like the one-sided or two-sided platforms described above) but rather platform capabilities that can be leveraged when developing new offerings (eg Google's Android operating system for smartphones and Amazon Web Services to build scalable, high-performance websites). Hence it is not only about the integrity among the offering's building blocks but also about the integrity between the platform and its 'heads'. A growing ecosystem of relevant complementors drives up the number of value-adding offerings, hence the inclusiveness of the offering portfolio. For complementors, the platform decision is also strategic, as it requires an investment in platform-specific capabilities and signifies a bet on the future evolution of the platform.

Amazon and Amazon Web Services: The evolution of platform business models at their best

Amazon's business model evolution in the course of the last 20-plus years, during which Jeff Bezos has continuously improved, fine-tuned and extended the company's platform approach, started back in 1994 as an 'online bookstore' with Bezos's vision to revolutionize the book industry. The Amazon online shop offered superior services like convenience thanks to 24/7 availability and home delivery on a platform that connected book sellers and book buyers directly and hence cut out the local retailer as intermediary. Bezos also introduced a sort of mass customization of Amazon's business model by making specific suggestions based on a customer's order history. In 2000 Amazon introduced the 1-Click ordering process.

Since the customer's payment and shipping information is already stored on Amazon's servers, it creates a checkout process that is virtually frictionless and achieves a high conversion rate from existing customers. Amazon filed the 1-Click patent in 1997; today its value is considered to be several billion dollars.[14]

The next steps of the evolution included the introduction of Amazon Marketplace in 2000, which enables third-party vendors to sell items along with the ones offered by Amazon on a commission basis. As different retailers can offer the same product at different prices, a market with internal competition is created. This extended the breadth and depth of Amazon.com's offering portfolio and created further transactional inclusiveness. But it also creates market insights that can help to fine-tune its own offerings.

Further services followed, like Amazon Prime in 2007, which initially allowed unlimited, free-of-charge express delivery for a certain membership fee. Today, as Amazon has also become one of the largest online platforms for content, the Prime offering includes unlimited music and movies streaming and free e-books for a $99 per year flat-fee membership. Prime has become an all-you-can-eat, physical–digital hybrid. To build up a complete ecosystem – as Apple did – offering everything from end devices (tablets, etc) and content (books, films, etc) to small service apps, Amazon also introduced its own devices to connect its 244 million active customers even more tightly to the Amazon platform, for example the Kindle reader in 2007 and the Fire smartphone, tablet and TV in 2014. And it even started to produce its own TV content: the soap *Transparent* won five Emmy awards in 2015.

In parallel, Amazon has built up Amazon Web Services (AWS), a leading cloud service provider, and along with it a completely new line of business. AWS, officially launched in 2006, today offers computing power, networking and databases, content delivery and other functionality to help businesses scale and grow. Everything is delivered as a service, on demand, with pay-as-you-go pricing. Since its launch, customer adoption has increased substantially, including many well-known start-ups like Pinterest, Netflix, Spotify and Airbnb. They follow the general trend of building new ventures not from scratch but on top of elastic cloud infrastructures and application platforms in order to scale the business growth when needed.

For 2015, Amazon posted a net income of $596 million. This was much more than analysts had expected for the 'high-spending company' and after a loss of $242 million the year before. Both Amazon's net revenue of $107 billion (2014: $89 billion) and its income were especially boosted by the AWS division, which reported revenues of $7.9 billion. The market capitalization of Amazon on 29 December 2015 was $325 billion.

Amazon's evolution has led the firm from being an online store for physical goods to a marketplace that enables third-party sellers, a cloud infrastructure provider, and eventually a content retailer and even a content producer. With that, Amazon is one of the few global platform companies today that can claim to be proficient in all flavours of a platform BM.

A platform BM is a good choice if a company can build a strong shared foundation that integrates a broad range of products and services, sets the rules and enables the users. Additionally, it has to be able to drive 'traffic and gravity', which is determined by the size and activity of its user base and potentially its surrounding co-innovating ecosystem. The advantages are economies of scale and scope based on network effects and the offering's integrity, which makes a customer's platform decision long-lasting. The disadvantages are that platforms that usually have a longer life cycle than the offerings at the top must comprise leading processes, a superior architecture and/or a substantially better cost position to become a de facto standard in the market.

Project business model

A project BM relies on highly customized products or services. These are typically developed by closely involving the customer during development and production. Even though the projects usually run over a longer time period and can include allotment contracts with milestones, they are still one-time contracts. Such customized business models are normally service-centric. Examples include a construction company's complex planning and building of a dam, which cover a vast number of engineering services, or an advisory group's consulting project, which has no tangible product at all. Since the customer is usually free to change providers for subsequent transactions, service companies naturally target the development of close relationships with a client during a project and the cross-selling of other or future services. For example, it is a generally accepted practice in the power generation business to switch vendors (like General Electric, Siemens and ABB) from one installation to the next, thus staying independent by running a balanced portfolio of vendor-facility combinations. Similarly, a listed company's auditor needs to be explicitly reconfirmed year after year and should be changed after a multi-year collaboration period to avoid biased integrity and to safeguard mutual independence.

A project BM is a good choice if a firm's competitive advantage stems from its capability and willingness to design and execute complex local projects for highly specific customer needs. The advantages include the manageable amount of complexity, the vendor's accumulation of customer-relevant knowledge through the collaboration during development and implementation (economies of scope), and the highly flexible cost structure with limited upfront investments. Disadvantages are the lack of scalability and leverage of the customer-specific service and project capabilities (which can only be deployed for one client at a time), and the typically volatile revenues.

Nüssli: Providing events with temporary structures

Nüssli is an international supplier of temporary structures for complex major sports and cultural events, trade fairs and exhibitions. The company provides customized, integral solutions from concept to final implementation.

For example, in 2014, one of the tournaments of the Women's Tennis Association was hosted by the Mexican city of Monterrey. Nüssli was tasked with installing a grandstand with an audience capacity of 2,400 seats and a VIP area for an additional 1,500 spectators. Furthermore, the company was in charge of providing light towers and camera platforms for the event. After the dismantling of the tennis arena used for the Davis Cup in Geneva, 180 tons of material were transported directly to Mexico for reconstruction. It took a 29-person crew 10 days to complete the event infrastructures.

In this BM, there is obviously no lock-in of the customer. Nüssli plans and builds the temporary event structure, and after the eventual dismantling of the materials the project is finished.

Solution business model

A solution BM is characterized by the combination of a highly customized individual offering and a comprehensive scope of integrated products and services. These holistic solutions solve a customer's problem holistically and include the project management along the entire life cycle ('one-stop shop').

They tend to be co-created with the customer, which requires some upfront investments by the solution provider. At the same time, the fact that the provider often takes over entire value chain functions leads to a lock-in of the customer. This bi-directional dependency between a vendor and a customer creates significant stickiness and can lead to mutual long-term partnerships. The offering usually comprises physical and digital components, such as technology, products (hardware and software), services and content. If the solution provider is unable to provide all the building blocks of the customer solution, it can also integrate third-party contributors or even competitors, leading to a multi-vendor landscape, which needs to be well orchestrated.

The pricing of such a solution is often based on a service level agreement (SLA). An example is Hewlett-Packard (HP), which offers managed office printing services. This means that HP – on behalf of its customer – runs complete fleets of printers, scanners, copiers, fax machines and so forth over a multi-year contract period. The customers only pay for the output (ie the number of pages printed). Included in the solution are additional value-added offerings – partially with on-site personnel – such as installation services, life cycle management, device usage monitoring, help desk support and consulting services.

A solution BM is a good choice if a firm or unit is able to deliver a highly customer-specific and inclusive solution via the orchestration of individual offerings and to establish a mutual, trust-based business relationship. Mastering the complexity of a solution business requires competences in multiple domains, namely managing the scale of the solution's product and system parts, the scope of the solution's service and content parts, and eventually integrating the various building blocks. This is particularly challenging when offerings are sourced from external vendors with a less customized business model, as the solution provider then has to manage an even larger portion of the offering individualization. Last but not least, leading project and risk management competences are a requirement. The advantages are an opportunity for a mutually trusting vendor–customer partnership to create a barrier against new market entrants (economies of customer integration), a strong differentiation via integrated solutions to prevent commoditization and price competition, and the potential for higher margins through the substantial service and content business part of the business model. The disadvantages are the model's inherent high complexity, which requires mastering various unique competences, the need for in-depth customer business and process expertise, and the challenging orchestration of various internal and external suppliers. Needless to say, the solution BM – like the project BM – requires pre-investments in the individualization of offerings.

Rolls-Royce: Power by the hour for airline engines

With Rolls-Royce's Total Care service offering,[15] an airline – as a customer – can buy 'operating aircraft miles' as a holistic solution ('brake horsepower by the hour') instead of purchasing engine products, paying maintenance fees and investing in infrastructure up front.

Rolls-Royce – as the provider – orchestrates the customer problem resolution process end to end across functions, divisions, partners and so forth, in order to deliver to its airline customers based on an SLA. As a result, the airline can now focus on its core competencies, and is given a more predictable and manageable expense stream, and partners with a supplier that is strategically aligned with the airline's own goals and incentives. This means that – in the old product business model – the more money Rolls-Royce made, the more often the engine had to be serviced. With the 'power by the hour' SLA, it is just the opposite: as Rolls-Royce makes more money, the less often the engine has to be serviced.

To offer this total solution, Rolls-Royce transformed itself from a product company with loosely coupled functional silos into a services-driven, SLA-oriented provider for total solutions and an integrated firm. Rolls-Royce orchestrates a business network for end-to-end process performance enabled by analytic capabilities to monitor and proactively respond to changes that could affect its SLA. Consequently, Rolls-Royce can achieve a predictable revenue flow and a stronger top line and margin position thanks to higher service profitability.

Options for radical transformation

In this chapter we developed a typology of business model types according to the degree of customization offered and the inclusiveness of the transaction. We outlined the characteristics, strengths and weaknesses of all four generic business model types. To conclude, Table 2.1 compares all four models. It seeks to support the analysis and positioning of a firm's (and its competitors') dominant business model, to provide a basis for reflection about the need for a transformation, and to help identify options for a promising future business model.

As elaborated at the beginning of this chapter, a variety of business model types can coexist and compete with each other within an industry. In Table 2.2, we provide examples of such competing business models in some of the industries that experience a particularly strong pressure to transform.

Table 2.1 Comparison of generic business model types

	Product business model	Project business model	Platform business model	Solution business model
Model-type characteristics	• The product itself offers a clear and discrete advantage in the competition (features, functions). • Services with complementing role. • Almost no recurring business transactions due to low inclusiveness of transactions and low customization of offering.	• Competitive advantage stems from excelling in a customer-individual local (customer-site) project business. • Almost no recurring transactions, but customer retention can be increased by specific activities (branding, etc).	• Competitive advantage through broad scope of integrated products and/or services. • Recurring customer investment chain due to architectural foundation and integration. • 'Traffic and gravity' around system platform impacts competitive edge.	• Competitive advantage stems from customer-individual and inclusive end-to-end problem solutions. • Co-created and integrated hybrid solutions. • Stickiness due to long-term-oriented value partnership • Orchestration of individually configured contributor networks.
Pros	• Economies of scale. • Well-understood business model; liked by seed/growth investors. • Relatively low level of complexity.	• Economies of scope; vendor accumulates customer-relevant knowledge while offering creation with customer. • Manageable amount of complexity.	• Economies of scale through network effects and offering integrity. • Favourite model of seed/growth investors. • Flexibility to continuously develop the offering aligned with evolving market requirements.	• Economies of customer integration. • Strong differentiation to exit price competition. • Potential for higher margin in service/content business.

Cons	• Need for substantial marketing investments to gain customer retention. • Relatively distant from end customer. • Vulnerable to platform BM.	• Substantial pre-investments in customer-specific capabilities.	• Platform system requires superior architecture and/or substantially better cost position to become de facto standard in market.	• High complexity; requires mastery of various competences. • In-depth customer process expertise needed. • Challenging orchestration of internal/external suppliers.
Examples	• Automobile OEM. • Machinery equipment. • Physical retailers (eg supermarkets).	• Consulting companies (plan, build phase). • Construction and civil engineering firms.	• Shops. • Online marketplaces. • Meta-platforms.	• Equipment fleet solution providers. • End-to-end process outsourcers.

Table 2.2 Examples of generic types of business models by industry

	Product business model	Project business model	Platform business model	Solution business model
Retail industry	• **Retail banking** (eg Bank of America): Mass banking with standard products (eg fund, loan) for private and business end customers.	• **Investment banking/ M&A consulting** (eg Goldman Sachs): Customer-specific projects to provide for example sell-side advice, cross-border M&A and merger transactions.	• **Crowdfunding** (eg Kickstarter): Online platform for entrepreneurs to fund initiative via a large pool of backers with smaller investments.	• **Family office** (eg HSBC Private Wealth Solutions): A private company to manage investments and trusts in the long run on behalf of a single family (plus personal services).
Travel industry	• **Hotel** (eg Hilton): Standard board and lodging services sold directly or indirectly to private or business clients.	• **Customized travelling** (eg iTravel): Online tour operator system platform that provides completely personalized holiday and unique travel experiences.	• **Accommodation agency** (eg Airbnb): Community marketplace that enables private apartment owners and travellers to interact and engage in commerce.	• **Corporate travel management** (eg BCD Travel): Full-service provider for travel-related solutions to meet the specific goals of corporate clients.
IT industry	• **Consumer software company** (eg Microsoft Office): 100 per cent standardized software for the mass market (locally installed).	• **System integrator** (eg Accenture): Manages complex customer-specific IT implementation and development projects (no hosting).	• **Standard business software company** (eg SAP): Standard software system platform, integrating different functions, on customer's premises or as a service (SaaS).	• **Managed cloud provider** (eg T-Systems): Integrates standard system platforms (SaaS/public cloud) with customer-tailored functionality (managed cloud).

Before we come to the core of this book – the study and management of the different transformation paths between the four business model types – we will briefly review the ongoing discussion about business models and explain how we contribute to this important debate.

Endnotes

1 For the 'stickiness' of business models see R G McGrath (2011) When your business model is in trouble, *Harvard Business Review*, January–February, pp 96–98. For 'core rigidities' compare G Hamel and C K Prahalad (1996) *Competing for the Future*, Harvard Business Press, Boston, MA.

2 'Lego' literally means 'I put together' in Latin and 'I connect' in Italian.

3 Despite the razor-and-blade business logic being widely credited to King C Gillette, this model did not actually originate with Gillette. Gillette's razors were expensive when they were first introduced, and the price only decreased after his patents expired and competitors started making them. See R C Picker (2010) The razors-and-blades myth(s), Working Paper No 532, September, Law School, University of Chicago.

4 C Anderson (2007) Freeconomics, *Economist*, 15 November.

5 This shared foundation of a platform BM can help to differentiate it from a product BM, which is characterized by its modular approach, with the fit-logic interfaces embedded in every module. Apple's iTunes platform acts as an integration hub and is clearly a platform BM. In contrast, Pampers Baby Portal, where parents can get information and coupons and can purchase Pampers online with special offers, is still a product BM, as the nappy product remains the core offering. Tesla's cars also remain a product BM despite the increasing digitization of the product (eg Autopilot functionality via software update); it could be classified as a platform BM as soon as the core of the offering's value proposition shifts to the platform, for example managing a multi-generation car fleet and providing end-to-end mobility processes.

6 This structure is based on M W Van Alstyne, G G Parker and S P Choudary (2016) Pipelines, platforms, and the new rules of strategy, *Harvard Business Review*, 94 (4), pp 54–62.

7 K Boudreau and L Jeppesen (2015) Unpaid crowd complementors: The platform network effect mirage, *Strategic Management Journal*, 36, pp 1761–77.

8 J-C Rochet and J Tirole (2006) Two-sided markets: A progress report, *RAND Journal of Economics*, 37 (3), pp 645–67.

9 Two-sided markets represent a refinement of the concept of network effects. There are same-side and cross-side network effects. Each network effect can be either positive or negative. For example, end-users sharing a PDF, or player-to-player contact via PlayStation 3, are a positive same-side network effect. A negative same-side network effect appears when there is competition between suppliers in online auction markets, or dates on Match.com. For example, with the network effects concept behaviour in software markets can be explained. See M W Van Alstyne, G G Parker and S P Choudary (2016) Pipelines, platforms, and the new rules of strategy, *Harvard Business Review*, **94** (4), pp 54–62, or J-C Rochet and J Tirole (2003) Platform competition in two-sided markets, *Journal of the European Economic Association*, **1** (4), pp 900–1029.

10 D Evans (2003) Some empirical aspects of multi-sided platform industries, *Review of Network Economics*, **2** (3), pp 191–209.

11 Does Deutschland do digital? Europe's biggest economy is rightly worried that digitization is a threat to its industrial leadership, *The Economist*, 21 November 2015.

12 A Gawer and M A Cusumano (2002) *Platform Leadership*, Harvard Business School Press, Boston, MA.

13 For platform-based 'ecosystem' innovation, see M Iansiti and R Levien (2004) *The Keystone Advantage: What the New Dynamics of Business Ecosystems Mean for Strategy*, Harvard Business School Publishing, Boston, MA; for ecosystem and collective health indicators see also M Iansiti and R Levien (2004) Strategy as ecology, *Harvard Business Review*, March, pp 68–78.

14 See http://blog.rejoiner.com/2012/07/amazon-1clickpatent/.

15 For a more in-depth discussion of the Rolls-Royce transformation, see C Linz and P Fiegl (2010) Business model transformation towards the service-oriented enterprise, in *Applying Real-World BPM in a SAP Environment*, ed G Chase, R Omar, J Taylor, A Rosenberg and M von Rosing, pp 55–84, Galileo, Bonn. For 2015, Rolls-Royce reported a pre-tax profit of £160 million on sales of £13.7 billion.

Moving from small tweaks to radical shifts   03

Hardly any other management concept has spread as quickly during the past decade as that of the 'business model' (BM). In the mid-1990s, academics started investigating this phenomenon, trying to understand *how firms do business on the system level*. Since 1995 around 18,000 articles (3,000 in peer-reviewed journals) have been published on this topic.[1] Currently, a certain level of shared understanding has been reached, namely that *a BM represents the firm's distinctive logic regarding value creation and appropriation.* A business model 'explains the way the firm operates and how it creates and captures value for its stakeholders' through the systemic configuration of activities, respectively through the discovery, creation and exploitation of opportunities driven by an entrepreneurial spirit.[2] Various authors have contributed to a better understanding of BMs by investigating dedicated aspects like business model dimensions, types, semantics, the design of (new) models and the performance of different models (including the creation of social wealth), and by applying the concept to the corporate level versus the business level.[3]

If we want to analyse a business model and its development, *five components* are usually of particular relevance. Four out of these five components go beyond the specific product or service that a business model provides:[4]

1 *The customer value proposition:* This is the offer of a company to its clients – the job to be done. It is the way a company offers to satisfy specific customer needs that alternative offerings don't address. The degree of *customization* is one important lever to influence the offering; another one is the *inclusiveness* of the transactions.

2 *The activities systems:* These are the value creation activities needed to realize the value proposition. Here we also have to answer the make-or-buy

question: which of these activities will we run by ourselves, or will our design of activities involve strategic partners who each bring unique expertise and resources to the system? Often such collaborations with complementors to our own activities are inevitable and decisive for the invention and realization of new solutions.[5]

3 *The governance:* Here we decide how the different activities are coordinated and interact with each other.

4 *The critical resources:* To create value, resources such as physical resources or human and social capital are necessary to run the activities. Organizational resources (like specific processes and management systems) are also needed to leverage the value-creating resources.

5 *Unique resources* (eg new knowledge, a specific capability, lock-in) can be the source of a competitive advantage.

6 *The monetization mechanics:* Here the profit formula, the way we earn money, has to be defined.

Up to now the discussion on business models has been more focused on the innovation of new business models in the context of start-ups. We know less about the BMs of established companies, for example how such companies change their BM over time.[6] And if there is research done on the change of BMs then it is more on the fine-tuning of existing business models, creating incremental change. But we see many established business models under heavy fire. For many companies small tweaks are not sufficient. The only option is to carry out a fundamental change, a radical shift to another type of business model. Owing to changes in the external business environment, or driven by internal factors, many companies need to challenge and potentially also change their existing business model proactively in order to remain competitive.

In the next section we give some background information on the evolution of the business model concept. Anyone who is less interested in the stages of this movement can omit this section and move on to the section 'Taking a dynamic perspective'.

Emergence of the business model concept

The emergence of the business model concept and the increasingly differentiated debate on the subject occurred in roughly four stages (see Table 3.1), namely the internet era (1993–1999), the innovation era (2000–present), the taxonomy era (2003–present) and the transformation era (2011–present).

This book will focus on the transformation of established companies' business models. However, because this era builds on knowledge and insights from previous eras, we give a short overview of the developments that have had an impact on the transformation era.

Business model internet era (1993–1999)

Business practitioners were the first to be interested in business models, which became a broadly discussed concept during the advent of the internet in the mid-1990s. The practical interest in the subject was driven by the start of the world wide web in 1993, which led to the 'dot-com era'.

During the dot-com era, a vibrant start-up scene introduced a flow of new business models for 'killer applications' at an unprecedented speed. As the technical backbone, the internet enabled the rise of web-based business models, like portals and search engines, in the first generation, and e-commerce in the second generation. At this stage, a key belief was that the virtual world would triumph over *bricks-and-mortar*: it was just a matter of building mind and market share very quickly. A spectacular case following this logic was the acquisition of the established media corporation Time Warner ($14.6 billion in sales, 67,500 employees) by the internet access provider AOL ($4.8 billion in sales, 12,100 employees) for $182 billion in January 2000. Steve Case, AOL's chairman and chief executive officer at the time, said: 'I don't think it is too much to say this really is a historic merger. We've transformed the landscape of media and the internet.' He failed.

But, in spite of the burst of the dot-com bubble in March 2000, entrepreneurs like Amazon's Jeff Bezos and eBay's Pierre Omidyar have succeeded with their radically new business models – their 'killer applications' – to win over the competition of larger, incumbent firms. This success was not built on the basis of better products or services, or ground-breaking technologies, but on their superior business models and their approaches to creating and capturing value.

Probably the most famous entrepreneurial leader at this stage, who also outlived the dot-com bubble's burst, was Michael Dell. In 1996, Dell started selling computers that could be configured by the customer over the web. It soon reported about $1 million in sales per day from dell.com. In 2001, Dell Inc reached a world market share of 12.8 per cent, surpassing Compaq to become the world's largest PC maker. In addition to direct sales via the internet and build-to-order capabilities, Michael Dell revolutionized the computer retailing business by designing a negative working capital model. Dell first collected money from its customers and only subsequently ordered

Table 3.1 Emergence of business model eras

	Business model internet era (1993–1999)	Business model innovation era (2000–present)	Business model taxonomy era (2003–present)	Business model transformation era (2011–present)
Trigger	• Internet as enabler for web-based BM. • Accelerated by rise of mobile phones and hand-held computers. • Rapid growth in emerging markets. • Ended by burst of dot-com bubble.	• Innovation backlog; cautious investments after dot-com bubble-burst shock. • New tools for innovative BM configuration. • Cheaper and more standardized components allow 'lean start-ups'.	• BM discussion fired up as start-up scene regains strength. • Soaring knowledge on BM leads to increased subject differentiation; one-size-does-not-fit-all. • Awareness that consistency within a BM type is critical.	• End of life cycle of certain business models. • New market opportunities (eg big data, cloud, Industry 4.0). • Need for business model and IT model alignment.
Prevailing logic	• The concept of a BM as a new unit of analysis. • Virtual world wins over bricks-and-mortar. • Companies in search for 'killer application' to challenge incumbents' BM. • Motto: 'Get big fast.'	• Business model design/creation can be done in systematic way. • Ecosystem helps to deliver a dynamic and comprehensive offer. • Exponential organizations leverage abundance.	• BMs can be grouped in types/classes based on common patterns. • BMs as a holistic composition of a purpose, activities and resources, governance mechanisms, and a monetization mechanic.	• Fine-tuning of the existing BM is not sufficient to manage the challenges. Only a radical shift and systematic strategic change from one BM type to another can help.

Approach	Conceptual BM approach.	Configurational BM approach.	Taxonomical and holistic BM approach.	Transformative BM approach.
Publications	• P Timmers (1998) Business models for electronic markets, *Electronic Markets*, **8** (2), pp 3–8. • R Amit and C Zott (2001) Value creation in e-business, *Strategic Management Journal*, **22**, pp 493–520.	• G Hamel (2000) *Leading the Revolution*, Harvard Business School Press, Boston, MA. • W C Kim and R Mauborgne (2005) *Blue Ocean Strategy*, Harvard Business School Press, Boston, MA • A Osterwalder and Y Pigneur (2010) *Business Model Generation*, John Wiley & Sons, Hoboken, NJ. • E Ries (2011) *The Lean Start-Up*, Portfolio Penguin, London. • S Ismail, I Malone and Y Geest (2014) *Exponential Organizations*, Diversion Books, New York.	• C Zott, R Amit and L Massa (2011) The business model: Recent developments and future research, *Journal of Management*, **37**, pp 1019–42. • C Linz and G Müller-Stewens (2012) Lösungsanbieterstrategien, *Zeitschrift für betriebswirtschaftliche Forschung*, **65** (12), pp 1–24. • O Gassmann, K Frankenberger and M Csik (2014) *The Business Model Navigator*, F T Publishing, Harlow.	• J Aspara, J-A Lamberg and H Tikkanen (2011) Strategic management of business model transformation: Lessons from Nokia, *Management Decision*, **49** (4), pp 622–647. • This book.

the components from its suppliers to build the computers. As the Dell example shows, business model innovation primarily relies on better integrating and renewing the different steps of the value chain to increase value creation and appropriation.

Business model innovation era (2000–present)

The shock of the dot-com bubble's burst led to a substantial innovation backlog, as investors became far more cautious than they had been before, and technology and product development costs were on the rise. In order to counter this backlog, prevent diminishing returns and secure growth, firms turned to new ways of doing business without fundamentally changing their business model.

An increasing number of concepts came up to support the process of business model innovation and configuration in a systematic way. For example, Hamel offered heuristics to challenge a firm's business model in a revolutionary way,[7] while Kim and Mauborgne developed new frameworks and tools to create 'blue oceans' of uncontested market space.[8] A very practical and integrated toolbox for a systematic business model design is the 'business model canvas' developed by Osterwalder and Pigneur.[9]

At the same time, a major change happened in the start-up scene that had a strong impact on the whole competitive landscape: the components and tools (from crowdfunding to big data analytics) of an internet-based business model became much more standardized and cheaper than before, and could be bought off the shelf. This meant it became faster and less expensive to implement a lean start-up idea,[10] which led to many very lean, agile and exponentially growing companies.[11] Take the example of the accomodation and home-stay platform Airbnb, founded in 2008, and compare it with a hotel company like Hyatt. Airbnb does not own any property and has a comparably very small number of employees but is already active in more than 34,000 cities around the globe. If Hyatt wants to grow, it faces the prospect of securing heavy investments to build and develop infrastructure, recruit and train people for each location and so on.

As we have seen, this stream of activities was focused on the modification and innovation of business models, but it did not differentiate between business model types. However, with the emergence of more and more new business models, it was increasingly obvious that there are different business model categories and that they played by different rules.

Business model taxonomy era (2003–present)

The increasing diversity of business models led to a demand for a more systematic perspective on this subject. The start-up scene regained its strength, but – in sharp contrast to the one-size-fits-all approach of the internet boom – researchers and practitioners began to become interested in the differences between the business models.

One example of such a new business model type is the 'freemium' model, where new competitors entered the market, offering similar services to those of the incumbents, but at a much lower price or even free. Think of the Swedish entrepreneur Niklas Zennström and his Danish colleague Janus Friis, who founded Skype in July 2003. By the end of 2004 they had already had more than 46 million downloads of their software and were among the first to prove that a start-up built on a freemium business model could outpace the incumbent telecom providers with their traditional, paid service business model. In September 2005 they sold their company for $3.1 billion to eBay.

With the development of business model taxonomies, types or classes along several dimensions, companies got the opportunity to choose between different options in a systematic way to find their most appropriate business model. For example, Gassmann et al. discovered 55 business model types that could be applied to 90 per cent of the world's most successful companies.[12]

The business model taxonomy era opened the way to much more radical changes in some industries: applying a different type of business model became a new way of entering a market and attacking the established competitors. However, these changes were mostly driven by small start-ups created from scratch around entirely new ways of value creation and appropriation, while it was assumed that incumbents had few alternatives other than sticking to their established business model.

Business model transformation era (2011–present)

In reviewing the discussion on business models up to now, we can make two observations. First, there is a clear dominance of structural topics regarding BMs: Which types? Which components? Which actors? Little is known about the management process of business models: How are they designed, implemented and operated? How is strategic change of business models managed? Second, the discussion is more about new business models attacking the incumbents, rather than about the transformation of an incumbent's business model.

However, business reality today is all about adjusting, changing and transforming business models. We currently see old and new incumbents increasingly being forced to transform their business model in order to stay close to their customers' changing needs and ahead of the start-up competition. These transformations can go in many different directions. Some firms move from product BMs to platform BMs by complementing their original products and services with a comprehensive offering for their customers. The German premium car producer Daimler, for example, has expanded its business of selling cars to offer integrated point-to-point mobility services that rely on a vast number of different means of transportation. Every business model transformation implies a major strategic change. In some cases the company even has to exit the old business model and enter a new one, with all the hurdles and roadblocks to overcome. Despite its widely recognized significance, research applying this dynamic view to business models – namely *business model transformation* – is still limited and typically focuses only on specific aspects. Very little research has been undertaken to study the change processes that occur in a holistic business model transformation,[13] which have been described as the most challenging issue in business model research.[14]

Taking a dynamic perspective

In this book, we take a dynamic perspective on business model transformation and set out to explore how a transformation path from an existing business model to a new one can be managed successfully. Owing to changes in the external business environment, or driven by internal factors, many companies need to challenge and potentially also change their existing business model proactively in order to remain competitive. It is therefore often not enough to develop the established model incrementally. Instead, radically transforming a company's or unit's business model despite the potential path dependencies into a new, more appropriate one is required. We call such a change of the generic type of business model a *radical business model transformation*. Managing such a radical business model transformation process is regarded as a key organizational capability.[15]

A radical business model transformation can be performed either as a full transformation (ie totally abandoning the former model and adopting a new model for the complete company) *or as a partial transformation* (ie adopting or adding a new type of business model but retaining the existing model as the dominant one in parallel – sometimes only for a specific transition period). For example, Netflix was using such a *mixed-model approach*. The dominant model was the platform BM of video streaming; but later it added a product BM by producing its own content. Daimler did it the other way around: its dominant model is the product BM of selling cars; with moovel it added a mobility platform BM. Of course, this new business model will influence the traditional model, because it redefines the purpose of a car from a transportation tool to a mobile living room. The car here is only one of many components in an inclusive mobility solution.

Such radical transformations are very challenging, as they often directly conflict with the dominant culture of the company. Managers in such companies are primarily focused on day-to-day operations and often realize too late that they need to transform their business model to secure their firms' long-term survival and prosperity.

Radical business model transformation is all about the systematic strategic change process of switching from one business model type to another in order to gain or regain a competitive advantage. As mentioned before, radical business model transformation thus differs from business model innovation, which focuses on the modification of single business model dimensions *within* a given business model type but not necessarily on the change *from one type to another*. Business model innovation and radical transformation diverge, because they deal with different phenomena but have a small area of overlap, namely when an innovation is so far-reaching that it goes beyond adaptation within an existing business model type and leads to a new type of business model. *A radical business model transformation requires an integrative and well-orchestrated adaptation of the front end (value proposition, offering and customer interaction), the back end (activities, critical resources and capabilities) and the monetization mechanics (cost and revenue structure).*

The leading question that emerged during the development of this book and guided us during our discussions was the following: 'Are you thinking radically enough?' We analysed and discussed hundreds of cases in which business units and companies have either completed a business model transformation or are still in the process of changing their business model to a new type. In so doing, we identified a large number of cases in which a business model's front end, back end and monetization mechanics were modified to a certain extent, but the business model type by and large remained the same. This always occurs if the business model transformation does not go far enough. For example, if a magazine publisher offers previously printed content on mobile devices, this is not sufficient to call it a radical business model transformation. Instead, if the value proposition is extended by adding third-party content, an architecture-based platform is established, and the publisher decides to adopt a subscription-based pricing scheme, it can qualify as a radical business model transformation. More recent history tells us that many firms are still reluctant to engage in such radical transformations and prefer the more incremental innovation path. However, there is a big risk that these steps only obscure the view of the real issues without solving them. The publisher that launches its content online might feel this is a sufficient answer to the pressure from online competitors, but without a full business model transformation it will sooner or later run out of money, as users consume content free without any alternative revenue channels being built up.

For example, the German Bauer Media Group, founded in 1875, has systematically transformed its business model. Successful print magazine concepts were transferred to the internet, to better link printed and digital media and build up communities. For example, in 2000 the group launched the people magazine *heat*, which encompasses the internet portal heatworld.com and the radio station heatradio. It established new online brands like the portal *The Debrief* for the 'constantly connected young female' in the United Kingdom or the health portal *Praxisvita* in Germany. To bundle and manage the digital portfolio it launched a new operating unit, Bauer Xcel Media. In 2014 this unit contributed sales of €94 million to the €2.3 billion sales of the group.

The objective of this book is to encourage managers to think about and engage in radical business model transformation by showing how to make use of the DNA of an existing business model while successfully entering new territories. In Part Two, we introduce the concept of 'crossing' between business model types, which clarifies that there is a demarcation line that needs to be crossed if you truly want to transform your business model radically into a new type. We also illustrate that such changes need to be driven in a synchronized and balanced manner across all relevant business model transformation levers.

Endnotes

1   B W Wirtz, A Pistoia, S Ullrich and V Göttel (2016) Business models: Origin, developments and future research perspectives, *Long Range Planning*, **49**, pp 1–19.

2 B Demil, L Xavier, J Ricard and C Zott (2015) Introduction to the SEJ special issue on business models: Business models within the domain of strategic entrepreneurship, *Strategic Entrepreneurship Journal*, 9, pp 1–11.

3 Various authors contributed to today's better understanding of BM, for example: 1) *dimensions:* C Zott and R Amit (2007) Business model design and the performance of entrepreneurial firms, *Organization Science*, **18** (2), pp 181–99; 2) *types:* O Gassmann, K Frankenberger and M Csik (2014) *The Business Model Navigator*, FT Publishing, Harlow; C Linz and G Müller-Stewens (2012) Lösungsanbieterstrategien, *Zeitschrift für betriebswirtschaftliche Forschung (zfbf)*, **65** (12), pp 1–24; 3) *semantics:* A Osterwalder and Y Pigneur (2010) *Business Model Generation: A Handbook for visionaries, game changers, and challengers*, John Wiley & Sons, Hoboken, NJ; 4) *the design of (new) models:* C M Christensen (1997) *The Innovator's Dilemma: When new technologies cause great firms to fail*, Harvard Business School Press, Boston, MA; Osterwalder and Pigneur, *Business Model Generation*; and 5) *the performance of different models:* A Afuah (2004) *Business Models: A strategic management approach*, Irwin/McGraw-Hill, New York. They have also contributed by applying the BM concept to the corporate level versus the business level: R A Burgelman and Y L Doz (2001) The power of strategic integration, *Sloan Management Review*, **42** (3), pp 28–38; H Chesbrough and R Rosenbloom (2002) The role of the business model in capturing value from innovation: Evidence from Xerox Corporation's technology spin-off companies, *Industrial and Corporate Change*, **11** (3), pp 529–55; G Müller-Stewens and M Brauer (2009) *Corporate Strategy and Governance*, Schäffer-Poeschel Verlag, Stuttgart.

4 G Müller-Stewens and C Lechner (2016) *Strategisches Management*, Schäffer-Poeschel Verlag, Stuttgart. See also M W Johnson, M C Christenson and H Kagermann (2008) Reinventing your business model, *Harvard Business Review*, **86** (12), pp 59–67.

5 K J Boudreau and L B Jeppesen (2015) Unpaid crowd complementors: The platform network effect mirage, *Strategic Management Journal*, **36**, pp 1761–77.

6 B Demil, L Xavier, J Ricard and C Zott (2015) Introduction to the SEJ special issue on business models: Business models within the domain of strategic entrepreneurship, *Strategic Entrepreneurship Journal*, 9, pp 1–11.

7 G Hamel (1996) Strategy as revolution, *Harvard Business Review*, **74** (4), pp 69–82.

8 W C Kim and R Mauborgne (2005) *Blue Ocean Strategy: How to create uncontested market space and make the competition irrelevant*, Harvard Business School Press, Boston, MA.

9 A Osterwalder and Y Pigneur (2010) *Business Model Generation: A handbook for visionaries, game changers, and challengers*, John Wiley & Sons, Hoboken, NJ.

10 E Ries (2011) *The Lean Start-Up: How constant innovation creates radically successful businesses*, Portfolio Penguin, London.

11 The term 'exponential organization' comes from S Ismail, I Malone and Y Geest (2014) *Exponential Organizations: Why new organizations are ten times better, faster, cheaper than yours*, Diversion Books, New York.

12 O Gassmann, K Frankenberger and M Csik (2014) *The Business Model Navigator*, FT Publishing, Harlow.

13 F M Santos and K M Eisenhardt (2009) Constructing markets and shaping boundaries: Entrepreneurial power in nascent fields, *Academy of Management Journal*, **52** (4), pp 643–71. They developed a typology of BM adjustments in terms of reconfiguring value networks, namely relinking, repartitioning, relocating and reactivating. Or see M Sosna, R N Trevinyo-Rodríguez and S R Velamuri (2010) Business model innovation through trial-and-error learning: The Naturhouse case, *Long Range Planning*, **43** (2/3), pp 383–407. Their case study of a Spanish food retailer analyses the BM transformation process and distinguishes four phases: 1) the initial BM design and test; 2) the BM development (as a trial-and-error learning process); 3) scaling up with a suitable BM; and 4) sustained growth. However, no research has yet investigated the transformation path of transforming one business model type into another.

14 A G Pateli and G M Giaglis (2004) A research framework for analysing eBusiness models, *European Journal of Information Systems*, **13** (9), pp 302–14.

15 D J Teece, G Pisano and A Shuen (1997) Dynamic capabilities and strategic management, *Strategic Management Journal*, **18** (7), pp 509–33; D J Teece (2010) Business models, business strategy and innovation, *Long Range Planning*, **43**, pp 172–94.

PART TWO
How to lead a radical shift of your business model

If a business model is under pressure, a firm has three options: first, it can exit the business (by closing or divesting); second, it can try to optimize and innovate the current business model in order to bring it closer to its customers' needs and requirements; third, it can start searching seriously for a better-suited type of business model. From a management point of view, option three is probably the most challenging but also the most promising. Migrating from one business model type to a more effective one in order to defend or regain a company's competitive edge means managing a deep strategic renewal process that includes a shift in the firm's dominant logic and cognitive mindset.

We refer to business model transformations as *crossings*, a term that emphasizes the fact that, in times of discontinuous changes in markets and industries, it often may not be enough just to improve or innovate a firm's current business model in an incremental way. Instead, leaders need the courage to cross the line to a radically new business model. But there are often two particular forces that impede the switch to another business model type: the established business model's exit barriers and the new model's substantial entry barriers. As a result, the risk of failure is quite high, but sometimes there is no other option to safeguard a firm's long-term viability. To mitigate the risk of failure, such transformations have to be prepared very carefully with respect to their specific managerial challenges.

Figure II.1 shows the basic framework of this book: the *business transformation board*. Based on the typology introduced earlier, we explain the different options leaders have who want to shift their business model in a radical way, by crossing one or even both of the following demarcations:

- *Business model equator:* Passing the BM equator implies a change in the degree of inclusiveness. North of the equator, we find business models based on comprehensive and highly integrated transactions that generate a continuous stream of cash flow. Conversely, south of the equator, business models rely mainly on discrete, stand-alone transactions.

- *Business model meridian:* Passing the BM meridian requires changes in the degree of customization. East of the meridian, business models are based on customer-individual offerings, while west of the meridian they rely on standardized mass offerings (including mass customization).

The BM equator and the BM meridian can both be crossed in two directions: from south to north and from north to south (from non-inclusive to inclusive, and vice versa), as well as from west to east and from east to west (from non-customized to customized, and vice versa). Furthermore, we observed cases not only of single-dimensional transformations (ie across the BM equator *or* the BM meridian) but also of two-dimensional transformations (ie across the BM equator *and* the BM meridian). The latter can be done in a direct, diagonal way or in a stepwise process of two one-dimensional crossings.

The business transformation board is a tool that helps to navigate the fundamental change process from the currently applied business model type to another one. Once a BM crossing has been chosen, the leadership team needs to engage in the actual transformation process. We have observed that a successful radical transformation requires changes in *three domains*:

1 *Front end:* Changes to the customer-facing front end. This includes the value proposition of the business model with the offering to the customer, and all activities that a customer sees and experiences.

2 *Back end:* Changes to the organizational activities required to run the business, but that the customer does not see. This includes changes in the critical resources (like capabilities or technologies).

3 *Monetization mechanics:* Changes to the way in which a company creates its revenue streams, and how it fosters profitability.

Changes in these three domains do not necessarily occur all at the same time. We have observed cases where firms began their business model transformation by changing only one or two of these domains. However, the radical transformation process should not end in such an unbalanced situation, as front end, back end and monetization mechanics are strongly interdependent. *If a firm wants to capture the full potential of a new business*

Figure II.1 The business transformation board

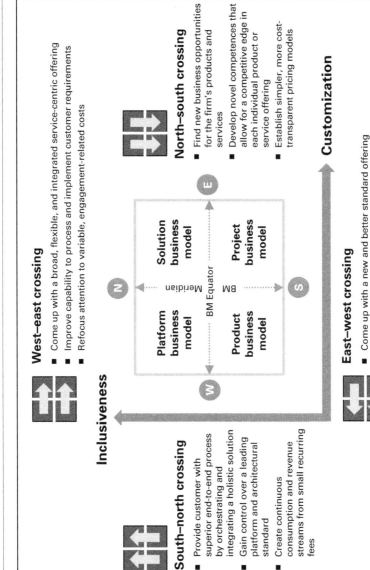

West–east crossing
- Come up with a broad, flexible, and integrated service-centric offering
- Improve capability to process and implement customer requirements
- Refocus attention to variable, engagement-related costs

North–south crossing
- Find new business opportunities for the firm's products and services
- Develop novel competences that allow for a competitive edge in each individual product or service offering
- Establish simpler, more cost-transparent pricing models

South–north crossing
- Provide customer with superior end-to-end process by orchestrating and integrating a holistic solution
- Gain control over a leading platform and architectural standard
- Create continuous consumption and revenue streams from small recurring fees

East–west crossing
- Come up with a new and better standard offering
- Transform services and content into reusable elements
- Actively manage the fixed costs

Inclusiveness

Customization

Platform business model

Solution business model

Product business model

Project business model

BM Meridian

BM Equator

N

E

S

W

model, it usually needs to cross the meridian or the equator on the front end and to align the two other domains to the new front end. Sometimes front-end changes are enabled or triggered by changes of the back end (eg new technologies) or by changes of the monetization mechanics (eg new subscription-based contracts with customers).

Additionally, within each of these domains, we may observe a gradual transformation, because many organizational systems and processes cannot be radically transformed at once and have to evolve over time. Thus, it is sometimes difficult to assess at which point a firm has actually crossed the BM equator or the BM meridian. In order to support managers with tracking progress and making sure that the transformation continues in the right direction, in Chapter 11 we introduce *business model profiles* that make it possible to assess the degree of inclusiveness and customization in a firm's front end, back end and monetization mechanics. In Chapters 4 to 6, we describe the one-dimensional crossings in detail and then discuss possible diagonal crossings across both dimensions.

Shifting the level of inclusiveness

04

Crossing the BM equator from non-inclusive to inclusive business models, or vice versa, requires a transformation of the different value drivers in each of the three transformational domains (see Table 4.1). Front-end adaptation includes how the offering is structured, how consumption happens and how the vendor is related to its customers. For back-end transformation, firms have to adapt the competences and linkages (eg partnerships) required to run the business model. Last but not least, the monetization mechanics require a shift in the frequency of the revenues, the time horizon of the total cost coverage, and the pricing model.

Transforming to more inclusive business models

When Apple launched the iPod in 2001, most people thought it was just another MP3 player, although a cool one, with the promise to store more than 1,000 songs on a pocket-sized device. Few people recognized that Apple had already started its transformation from a product category to a platform company. The iPod's value proposition could in fact only be achieved in combination with the iTunes platform, which makes it possible to manage music and buy it legally online while at the same time seamlessly integrating all music content. It is worth noticing that, when incumbent firms like Sony started to strike back against the iPod with their own product launches, they actually attacked Apple in the 'wrong' business model. They still perceived it as a product company, even though Steve Jobs's strategy was already geared toward platform plus ecosystem, as he stated in an interview in April 2003:

Table 4.1 Value drivers of north versus south BM transformations

Domains / Crossings	Front end	Back end	Monetization mechanics
NORTH — Comprehensive and integrative transactions	**Comprehensive and integrative value proposition** • Bundling of a critical mass of products and services to fulfil customer needs. • Frequent consumption. • Strategic, retention-oriented customer relations.	**Integrated (architecture)** • Leading proprietary or semi-open architecture. • Excellence in creating scope through horizontal network management. • Using network effects.	**Recurring fees** • Steady long-term revenues (eg subscription, SLA). • Steady long-term revenues (eg subscription, SLA). • Long-term cost coverage (profitable customer life cycle).
South–north crossing	*Provide superior end-to-end process by orchestrating and integrating a holistic solution.* *Offer superior customer experience.* *Establish a retention-oriented customer engagement approach*	*Gain control over a leading platform and shared architectural standard.* *Broaden firm's competence base (horizontal) and build up ecosystem of complementors.* *Drive more frequent innovations in the offering.*	*Create continuous consumption and revenue streams from smaller recurring fees.* *Build up an integrated pricing with subscription-based consumption models.* *Focus on profitable customer life cycles.*

North–south crossing

- Develop a convincing value proposition for stand-alone offerings.
- Find new business opportunities for the firm's products and services.
- Emphasize new customer acquisition.

- Develop novel competences that allow for a competitive edge in each individual product or service offering.
- Establish close interfaces with suppliers.

- Build short-term cash planning.
- Estimate cost coverage for product or service life cycle.
- Establish simpler, more cost-transparent pricing models.

SOUTH

Stand-alone transactions

Singular value proposition

- Having a very focused offer.
- Happening as a single, independent transaction.
- Transactional, temporary customer relation.

Stand-alone (architecture)

- Leading innovation and process competences.
- Excellence in optimizing efficiency through vertical supplier management.

One-off sales

- One-time revenues (eg allotment contracts).
- Short-term cost coverage (profitable transaction).
- Cost-transparent pricing.

> With the introduction of the new iTunes Music Store, we've now built the first
> real complete ecosystem for the digital music age... We've got a way to buy
> music online legally... We've got a way to manage music with the iTunes
> Jukebox... We've got a way to listen to music on the go with the iPod... So
> we've really got, from one end to another, a complete solution for digital music.[1]

Through its integrated and comprehensive offering, which consists of hardware, software, content and the platform, Apple was able to offer an end-to-end process for digital music, create a reason to stay in the Apple ecosystem ('lock-in') and make it hard for other firms to compete in the individual segments against Apple's integrated offering. As we know, the story continued with the iPad, the iPhone, the Apple TV, the Beats Electronics streaming service, the Apple Watch and so on – always integrated with the iTunes platform and its App Store as the central hub. The more content and the more personal devices this digital ecosystem comprises, the stronger the benefits of staying with Apple for the next purchase too.

Ride-sharing company Uber is currently disrupting the mobility industry. Uber orchestrates and aggregates many local and individual mobility service suppliers into an integrative offering and runs the transportation process end to end as conveniently as possible for its users. Such new entrants challenge the status quo in an established market – in this case the taxi industry. But can an established company also challenge the industry rules despite not having the greenfield advantage that all start-ups have, namely beginning from scratch without a legacy?

Daimler – as a traditional car manufacturer – is also worth a closer look. In 2008 the company launched its car2go car-sharing service. To cater to broader social change (ie the sharing economy), it decided to offer a flexible and environmentally sustainable car-sharing service. Following a one-off registration process, customers were able to hire the cars spontaneously in passing, or pre-book and use them for as long as desired. The service charged by the minute, with reduced hourly and daily rates. After usage, vehicles could be left at any public parking space within the city limits. The car2go platform became a big commercial success and is available in more than 30 cities in Europe and North America. Operations in China started in 2015. Nevertheless, Daimler realized that customers' needs are evolving further, toward integrated end-to-end mobility solutions that offer the best way to get from A to B, independently of whether a customer is willing or able to drive a car. Hence in July 2012 Daimler launched its Daimler Mobility Services AG with the moovel mobility services platform. The CEO of moovel declared: 'moovel's purpose is to provide people in cities with every possible mobility option. This will allow us to always offer the best way to get from A to B by using public transportation, taxis, limousines, rental cars, rental bikes, car-sharing, trains, long-distance buses, or flights. We invite everyone who can contribute to this purpose to join us.'[2] With the introduction of moovel, which integrates various mobility providers, facilitates their interactions and runs the mobility processes with superior user experiences at scale, Daimler transformed again, from a one-sided business model with car2go as an isolated offering to an open and more inclusive mobility platform business model. Daimler's moovel is currently acquiring a large number of complementors for its platform in order to offer customers ever more flexible point-to-point mobility. Further internationalization of the service beyond Germany and the EU is happening right now.

With Apple and Daimler, we have now seen companies shifting from a product BM to a platform BM by establishing themselves as operators of a new, integrated, end-to-end service that provides superior user experience with the ambition to set a new industry standard. The attractiveness of such a move is comprehensible: products produce more or less only a single revenue stream, while platforms can generate many.[3]

When companies move from a project BM to a solution BM, they want to offer customers not only individual products and services but more inclusive solutions combining multiple product and service components to address the client's broader problems and hence gain higher margins than in their traditional, more focused business. Take as an example Sociedad Ibérica de Construcciones Eléctricas, SA (SICE), a Spanish construction company that transformed itself into a solution provider for toll collection. To always provide the best customer solution, the company not only relies on its in-house offerings but also leverages superior offerings from other vendors. Its mission is 'providing added value services through the integration of a range of in-house and third-party technologies and systems, always with the aim of offering the best solution tailored to each customer'.[4] Based on its vast experience in construction projects, it entered the market for toll collection and works on all phases of a project, from design to operation. Bilfinger Berger, which develops, builds, maintains and operates facilities and structures for the industrial, energy and real estate sector and has more than 70,000 employees worldwide, took a similar path. It plans and builds real estate and additionally offers to run these buildings over their entire life cycles. Bilfinger Berger ensures, for example, that a refinery operates reliably, or it runs facility management for entire companies. Its solution BM combines two complementary characteristics, namely engineering competence and service mentality. In 2010, about 80 per cent of its sales came from services and only 20 per cent from construction; in 2014 its total revenue was €7.7 billion.

The transformation toward more inclusiveness was even more radical in the strategic transformation of the Siemens Group's Industry Division. Building on its historically strong project business acumen with regard to wind turbines, smart grid and building technologies, among others, Siemens launched the platform Siemens Cloud for Industry in March 2015 to run co-innovation projects with the customer on top. Siemens – together with its customers – builds customer-specific industry solutions for complex Internet of Things use cases on its platform. Klaus Helmrich, managing board member of Siemens AG, declared: 'The establishment of the new cloud platform will make a significant contribution to driving forward the digitalization of automation. Powerful services for analyzing data from industry are an important part of our digital enterprise strategy.'[5] In this respect, Siemens becomes a platform provider and at the same time operates in a project BM when it comes to building customer-individual industry solutions on top. With the ecosystem approach that also has an open standard for connectivity (OPC), it is possible for customers, third-party original equipment manufacturers, and application developers to build new solutions to optimize asset performance, energy and resource consumption, and maintenance services for machines and plant. A growing ecosystem of relevant complementors is driving up the number of value-adding offerings and hence the inclusiveness of the offering portfolio – and, with that, the gravity of the platform.

If a company aims to transform its business model from south to north, it needs to increase the degree of inclusiveness. This implies that the company moves from single, stand-alone transactions to more comprehensive, integrated transactions and has a more enduring customer relationship. To achieve this, the introduction of a shared foundation is needed, which architecturally integrates a comprehensive set of products and services from various stakeholders in the particular ecosystem. The customer is only willing to accept the resulting stickiness if the incremental benefit of the provided end-to-end process outperforms alternatives (eg through network effects, user experience, scope of functionality). The new process can be standardized or customer-specific.

The move *from a product BM to a platform BM* often implies that firms introduce additional services for new standardized processes on top of a digital platform to win new customers. This makes the portfolio of offerings more comprehensive and increases the innovation rate, especially when the platform provider also grants third parties the right to add complements and link them to the platform's customer base.

Similarly, the move *from a project BM to a solution BM* relies on the introduction of a shared foundation to integrate across various services and products, but here the goal is to engineer and mostly operate customer-individual processes. In this context, products function as an enabler for the process offered as a service. The firm needs to leverage its established customer relationships to introduce such a holistic solution, which solves a specific customer problem.

A successful south–north crossing in the business transformation board (see Figure II.1) requires: 1) *an adaptation of the customer-facing front end from a singular value proposition to a comprehensive and integrated value proposition*; 2) *a transformation of the organizational back end from standalone to integrating architecture by establishing a platform foundation and ecosystem*; and 3) *a shift in the monetization mechanics from one-off sales to recurring fees with SLA- or subscription-based payment schemes.*

Front-end adaptation: From singular to comprehensive value propositions by providing superior integrated end-to-end services

To change from a non-inclusive business model to an inclusive business model, a company needs to move beyond the established value proposition focused on a single product or service and – going forward – focus on *providing superior end-to-end processes as a service by orchestrating and integrating a holistic solution*. This holds true independently if the process is highly standardized and scalable, as exemplified by the Apple, Uber and moovel cases, or if it is customer-specific and often complex, as we have seen with SICE, Bilfinger Berger and Siemens, all of which provide individual solutions by means of last-mile projects with tight customer integration. We know that the incremental benefit of the provided end-to-end process must also outperform alternatives in the medium term to make customers accept stickiness in the vendor's offering.

The concept goes beyond the experience directly linked to the offering itself, as Nike+ demonstrates. Its platform leverages data from a sensor in the running shoe and hence allows athletes to track their performance statistics and improvement over time, as well as connect with fellow runners and share routes. Nike CEO Mark Parker declared in February 2012: 'NIKE+ allows us to connect the physical world of sport with the social elements of digital to create a better sport experience for every athlete. It's about much more than a shoe. It represents a shift for Nike.'[6]

Another key success factor for successful customer relations is determined by the *ability to offer a superior customer experience at every single customer touch point*. The upswing of multichannel marketing and commerce approaches, which help to secure a consistent brand experience during the client journey across all physical and online interaction channels, underpins the importance of superior experience.

When it comes to the sales approach, the firm needs to shift its attention from customers' single and immediate demands to their long-term or at least medium-term needs. This shift includes *applying a retention-oriented customer engagement approach* in which all front-end activities are focused on building and sustaining the customer's loyalty. Despite the rise of online channels, the importance of a direct sales force has not diminished. Even in a platform BM like software as a service (SaaS), a relatively high revenue proportion still comes from traditional sales. Instead of 'closing deals', it is all about 'opening deals', which means providing the advantage of continuing the relationship with the same vendor over a series of future transactions. When heading toward a platform BM, the focus should be on positioning the foundation first, followed by the sale of extensions and complements. When heading toward a solution BM, the firm needs to establish tight customer–vendor partnerships with a value-based, multi-year sales model. Often a shift in sales focus to new buying centres is also required. In the Xerox case, the buying centre changed from facility management, which purchased printers, to the CIO, who subscribes to high-value process management services. Viable instruments for a retention-oriented engagement approach are actively managing renewal rates when it comes to subscription-based platform businesses and continuously securing alignment with customers' goals. For example, Rolls-Royce's power-by-the-hour service aims to maximize planes' flight times, which aligns tightly with the airlines' strategic intent. In return, Rolls-Royce is more likely to accept pre-investments for customer specifications if medium-term revenues can be expected, for example via a multi-year contract.

Heading northward, the company's sales reporting and incentive systems also need to be aligned with each other. The metrics to track progress should centre on growth in successfully engaged customers in terms of both engagement and offering satisfaction. Instead of metrics like net new customers or quarterly sales quotas, the focus should be on the renewal rate or ultimately compound growth rate, namely new customer acquisition rate minus churn rate.[7] Incentives should be aligned and even cross-linked across all customer-facing teams to serve the same overarching intent: the enduring customer relationship. It is important to ensure that people really understand how the company makes money and which levers and behaviours will drive its margin. At Netflix, in the early years, employees used to focus too heavily on subscriber growth, without much awareness that the expenses often ran ahead of it. Hence, the company had to invest in buying DVDs, installing distribution centres and ordering original programming, all before collecting any money at all from new subscribers. Employees needed to learn that, even though revenue was growing, managing costs and efficiency really matters. And, if the company has a bonus plan, people have to understand the strategy behind the bonus plan exactly, as well as what they should be doing to increase their bonus.[8]

In summary, in the front end a south–north transformation requires new sales team capabilities (from offering features or functions to processing expertise), new goals and incentive systems (from quarterly quotas to strategically aligned relationships) and, last but not least, a new overall culture (from closing deals/'hunting' to opening deals/'farming').

Back-end transformation: From self-contained value creation to network integration by establishing a platform foundation and ecosystem

When changing from a non-inclusive to an inclusive business model, a company's competitive advantage is no longer rooted only in its ability to innovate and optimize its offerings. The firm needs to *establish and gain control over a leading platform that acts as a shared foundation integrating architecturally diverse offerings in order to provide a seamless end-to-end process*.[9] In other words, the company's core competence shifts from creating its own outcomes (vertically integrated), in the form of products or projects, to orchestrating and assembling offerings across a network of suppliers to provide integrated end-to-end processes (horizontally integrated). If it is to earn such an orchestrator role, the customer must perceive the platform provider's contribution to the average market requirements as relevant; this contribution should include a strategic part of the end-to-end solution. The design of this integrating architectural foundation needs to fit the specific requirements of the business model to reach transactional inclusiveness. With the transformation goal of being a platform provider for standardized processes that seeks scalability triggered by network effects, the foundation must be geared toward heavy offering integration and massive user orchestration, be it vendors, buyers or complementors. If the firm is heading toward being an individual solution provider for customer-specific processes, the foundation first and foremost needs to secure the integrity of the customer solution, which means that all parts work hand in hand and solve the customer problem holistically. Therefore, in the tailored approach, a platform is needed that also allows building – on a project basis – customer-specific solutions on top, as we have seen in the example of Siemens Industry. In any case, the firm has to decide whether to establish a proprietary or (semi-)open architecture standard. Proprietary standards are only a viable option for companies that have the competences and resources to create a de facto standard on their own. Alternatively, a group of companies can join forces to develop a common standard or leverage an existing (semi-)open standard. Google's open Android operating system for mobile phones serves as an example. Android has become a dominant design in the market because it signifies major progress over the previous situation in which every mobile phone producer had to develop its own operating system and applications. It stands in contrast to Apple's proprietary approach, which includes iOS, OS X, tvOS and so on. Either way – going for an open or a proprietary standard – companies heading northward must reach and maintain a certain level of influence over the architecture to ensure the business model's financial sustainability. Consequently, this can even lead to situations in which firms promote an architectural standard that they can control instead of joining an open standard as just another consortium member.

Heading northward requires a company to *broaden its competence base* into new and complementing areas, be it via its own R&D activities or by recruiting experts from other industries or acquiring companies, for example Apple's acquisition of Beats International to enter the music and video streaming services market. The more complex the customers' requirements, the more difficult it becomes to provide all these offerings with a single company's limited resources and capabilities. In this case, firms should *build up an ecosystem of partners* that can complement the portfolio (eg via add-ons or services) and provide customers with a comprehensive offering integrated through the common architectural standard. In order to grow the partner ecosystem, firms need to introduce professional management to win and retain complementors, foster cooperation with and among the partners (eg co-innovation) and potentially expand the cooperative profit-sharing model.[10] All these aspects require effective and efficient processes, systems and structures, including processes for quickly getting partners on-board. On the one hand, partnerships can become the basis for additional revenue streams, for example when partners can be charged for applying the architectural standard. On the other hand, the situation should be avoided where complementors become too powerful and begin absorbing substantial margin potential from the ecosystem. Building 'gravity' around a platform, which means attracting others to build their offerings or even businesses on top of a platform, requires firms to expose to others what they can do best and to add the highest value. Key advantages of having gravity through a strong partner ecosystem include economies of scale based on network effects, which make platform decisions sticky. This also leads to a major challenge when transforming north toward platform-based 'ecosystem' innovation, namely the increasing complexity, as the number of collaboration interfaces with other suppliers and partners can grow exponentially, and hence the effort to manage the ecosystem.

LEGIC, part of the Swiss-based Kaba Group, is a provider of identification technology, for example access control to open and lock doors. The company transformed its business model from a product BM with its key-and-lock-type offering (smartcards and lock readers) into a platform BM for mobile ID solutions (smartphones, lock readers), plus the trusted service platform for smartphone authentication (via credentials), and a kit for developing customer-specific smartphone apps. As a result, a hotel can offer 'mobile-access-no-need-to-wait' service via its own hotel app, and guests can skip the check-in at the front desk and head directly to their room. For future bookings, the app helps the hotel cut out online booking agents and drive margin improvements via direct bookings. The key to platform success was LEGIC's ecosystem of mobile network operators, which provides secure access to the users' SIM cards to manage the credentials.

Most companies transforming from south to north sooner or later also start to offer the management of the integrated end-to-end process. The provider takes over the contracting of the operations and the responsibility for the process from the customer, who outsources it. This means a radical shift from internal process management – in other words, managing one's own operations and processes – toward managing a certain part of the customer's operations and processes on its behalf. We have seen that Xerox runs document-intensive processes, Bilfinger Berger entire facilities, Amazon Web Services elastic cloud infrastructures, and moovel end-to-end mobility processes for their customers, which requires an in-depth understanding of the customers' use case and end-to-end process. When establishing such an operation's back end from scratch, this implies a major undertaking because it requires new skills and competences and a major investment. As the (in-sourcing) operator is also in charge of maintenance, support and new functionality, a firm moving into operations needs to build the required capabilities in-house, acquire companies or partner with third-party providers (eg specific application management competences as cloud provider, which differ by application type). Beyond the offering's core functionality, context factors like service availability, disaster recovery and security now also need to be established. As the legal responsibility for the design, suitability and performance of the outcomes will be with the contractor, the risk moves from the client to the provider, and therefore professional risk management has to be built up, or the existing risk management has to be adjusted to handle risks of a different magnitude. Especially when delivering against a service level agreement (SLA), firms furthermore need to implement measuring and analytical capabilities, which are appropriate to gain performance transparency and to proactively respond to changes that could affect their service level and hence impact their customers' success. Customers expect the service to be delivered by a single contact to the agreed quality. When parts of the delivery chain are subcontracted to third-party providers, an even tighter control system should be put in place, because the contractual obligation remains fully with the platform or solution provider, for example when partners operate data centres but the SLA remains with the platform provider. When taking on the management of the integrated end-to-end process – in other words the operations and providing a service to the customer as well – the firm should use the opportunity to *drive more frequent innovations in the offering* and improve operations. Agile approaches allow the release of new offering versions much more quickly than ever before by shortening learning cycles with iterative customer feedback.[11] New integrative approaches help overcome functional silos and foster tight collaboration between product management, development, quality assurance and operations for a better customer experience and faster time to market.

Monetization mechanics shift: From one-off sales to recurring fees by establishing SLA- and subscription-based payment schemes

When moving northward, a firm has to change gear from a one-off sales approach to recurring revenue streams over a series of transactions. This requires *creating a continuous consumption and revenue stream* and potentially also the introduction of service level agreements (eg Adobe software in the form of service uptime, Liebherr Mining in the form of operating hours, Rolls-Royce plc in the form of fixed engine maintenance cost over an extended period of time, called 'power by the hour'). As discussed before, new controlling, reporting and incentive systems need to be established to reflect the focus on building and sustaining the customer's loyalty, for example measuring and incentivizing growth in successfully engaged customers as compound growth rate. The firm's billing function also needs to be technically ready to manage the high volume, which stems from a series of business transactions over time. Last but not least, new pricing models are required to better support service consumption over time, as well as a series of transactions.

When moving northward, there is a need to adapt pricing models. The pricing of both the product and the project BM can be described as relatively transparent for its core offering and is often broken down even further into prices for individual components. By contrast, the platform and solution BM, with their more comprehensive and integrative offerings, require a more *integrated pricing model*. As the offering is mainly consumed as a comprehensive service, price points of the underlying offering components are not revealed. These inclusive models often rely on a single overall price that includes the entire stream of consumption, or the pricing is determined on a per-use basis, which makes the solution or service price difficult to compare with competitive offerings. Therefore, cross-subsidization is not externally visible, for example when the cash flow from complements, extensions and upgrades covers the platform's development costs.

To transform from a one-off sales approach to a recurring revenue model, firms can implement *subscription-based payment schemes*. In contrast to the usage-independent monetization models with upfront cost, often ongoing support fees and potentially related infrastructure investments, the subscription-based models convert fixed cost into variable cost for the customer; hence all costs for providing the offering are on the vendor side. By paying the subscription fee, the customer is granted access to the product or service for a specified period of time or for a series of performances – most commonly on a monthly or an annual basis. Thus a one-time sale of an offering becomes a recurring sale. The renewal of a subscription may be periodic and could also be activated automatically. If customers' usage data are available, pricing can also be based on usage parameters, for example charging per transaction, event and so on. As alluded to in Chapter 3 with the Skype example, the freemium model provides services or content in limited form free, while access to premium features is restricted to paying subscribers only. When the price is linked to the effective consumption of the service level ('pay-as-you-go'), there can be predictable revenue flows and a more manageable expense stream, which can make a company more robust and able to overcome short-term economic periods of drought.

The LEGIC case demonstrated that identifying the right monetization model for the firm's platform BM was not an easy task, because at the beginning it was fairly unclear who was paying for what and in what fashion. When it comes to such pricing decisions, it is good to know which payment schemes are already known und understood to 'build bridges' (analogies) to the new monetization model. LEGIC worked closely with a number of pilot customers, including the Cromwell hotel in Las Vegas, and discovered that the smartcard pricing should be based on traditional consumption logic (the item) and that the installed base of door locks should be priced on an annual subscription basis (per lock per year). As we have seen, there is still an opportunity to shape customers' expectations and their cognitive anchors when entering the market early.

From a bottom-line perspective too, a shift to north can have a major impact, especially when the operations and management of the customer process are taken over. Whereas the outsourcing customer converts fixed costs into variable costs, the provider – operating the integrated end-to-end process on the client's behalf – has to make substantial infrastructure investments (eg data centres as a cloud provider). To meet margin targets, the total cost of operations (TCO) must be actively managed, because the majority of the costs accrue in the later phases of the asset's life cycle. Therefore, the *focus has to be on profitable customer life cycles.*

As we have seen, SAP is currently going through the biggest transformation in the company's history – moving from the traditional perpetual-licence model for on-premises software to the subscription model for cloud computing.[12] The key challenge is that revenues, earnings and stock price are almost certain to drop in such a transition from an on-premises software to a cloud business model, because at the beginning the subscriptions' smaller revenue increments are not sufficient to cover the corresponding cost of operations and sales. To bring the cloud business into the profit zone, a critical mass of the installed base must opt for the cloud subscription model. Based on its own software development plus major acquisitions of specialized cloud companies like Aribe, SuccessFactors and Concur, a broad cloud portfolio of SaaS and platform as a service offering (PaasS) drove a substantial shift in the company's profit and loss mechanics. Therefore when in the third quarter of 2015 SAP reported that cloud subscription revenue had soared 90 per cent to €600 million, and revenue for on-premises software licences was still growing by 4 per cent to about €1 billion, the stock markets' reaction was positive surprise.

Summary

The major challenge in a south–north crossing is the development of a highly inclusive offering where customers truly benefit. This will only be possible if we are able to build up and lead an ecosystem of complementors, and if we have control over a leading platform and architecture. This will not be easy, specifically with regard to manufacturers. Many manufacturers still think that they can offer all the necessary services to serve the customer holistically. But there is a substantial risk of overestimating themselves. Hence, proprietary thinking needs to be overcome and replaced by an open ecosystem mindset. In some cases, even cooperations with direct competitors are required to keep control over their share of the profit pool. An example is the acquisition of Nokia's digital maps business Here by carmakers Audi, BMW and Daimler. Another challenge will be that, while in the past manufacturers were used to steering a number of suppliers, waiting for new orders in a vertical relationship, they now have to keep a network of partners at eye level happy. The monetization of the business model has to be created by revenue streams from smaller, long-term recurring fees with subscription-based payment schemes. But the question will be whether the company has sufficient liquidity to overcome the period when the one-off sales fall away and the recurring fees have not yet taken off. As for the design of usage-based pricing schemes, the company has to have access to historical customer usage data.

Transforming to more focused business models

In the 1990s, auditing firms like Arthur Andersen, Deloitte & Touche, Ernst & Young, KPMG, Price Waterhouse and Coopers & Lybrand (called the 'Big Six') wanted to transform into 'solution providers' for their clients. The idea was to offer 'one-stop shopping'. The argument was that they could give better advice if they had a more complete picture of their clients. They undertook their transformation by diversifying either internally or externally into, for example, tax, legal and strategy consulting, as well as IT and financial services, and by installing a one-face-to-the-customer relationship that one of the partners managed. But doubts arose regarding whether this was in line with auditors' legally determined independence. How 'independent' was such an auditing firm if so much of its total revenue came from a single client? And could clients really trust the 'Chinese walls' between the service lines? After the Enron scandal, legislation was changed in order no longer to allow auditors to offer their clients advisory services. Arthur Andersen even collapsed in 2002 because of its involvement in the case. At the turn of the century, the Big Six had to revert to a project BM and refocus on the auditing business. Newly founded companies like Accenture and BearingPoint were spin-offs from Arthur Andersen and KPMG, which had divested their consulting businesses. Later companies, like the merged PricewaterhouseCoopers (PwC), started to re-diversify their service offering – obviously now tolerated by the regulator.

But why should a company ever decide to decrease the customers' dependency and move toward more loosely coupled customer relationships without such legal pressure as a driving force? Another possible reason for firms choosing such a path and succeeding in the transformation relates to the increased competition between the architectural standards, which makes it difficult to attract customers (and therefore the necessary traffic) to a platform. A firm may therefore benefit from refocusing on its individual offerings. An example we have seen is T-Mobile USA, which decided to stop the common practice of selling bundles of mobile phones and long-term communication service contracts as an inclusive telecom solution. Customers now pay the regular market price for their phones but are in turn offered far more attractive conditions for their usage. The market celebrated this move of unbundling, as it led to telecommunication services' pricing being much more transparent and ended the usual cross-subsidization between hardware and service.

In the detailed Netflix case study, competitive pressure was another reason for its latest business model transformation. The company runs a clear platform BM of subscription-based media services, but more and more competitors launched similar streaming services. The question was how to differentiate Netflix from the new competition. The answer was to develop proprietary content. At the beginning, this content is made available exclusively to the company's subscribers. Later the new content is licensed to other sales channels. This means that one foot stepped (back) into a product BM.

Alternatively, it might be not only the competition but also the customers themselves who initiate a move from north to south. We found examples of customers developing their own bundling activities. For example, for a long time the travel industry relied on its often proprietary booking systems. Today, travellers demand and gain access to hotel, airline, train, activity and other booking systems that allow them to compile holiday packages themselves. Travel agencies suffer greatly from these developments and need to refocus on developing a unique selling proposition with single services or offerings.

Finally, moving away from an architecture-based business model can become necessary if a business risk exceeds a certain threshold. Companies applying a solution BM are often liable for all offerings: their own as well as those of their partners. With increasing complexity, the related risk and the costs of building reliable architectures may become so extensive that the ecosystem is no longer manageable at an acceptable risk level.

No matter what the reasons for a north–south transformation, a company undertaking it will have an 'unfair' advantage over the new competitors applying a product or a project BM. This advantage is based on the previous experience with a comprehensive offering that allows a company to identify the most attractive product or service components that fit the company's DNA best. This knowledge is much harder to obtain without prior experience in a platform or solution BM.[13] However, such a north–south transformation is also impeded by strong exit barriers. These include long-term legal and moral obligations, which can lead to litigation issues and loss of reputation because of their interlacement with customers and business partners.

A successful north–south crossing on the business transformation board (see Figure II.1) requires: 1) *an adaptation of the front end from a comprehensive and integrated to a singular value proposition*; 2) *a transformation from an integrative architecture to a stand-alone back end*; and 3) *a shift in the monetization mechanics from recurring fees to one-off sales.*

Front-end adaptation: From a comprehensive and integrated to a singular value proposition

If a company decides that a move toward a less inclusive business model is beneficial, it needs to refocus on each individual offering, and to this end it has to *develop a convincing value proposition for unique, stand-alone products or self-contained projects* with superior methodologies. The entire communication with the customer has to change to explaining and ultimately selling distinctive product or service features. Some firms, like T-Mobile, have even used the unbundling of their offering as a means to differentiate themselves from their competitors. Netflix does it by producing outstanding content with the best actors and directors, and it receives many awards. The political drama *House of Cards* is an example of this. The user data that the company has from its millions of subscribers give it the information it needs for the right investment target.

Following on from the above, the company has to adopt a consumption model based on single, independent transactions when moving southward. This puts additional strain on the company to *find new target groups and business opportunities for its own products and services* to keep the transaction flow running. Netflix did it by selling content like *House of Cards* through many other sales channels, including free TV (ProSiebenSat.1

Media) and pay TV (Sky Atlantic HD) or by selling the content as a DVD or Blu-ray disc or offering only the soundtrack as a stand-alone product. Company leaders' experience of the platform or solution BM might help them identify and tackle the most promising segments of the profit pool.

Moving from integrated to single transactions requires fewer contractual and moral obligations but also a broader, new business transaction funnel. In a product or a project BM, the period after the transaction is as important as the one before, as there is a substantial risk that customers will switch vendors once a transaction has been completed ('one-offs'). Additionally, the life cycle of products or services (dominating a product or a project BM) is on average shorter than the life cycle of the architecture (dominating a platform or solution BM). Consequently, a firm has to *emphasize new customer acquisition* while still fostering transactions with existing customers. Given that the company has close relationships with its customers before the transformation, it might achieve this far more easily than its competitors.

Back-end transformation: From an integrative architecture to a stand-alone back end

Moving from north to south means moving from running a holistically integrated system based on a leading architecture toward managing a portfolio of independent products or services that offer clear competitive advantages. At the same time, disengaging from the platform dependencies and service level agreements can lessen the business risk. A transformation from a solution BM to a project BM, for example, is a move to deliver single customer-individual projects that still have project management complexity but no predominant architecture risk. Accordingly, the company has to develop novel, often functional, *competences that allow for a competitive edge in each individual product or service offering* while exercising its abilities to integrate and manage complexity. In many cases, the data and information collected in a platform or solution BM make it possible to identify the competences that are most valuable to the customers and to develop them more thoroughly as part of the business model transformation. The challenge for Netflix was to get in touch with the most established actors, producers, screenwriters and composers and to convince them to invest their time and efforts in a television series instead of a new Hollywood movie. Completely new competences were required to orchestrate these people as reliable 'suppliers' to such a relatively long-lasting project.

In other words, a north–south transformation also requires a careful reassessment of the linkages to other companies. The company needs to switch from a horizontal system of value creation with eye-level partners to vertical supplier management. Collaborations with complementors thus need to be significantly reduced. However, the company's original, central role in a network may allow it to identify the areas that provide the highest level of value appropriation. At the same time, southern business models need the vertical optimization of the complete value chain and thus require firms to *establish close interfaces with suppliers*. All collaborative processes need to be refocused on improving effectiveness and efficiency.

Monetization mechanics shift: From recurring fees to one-off sales

Payments in non-inclusive business models are much less frequent. *Accordingly, cash planning needs to become more short-term.* It is often based on one-off big-ticket sales and driven by quarterly quotas. Moving southward means that each transaction has to cover all related costs. This requires a revision of the controlling and measurement systems and processes from a focus on integrated businesses to a focus on isolated offerings. Therefore, it is necessary to *estimate what costs occur over a product's or a service's life cycle* and ensure sufficient margins. Netflix invested about $100 million just in the production of two seasons of *House of Cards*, consisting of 26 episodes. The only chance to make such a huge investment profitable is if you already have a very strong customer base and furthermore if you are able to get access to additional sales channels. That is what the company did, as we mentioned before.

By moving southward, a firm might reduce the cost of sales, as complex negotiations for long-term (service level) agreements are no longer required. This should also be linked to the *development of simpler, more cost-transparent pricing models*. In platform or solution BMs, we often observe mixed calculations that are not really transparent to the customer. Conversely, a product BM's prices are fully transparent and easily comparable with those of competitors. Even though a project BM's pricing can also be quite complex, projects still have defined start and end points and a clearly defined scope (eg number of consulting person days), which creates a certain level of transparency for the customer.

Summary

The major challenge in a north–south crossing is finding new business opportunities for the firm's products and services that will provide the company with a lasting competitive edge. But the question will be whether the company is really willing to leave the architecture or platform behind as its legacy, and whether it can live with the related sunk costs. Finally, the company has to ensure that is has sufficient cash reserves to deal with the initial declines in revenues because of the switch to simpler, more cost-transparent pricing models per offering.

Endnotes

1 See http://technologizer.com/2011/12/07/steve-jobs-on-the-itunes-music-store-the-unpublished-interview/.

2 M Hecking (2012) Wir wollen das Amazon der Mobilität werden, *Manager Magazin*, 26 September.

3 F Zhu and N Furr (2016) Products to platforms: Making the leap, *Harvard Business Review*, **94** (4), pp 72–78.

4 See http://www.sice.com/en/about-sice/corporate-information.

5 See http://www.siemens.com/press/pool/de/pressemitteilungen/2015/digitalfactory/PR2015030152DFEN.pdf.

6 See http://www.itweb.co.za/index.php?option=com_content&view=article&id=51891.

7 Churn rate = fraction of customers in any period who fail to remain engaged with the company's offering.

8 P McCord (2014) How Netflix reinvented HR, *Harvard Business Review*, January–February, pp 71–76.

9 The high level of integration ensures the functional integrity of the total offering by ensuring that everything fits together, interoperates and forms an integrated whole.

10 M Iansiti and R Levien (2004) Strategy as ecology, *Harvard Business Review*, March, pp 68–78.

11 Agile approaches include design thinking with its iterative feedback cycles, agile development approaches such as SCRUM and KANBAN, and the lean-start-up methodology with its learn–build–measure loops.

12 See http://diginomica.com/2014/09/15/luka-mucic-saps-cfo-talks-cloud-business-model/#.VjSxKE2FPIU.

13 For example, on the Amazon marketplace third-party sellers can offer their goods, but what happens if the platform owners 'essentially run the platform as a lab, letting people innovate and compete against one another, and then cherry-pick the best products for themselves and capture the value'? See F Zhu and Q Liu (2015) When platforms attack, *Harvard Business Review*, **93** (10), pp 30–31.

Shifting the level of customization

05

Crossing the BM meridian from non-customized to customized business models, or vice versa, requires transformations in a firm's front end, back end and monetization mechanics. In contrast to Chapter 4, where crossing the BM equator has been discussed, the value drivers here are different (see Table 5.1). First, in respect of front-end adaptation, these include the specifications, unique selling propositions and scope of the sales channels. Second, regarding the back-end transformation, firms have to adapt the production and development approaches required to run the business model. Finally, the monetization mechanics require a shift in the pricing and in the way margins are obtained.

Transforming to more customized business models

FUNDES used to be a very successful non-profit organization that offered standardized support and education to small South American companies in order to help them integrate their products into the supply chain of large multinationals. The firm relied on donations, especially from one particular donor. When this donor decided to withdraw, FUNDES had to look for new ways to finance its social mission of improving the perspectives for these small entrepreneurs. It had to shift its business focus to the large multinationals, which had sufficient money but were not interested in the standardized services that FUNDES had previously offered. While they saw the potential to create value for themselves and for the small firms, they asked for highly individual support to manage their supply chains.

Table 5.1 Value drivers of west versus east business model transformations

Crossings / Domains	WEST Standardized offering	West–east crossing	East–west crossing	EAST Individualized offering
Front end	**Standardized value proposition** • Limited range of product-centric offering specifications. • Features or cost advantage as USP. • Multiple sales channels.	• Come up with a broad, flexible and integrated service-centric offering. • Improve ability to adopt hybrid offering to individual needs. • Install direct access and dialogue with the customers.	• Come up with a new and better standard offering. • Implement a low-touch, scalable sales approach. • Develop a broad range of complementary offline and online sales channels.	**Individual value proposition** • Broad and flexible service-centric offering specifications. • Adaptability to customer needs as USP. • Focused sales channel.

Back end

Scalable production structure
- Scalability of production and realization processes.
- Excellence in standardizing and packaging modular components.

- Adapt production to customer needs by making it more flexible.
- Improve capability to process and implement customer requirements.

- Replace human resources with machines.
- Transform services and content into reusable elements.
- Develop a knowledge management system and a culture of knowledge sharing.

Flexible service structure
- Adaptability of production and realization processes.
- Excellence in processing and implementing customer requirements.

Monetization mechanics

Cost-driven pricing
- Competition-based target pricing.
- Margins driven by economies of scale and market power effects.

- Move to a pricing model, where the price reflects the customers' willingness to pay for customization.
- Refocus attention from fixed to variable, engagement-related costs.

- Identify a competitive price.
- Actively manage the fixed costs.

Demand-driven pricing
- Price represents customers' willingness to pay.
- Margin driven by variable cost coverage.

Generally, by crossing the meridian from west to east, a firm wants or has to enter market segments that do not allow for standardized, large-scale offerings. The customers in these market segments demand individualized products or services and are willing to pay for them. Even sophisticated mass customization strategies cannot fulfil the specific needs of these customer groups. From a company perspective, it is also important that there is a wide variety of different customer use cases securing a sufficient market size.

In many cases, increases in customization are accompanied by increasing the service component. Accordingly, they often imply a transformation from 'services around product core' to 'products around service core'.[1] This provides continuous revenue streams, requires fewer investments in assets and has higher margins. Involvement in operational services often opens doors to future orders (spare parts, upgrades, improved product designs, etc). It is important to ensure that the customer offering comprises the right mix and an effective interplay of products and services. In such *hybrids*, services make it possible to customize offerings in a flexible way, within a shorter time-frame and for an even closer link with the customer. In many cases, the outcome is the result of a co-creation process where the customer is highly engaged in developing the project or solution.

The challenge with customization is to find the right balance between increasing the customer specificity and flexibility while simultaneously limiting adaptation costs. For instance, customization usually leads to a strong increase in labour costs relative to the total costs. On the offering side, this balance can usually be achieved via a certain degree of modularization accompanied by individualizing services. However, the contradictory forces of a front-end pull for customization and a back-end push for standardization have to be managed carefully. To achieve effectiveness and efficiency in engagement with the customer, the engagement-related costs should be monitored very closely. This puts particular strain on the project teams, which need to have the ability to handle statements of work, change requests and claims professionally.

Transforming away from scale toward smaller, more individualized markets may be a defensive strategy, for example when competition in the mass market increases and the margins decrease, but it can also be promising as an offensive strategy when firms identify the emergence of an uncovered segment of potential clients who are looking for a unique and sophisticated offering. Particularly for transformations from a platform BM to a solution BM, such a proactive move has to be taken early enough, because late entrants in these unexplored market segments will have a much harder time finding clients that prefer an integrated solution.

To transform *from a product BM to a project BM*, firms may either individualize their mass-market offerings by substantially increasing the number of specifications from which customers can choose, or introduce value-added services to apply their products to the client's unique context. ABB, for example, introduced client-centric project services in complex and highly hazardous process industries. This organization found that maintaining a significant in-house engineering capability is difficult to justify in today's business environment, but that operators still want access to a full range of experienced engineers when needed. ABB fills this need through its extensive range of engineering specialists with operational experience.

The ability to sell integrated solutions requires completely new organizational structures and capabilities.[2] If a firm transforms *from a platform BM to a solution BM* it has to adapt not only the range of products and services but also the underlying architecture to its clients' specific needs. This means selling a problem resolution process – geared toward specific customer business processes and taking the entire life cycle into account – instead of selling standardized components of a system or platform. Solution providers have to manage a highly complex network of comprehensive and integrated products and services in a way that is closely aligned with the client's specific needs. Therefore, it is often not sufficient to engage in planning and building the solution, but firms also need to begin running certain business functions on behalf of their clients.

A successful east–west crossing on the business transformation board (see Figure II.1) requires: 1) *a front-end adaptation from a standardized to an individual value proposition*; 2) *a back-end transformation from a scalable production structure to a flexible service structure*; and 3) a *monetization mechanics shift from cost-driven pricing to demand-driven pricing*. The implementation of such a crossing has to be supported by an aligned organizational structure comprising front-end customer-facing units, back-end capability providers and a corporate centre delivering coordination and leadership.

Front-end adaptation: From standardized to individualized value propositions

A product BM or a platform BM benefits from a small number of offering specifications that allow for standardization and economies of scale. Conversely, project BMs and solution BMs are only successful if they *provide a broad, flexible and integrated service-centric offering*. Most firms make substantial efforts to integrate forward into service components, including consultancy advice, guarantees of systems reliability and responsiveness, and services to operate, maintain and finance a project over its full life cycle.[3] From a customer perspective, the value of such an offer must be greater than the sum of its component parts.

Consequently, it is necessary for firms to identify the dimensions in which customers particularly value flexibility and offer the highest possible number of choices, while keeping other dimensions more standardized and scalable. Former mass-market producers have both strengths and weaknesses in this regard. While they possess the proven ability to scale and leverage, their identity and brand image can be an impediment to transformation success, as these could limit employees' openness as well as customers' expectations regarding individualized projects or solutions. In order to deal with this challenge, firms have to build project and risk management capabilities. In the case of the University of St Gallen's executive education programme, we have seen that customers have had good experiences with the standardized open enrolment programmes where the faculty was able to introduce novel insights from multiple industries to the participants. However, potential clients for custom programmes were sceptical that these faculty members also possessed the right background and competences to provide individualized, firm-specific teaching. To address this scepticism, the Executive School has developed a team of 'impact architects' to act as the single face to the client and subsequently managed the internal adaptation of the teaching content with the faculty members concerned. When transforming from a platform BM to a solution BM, firms may even offer additional third-party products and services in order to address a client's needs. For example, to provide the necessary business consultancy service, firms can either form a strategic alliance with a professional service firm or develop these skills in-house.

When moving east, a firm's unique selling proposition suddenly no longer relies on cost advantages or product or service features; instead, customers largely base their buying decisions on the firm's *ability to adapt its offering to their individual needs*. This adaptation requires close coordination and integration with the customer (eg through co-innovation processes). During the transformation of FUNDES, it was particularly challenging to develop people and processes that were experienced and aligned with the needs of large multinationals, as the firm had previously focused on providing standardized support services to small regional companies in South America. In particular, marketing and sales employees had to develop novel skills and an entirely new culture, as the key to success was now to listen to large customers' needs and develop individual value propositions for the integration of small suppliers into their supply chain. Such a tight link can lead either to vendor dependency, as the individualization effort requires customer-specific upfront investments (project BM), or to a mutual and bi-directional dependency between the vendor and the customer through the benefits to be achieved by remaining with the same vendor (solution BM). Based on such a mutual dependency, a trusted advisory role can be earned if a company is able to provide neutral advice that is in the customer's best interest.

Transforming a business model to make it more customized also requires firms to refocus their sales channels, as broad and anonymous customer contacts usually fail to provide the insights required to truly adapt an offering to the customers' individual needs. Instead, companies have to *establish direct access and a dialogue with the customers.* Depending on the business, this dialogue can be achieved through personal interactions between the vendor and the customer representatives. Alternatively, firms may introduce technical solutions that allow customers to express their individual needs. The hotel chain citizenM, for example, introduced tablet PCs to make it possible for their customers to individualize their hotel experience (eg lighting, sound, climate, services) according to their mood or travel purpose.

In addition to establishing a channel for communication, it is necessary to develop holistic customer key account management. One account executive should be responsible for making decisions such as structuring a deal or ensuring delivery. Furthermore, the incentives for the product sales and the service sales organizations should be cross-linked in order to serve the same overarching intent, namely understanding and fulfilling the customer's demands. Ideally, an integrated or virtual account team[4] – consisting of a representative from each customer-serving team – should provide the customer with competent advice and a single face to the customer at every point in time throughout the entire engagement life cycle.

Back-end transformation: From scalable production to flexible service structure

In order to produce customized offerings, firms need to change their operational back end substantially. While they previously benefited from stabilizing and formalizing their production processes, they have to *adopt production to customer needs by making it more flexible.* This is particularly challenging for firms transforming from a product BM, in which the change, for example in production lines, is usually very expensive. Such a transformation often requires high investments in a novel infrastructure that caters to the need to adapt production and realization processes to individual customer demands. The recent progress in the field of 3D printing technology and robotics may create novel opportunities for companies to increase the level of customization of their goods.

In addition to the more flexible production systems, modularization approaches may also provide the necessary flexibility. Unlike mass customization, where customers can choose from a sometimes vast number of options, modularization primarily means breaking down an offering into small parts. Customers can then decide which parts they want to individualize and where they want to choose from standardized options. Clearly defined interfaces ensure that even the customized parts fit neatly into the overall product (or service). This helps firms and their customers control and limit the individualization cost. However, there are, of course, limits to standardization and replication, as customers may find that their individual needs have still not been sufficiently satisfied and that they want their product or service designed from scratch.

To move east, firms also have to *improve the capability to process customer requirements and implement them*. Sometimes, for example, this can be achieved by replacing traditional research and development activities through co-creation, where customers are closely involved (making them 'prosumers'). This is quite a fundamental change for processes and also for employees. Some high-end watch brands, for example, build teams comprising a customer and an experienced clockmaker. The two work together closely to design and redesign a highly individual masterpiece that usually costs several hundred thousand dollars. As a digital alternative to this highly human-intensive design process, firms may apply service-oriented software principles. For example, when customers compile their own software by using model-to-code business process management tools, the final solution is co-innovated.

Monetization mechanics shift: From cost-driven to demand-driven pricing

With increasing degrees of customization, firms also need to change their pricing logic. Given that the demand for an individualized product or service is less objective than that for a more standardized product or service, market competitors are less influential for the pricing. Instead, firms have to *identify the price that reflects the customers' willingness to pay for the customization* of individual projects or solutions. Often, a first step toward a new pricing model is to charge for the tangible modular components and the individualization services and adaptations individually. In a subsequent step, firms may offer individualized projects or solutions that no longer identify the individual prices of the components and the customization effort. This can have advantages and disadvantages, as the case of the University of St Gallen's executive education programme showed. When moving from standardized to more individualized programmes, it also started introducing packages that included the teaching as well as the customization effort. However, it had to realize that clients, particularly those with less experience in running in-house programmes, had little knowledge of what services they needed and what they could do themselves. They then asked for additional help and support but were reluctant to pay for them. In order to deal with this challenge, contracts were designed more flexibly but also clearly referred to potential add-on cost. Additionally, client monitoring was introduced, and the pricing model is now designed individually to better take the specific context and potential needs of the customers into account.

A business model transformation from west to east also changes the logic underlying the margins and profitability. Firms need to *refocus their attention from fixed costs to variable, engagement-related costs*. For example, Rolls-Royce competes by providing airlines with 'power by the hour'. Its jet engines are sold along with the services to maintain and upgrade them. To ensure that the engagement with the customer is profitable, the engagement-related costs are monitored closely. In particular, it needs to be clear to all parties which individual adaptations are part of the project and solution contract and which additional customization demands will lead to additional charges.

Summary

The major challenge in a west–east crossing is to find market niches in which standardized products do not yet cover the customer needs and where customers are willing to pay for a broad, flexible and integrated service-centric offering. If such niches exist, the question is then whether the company has the necessary in-depth understanding of the customer's demands to produce real tailor-made projects or solutions. Providing a customer-individual offering also means that the company now has to improve the capability to process and implement customers' individual requirements and take full responsibility to meet these requirements in a service level or project agreement. Finally, the company has to adjust its reporting systems to be able to control the variable engagement-related costs.

Transforming to more standardized business models

Customization can sometimes be quite frustrating. Despite much time and effort having been invested in an individual solution, customers may immediately start making adaptations to this solution once it has been handed over. This was what Jason Fried experienced after founding 37signals, a three-person, Chicago-based web design shop, in 1999. In order to manage the increasing number of projects and complexity of their growing service business, the two founders decided to develop a simple project management software for their internal use. The simplicity of the software impressed 37signals' clients, who started asking whether they could buy it for themselves. The two founders decided to improve the software and started selling it under the name Basecamp. A year later, the software was more profitable than the web design business, and 37signals stopped being a project business and started being a product business. Today, tens of thousands of small businesses use 37signals' software, and the company hasn't built a website – other than its own – since 2006.[5]

A similar case is that of Blume2000. The company started in 1973 as a traditional, stand-alone flower shop in Hamburg. The salesperson arranged fresh flowers, a perishable product, on the spot to meet the individual client's needs. In 1989, the Herz family, owner of the successful Tchibo coffee chain stores, took control of the company, and Blume2000 added 54 stores over 17 years. Furthermore, it continued to push the company's growth by introducing the franchise concept in 1991. Today, the company has a production and logistics centre that delivers flowers to more than 200 shops and to millions of end consumers. Unlike traditional flower shops that invest time in the creation of individual bouquets for customers, Blume2000 sells a limited number of previously arranged bouquets through its online and offline stores. These bouquets are produced centrally and in large quantities. Constant turnover allows the company to provide a seven-day freshness guarantee. Additionally, the bulk purchasing of flowers gives the company a cost advantage of about 20 per cent, which can be passed on to its clients. Finally, a sophisticated enterprise resource planning (ERP) system creates transparency for all the partners on the common platform and speeds up the ordering processes. The ERP also provides market insights from the stores, which are used to predict future demand and to optimize the online offerings.

Infosys was founded in 1981 as Infosys Consultants Pvt Ltd in Pune. In the 1980s, Infosys focused on offering customer-individual projects delivered on-site. Specifically the years after Infosys's IPO in 1993 were a period of hyper-growth, taking it from $5 million revenues in 1993 to $203 million in 2000 and reaching $1 billion in 2004. As a result of the commoditization of classical IT outsourcing and the increasing margin pressure for IT projects, Infosys started around 2000 transforming from project services towards productized offerings. In the back end, this required a radical shift from the IT service provider's traditional focus on resource management – namely to effectively allocate project managers, consultants and IT experts in order to co-create an individual IT solution with the customer – to building up intellectual property. The first result of this productization strategy was a software product for the banking industry, today branded as Finacle. For the first time, Infosys managed to convert the knowledge for a customer-individual branch banking solution into more general software that any bank could use. With the help of experienced engineers it established a flexible and scalable architecture, which made it harder for competitors to replicate its productization strategy: functionality was easy to copy, but flexibility was not. A dedicated product management function was also established, which was led by a banker not a software engineer. Last but not least, the Infosys leadership team adapted the monetization mechanics. They strategically shifted from time-and-material-based projects with their inherent variability and seasonality to one-time upfront licence payments for the software products; additionally, they offered in software product deals, which were typically larger as well as more transformational in nature, their services for strategy consulting, implementation and maintenance. The reporting was also adapted, which meant moving away from Infosys's project-oriented PSPD model (predictability of revenues, sustainability of such predictability, profitability of such realized revenues and de-risking) towards product-centric key performance indicators geared towards fixed cost degression. As Finacle was able to set an industry standard, Infosys decided to expand its product portfolio and invest further in intellectual property. Multiple acquisitions like Skava and Panaya accelerated this strategic path and, with EdgeVerve Systems in July 2014, Infosys gained a second enterprise-scale product. Today the product and platform portfolio contributes around 5 per cent of Infosys's total corporate revenues.

If a firm decides to cross the BM meridian from east to west, it needs to change gear from an individualized business model with a large variety of unique client cases to an industrialized business model with standardized offerings. This process is often referred to as productization. The race is then on with regard to scalability, which requires capabilities to mass-produce, mass-customize and mass-market, while very complex manufacturing, engineering and project management competences become less important.

Such a move may occur defensively if a company comes to the conclusion that there is no further scope for tailor-made solutions, because the mass-market offerings meet most of the customer needs and are cheaper. As a result, the customer base for the individualized business model may shrink, and there might be no way to push the market toward higher-end customers. Conversely, there is also an offensive option, when firms use their in-depth customer knowledge to discover an opportunity for standardizing their existing offerings better, or when they see an opportunity to leverage parts of their heritage competences and skills in the mass market. For example, if a firm has built a highly integrative customer-individual architecture for client solutions, this can be the starting point to scale up the business by standardizing the architecture in the form of a platform that can be launched on the mass market. Strong partner network orchestration skills may be another potential key asset to be leveraged if firms transform from a solution BM into a platform BM. However, this also depends on the partners' ability to deliver scalable products or services.

A successful east–west crossing on the business transformation board (see Figure II.1) requires: 1) *an adaptation of the front end from a customer-individual to a standardized value proposition*; 2) *a transformation from a flexible service structure into a scalable production structure*; and 3) *a shift in the monetization mechanics from a demand-driven to a cost-driven pricing model*.

Front-end adaptation: From an individual to a standardized value proposition

Many companies fail to transform from east to west because they think it is enough to mass-produce an offering. However, to successfully compete with the established players in the mass market, firms have to *provide a new and better standard offering* that covers a higher percentage of the relevant customer needs, as has been common up to now. Therefore, they have to out-innovate the existing products and services with a superior value proposition. The focus should be on innovations in the core offering that leverage a firm's heritage skills, like market insights, project management and service competence. In the most successful cases, firms start offering products or services that were previously not available on the mass market at all. Examples include banks that start providing easy-to-use stock trading functions to all their customers, thus breaking the logic that stock market activities are the privilege of high-net-worth individuals with a customized investment strategy. In comparison with the established players, firms that transform from east to west know the potential customers' needs very well. This familiarity allows them to identify the areas in which customers particularly value flexibility and those parts of the offering that can be easily standardized.

Moving west means engaging in a highly standardized interaction with a large number of customers. These customers primarily value specific product or service features or cost advantages. Therefore, a *low-touch, scalable sales approach* has to be implemented, and 'non-standard' customers need to be rejected to keep the sales costs low. A customized business model is usually based on a single sales channel, which allows a deep and continuous customer–vendor dialogue. This needs to be replaced by a *broad range of well-connected complementary offline and online sales channels.* Such omnichannel, or multichannel, strategies allows firms to increase the touch points to their customers. Some customers like to visit stores to obtain an overview of all the available offerings but then expect a firm to deliver its products to their home. Other customers like to shop online but prefer to pick up their goods at a store. Given the multitude and complexity of possible customer–vendor interactions, it is vital that prices, offerings and the overall brand experience be consistently aligned across all these channels.

Since communication becomes more indirect when the number of served customers shows a significant increase, a company has to build a strong brand for its offerings. The users of solutions that were customized in the past in particular have to be convinced that the new standardized products or services are appropriate for most of their needs. Such branding activities often occur digitally. They require advertising new offerings on the web, creating a customer experience through the web and interacting with customers via social media.

Back-end adaptation: From a flexible service structure to a scalable production structure

In order to achieve a high level of scalability, firms need to change their production or realization processes. For their original customized business model, they will probably have built strong, individual manufacturing competences. Through the transformation, these suddenly lose most of their value. Instead, firms need to establish a factory-style production that *replaces human resources with machines* and relies on a high level of automation. This automation not only concerns the internal processes but also needs to be established in supplier relations. In order to secure economies of scale, firms need to consider shifting toward just-in-time delivery contracts with their suppliers and to ensure effective interfaces between the production, planning, ordering and logistics systems.

When shifting from an adaptable toward a scalable production process, firms need to make their knowledge assets available on a large scale to many different potential customers. This requires the 'productization' of knowledge into building blocks or modules. Examples include services that are turned into a template, a standard methodology or even a software tool. To productize knowledge, you need *to transform services and content into reusable elements* and make them repeatable and reproducible. Such productization can be done inside out by focusing on the existing knowledge and how it can be divided, which predetermines what a customer's offering will look like. The key challenge of this approach is to predict the use case demand to avoid major modifications for each customer. Alternatively, productization may also occur outside in. In this case, a firm relies on its previous experiences to determine what the ideal offering will look like from a customer's perspective and to deduce which knowledge building blocks are required. On this basis, it can then assess the knowledge that the firm already possesses and the knowledge it needs to acquire. The online learning platform Moodle is an example of such a productization approach, as formerly individually resolved learning projects are now executed through open-source knowledge capturing.

However, having such standardized knowledge building blocks available is not enough. Firms also have to make sure that they can be accessed fast and efficiently across the entire company ('knowledge markets'). This is especially crucial when – in an international business context – local reuse through a subsidiary of a company is only legal if the intellectual property resides globally with the firm group's central repository. Additionally, content governance is essential to ensure the quality of packaged knowledge by ensuring 'semantic consistency', which creates value by seamlessly integrating the content and leveraging the synergies between the building blocks. The whole is more than the sum of its parts. Still, it is important to emphasize that successful productization not only requires *solid knowledge management but also a culture of knowledge sharing*.

Monetization mechanics shift: From demand-driven to cost-driven pricing

A move from east to west requires firms to invert their monetization mechanics, as they may no longer focus on their customers' willingness to pay but rather on the price level that the competitors in the mass market set. Accordingly, they first have to decide which market niche to target. Based on this decision, they may *identify a competitive price*. This price is then the basis for developing the offering.

In a non-customized business model, fixed costs drive the margins. In order to foster profitability, firms need to start *actively managing these fixed costs* by, for example, creating economies of scale and realizing market power in negotiations with suppliers. Additionally, they have to take advantage of the cost reduction effects of reusable standard assets. Moving west involves substantial make-or-buy decisions. Owing to the cost pressure, a firm may no longer be able to cover its full value chain alone. Instead, it may need to focus on those activities for which it has actual core competencies in order to secure a sustainable competitive advantage. All other activities, where leading competencies are missing and which are not critical to differentiation in the market, can potentially be outsourced to improve customers' value for money.

Summary

The major challenge in an east–west crossing is to come up with a new and better standard offering. The company has to learn how to commercialize a mass business through (mass) marketing. But it also has to be able to productize knowledge into building blocks or modules and industrialize the former individual services. Finally, it will be critical for the economic success of the transformation to grow rapidly to realize enough economies of scale and improve the margin by managing the fixed costs.

Endnotes

1 For a study on increasing service orientation enabled by technology, see J Bughin, M Chui and J Manyika (2010) Clouds, big data, and smart assets: Ten tech-enabled business trends to watch, *McKinsey Quarterly*, August, p 36.

2 A Davies, T Brady and M Hobday (2006) Charting a path toward integrated solutions, *MIT Sloan Management Review*, Spring, pp 39–48.

3 A Davies, T Brady and M Hobday (2007) Organizing for solutions: System seller vs systems integrator, *Industrial Marketing Management*, 36, pp 183–93.

4 Regarding the implementation of virtual account teams in major accounts, see for example T R Bacon (1999) *Selling to Major Accounts: Tools, techniques, and practical solutions for the sales manager*, Amacom, New York.

5 J Warrillow and J Fried (2010) The service-to-product switch, *Globe and Mail*, 20 October.

Sequencing multiple radical shifts

06

In the previous chapters, we deliberately focused on business model transformations that cross either the BM equator or the BM meridian. However, if the environment and competitive position of the firm is marked by fundamental, discontinuous changes, such a one-dimensional crossing may not be sufficient for it to survive and prosper in the long run. In this case, three optional paths are available, as firms may opt for a stepwise transformation that is clockwise or counter-clockwise or for a direct, diagonal transformation (see, for example, Figure 6.1). Such moves are evidently more challenging, because the company has to cross the meridian *and* the equator. In this chapter, we discuss the particular challenges of these multidimensional moves and provide some suggestions to manage them successfully.

Take the case of Singapore Post. Like many other national post companies, Singapore Post was faced with a strong structural decline in demand for its basic mail services, the traditional postal business, following the boom in internet-based alternatives (e-substitution), lifestyle changes and market liberalization. The decline is reflected in lower mail volumes and post office transactions. In 2011 the company launched its ambitious 'Ready for the Future' transformation programme. Following the vision to be the 'regional leader in e-commerce logistics and trusted communications', it managed the transformation from a domestic postal operator to a regional player in e-commerce logistics offering an end-to-end e-commerce logistics solutions platform in Asia Pacific. To manage such a fundamental change, the company had to invest heavily in human resources (communication down the line, hiring of new talents, leadership training, etc) and in IT and operations. On the one hand, the company improved its old core business by integrating transactional services in a digital platform. This offers a unified user experience for the customers across self-service automated kiosks,

Figure 6.1 Three transformation paths (example: from the product BM to the solution BM)

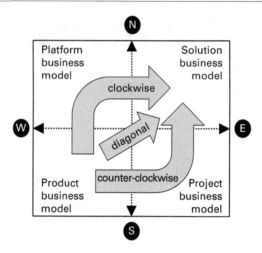

mobile phones, tablets and personal computers. On the other hand, to help its customers' businesses expand their e-commerce operations across multiple marketplaces and countries in a scalable, sustainable model, the company invested in technologies like online security, scalability, marketing and omnichannel to provide integrated end-to-end solutions. It also strengthened its regional e-commerce logistics by making several acquisitions and joint ventures overseas to extend its web solutions business to new online markets in Asia.

Directness: Diagonal versus stepwise shifts

The first question to ask is whether a multidimensional move can be managed in one direct, diagonal step or whether it requires two sequential steps – one horizontal and one vertical – owing to the manoeuvre's managerial challenges. In the Knorr-Bremse Rail Vehicle Systems case, it was clear from the beginning that it had to be a one-step transformation. The firm came from a world of producing and selling single brake control units to railway companies. To keep the direct customer contact and not be downgraded to a deliverer of components, it was obvious that the company had to come up with a much more comprehensive offering that needed to be customized to the specific needs of each railway company. In order to remain competitive, Knorr-Bremse had to fundamentally transform its business model to offer individual products and services across the whole life cycle of the railway system.

Such a direct, one-step move has the advantage that a firm only needs to undergo a single change effort. The goal of the business model transformation is clear from the beginning, and the entire company can be aligned on the move forward. However, the managerial complexity is very high owing to the multitude of simultaneous changes that are required to initiate, manage, control and terminate the transformation initiatives. Besides the more tangible projects to adapt systems and processes, the management team also has to guide the organization through a fundamental cultural change that gives the employees very little stability to hold on to.

Two sequential steps may intuitively appear less complex and easier to manage, as they limit the transformation to one dimension at a time. It might take longer, but the change effort and complexity per move are lower, which makes the operational risk easier to manage. However, the decision makers also need to be aware of the downsides and perils of this approach. A business model transformation is always a major change effort and puts considerable strain on the employees. When the company initiates a crossing of the BM equator or the BM meridian, the organization will (ideally) adapt its front end, back end and monetization mechanics as needed but will particularly appreciate and cherish those aspects that remain stable. These may even become the central pillars of identification during times of change. If, in a second step, the management sets out to change these as well, the organization may resist another transformation, holding the firm locked in halfway through a transition.

We can conclude that, if a two-dimensional transformation is required and if the company has the ability to adjust to the new rules of the game in a relatively short amount of time, a diagonal crossing might be a good approach. However, if the company requires many novel resources and competences to arrive at the targeted business model, a stepwise approach might be the better choice.

Sequence: Clockwise versus counter-clockwise shifts

If the company decides that a stepwise approach is better suited to its business model transformation, decision makers have to decide in which sequence to transform: clockwise or counter-clockwise. For example, the transformation from a product BM to a solution BM requires increases in transaction inclusiveness and offering customization. If a company decides to pursue a clockwise path, it first needs to increase the inclusiveness of the transaction by developing a comprehensive and integrated value proposition, establishing an integrative architecture and introducing recurring fees. Such a move is often easier for larger organizations, which have the scope and networks to develop and manage a comprehensive offering. The advantage of this path is that the company can already build up the architecture in the first step, which implies that leaders then 'only' have to add the competences to individualize their business. However, there are two challenges to be aware of when pursuing a clockwise transformation from a product BM into a solution BM. First, while size helps a firm transform from south to north, it tends to limit flexibility and thus impedes the ability to customize the offering. This is even more applicable if the transformation from a product BM into a platform BM requires many different partners' involvement. Such partnering contracts are often strictly formalized and require great mutual efforts to adapt them. In some cases, firms may even have to change partners if those that offer the standard solution are not flexible enough to accommodate individual customer requests in a solution BM. Second, the better the newly established platform, the higher the risk that customers are able to configure an individual solution themselves that satisfies their needs. This could render the second step obsolete, and the company could lose the opportunity to sell its customized services.

Conversely, if a company pursues a counter-clockwise transformation path, it first has to provide an individualized value proposition, develop a flexible service structure to implement customer requirements, and focus on demand-driven pricing schemes. In a second step, it may then begin expanding its core offering to increase the inclusiveness and bind its customers more tightly into a comprehensive and integrated solution. The first step is often easier for smaller firms to pursue, as, by definition, they can adapt to customer requirements more flexibly. However, traditionally, these firms struggle in a second step when they need to build an integrative platform or system and develop a thriving ecosystem of complementary offerings around it. Owing to their limited resources, small firms also run the risk of concentrating all their resources on one or just a few customers. Even if they succeed in the first place, they often lack the capacity to roll out the solution BM.

Theoretically, diagonal transformations are also possible in other directions than from a product BM to a solution BM. However, we did not observe such cases. A possible reason for this might be that the higher the level of inclusiveness and customization achieved, the higher the lock-in effects that hinder firms from moving southward or westward. Overcoming these lock-in effects might require so many resources that there is no capacity available to engage in additional transformation efforts.

It is important to note that not all two-step transformations paths are planned from the beginning. Some companies engage in a trial-and-error approach, in which they transform into one direction first and, if this does not provide the expected results, later turn their attention toward another transformation dimension. A good example is Liebherr. The company is one of the world's leading manufacturers of construction machinery, employs a workforce of about 41,000 and had a turnover of €8.8 billion in 2014. Early on, Liebherr identified the need to transform its business model. It used to be an original equipment provider with a product BM of selling machinery. In response to fierce competition and shrinking margins, it decided to move northward by taking on additional tasks within the mining process – from excavation and loading to transportation – by integrating maintenance into its heavy equipment and offering value-adding services like project finance and IT solutions. However, this platform-style business model was soon under pressure, as competitors quickly replicated Liebherr's portfolio of comprehensive and integrated products and services. They thus decided to engage in another transformation by carefully observing the changing customer needs and by adjusting their offerings to these needs. This time, Liebherr changed even more radically. It had realized that the customers did not want to invest heavily in assets but rather wanted to use construction machinery when they needed it. Liebherr thus took over the complete equipment management responsibility by employing on-site personnel. Customers were charged for the 'availability cost' and the 'operating hours', often as part of service level agreements over a period of 8 to 10 years. Liebherr thus ended up with a solution BM where it now develops customer-individual bundles of integrated products and services with the aim of solving a specific customer problem.

Conclusion and outlook

Transforming a firm's business model is a very challenging endeavour, and it is often very risky, not only for the company but also for those brave, entrepreneurial leaders who initiate and manage such transformations. In most cases there will be a lot of initial resistance and criticism from multiple stakeholders. Investors may fear the considerable investments, which could hurt profitability for some years before the transformation is completed successfully. Employees may be worried about lacking the necessary competences to participate in the new business model. Loyal customers may critically observe whether the firm will still be able to fulfil their needs with the new business model. Last but not least, the transformation leaders themselves can never be sure whether they will remain in their role long enough to take credit for the transformation's success. These criticisms can only be addressed if leaders develop a compelling strategic case for why a transformation is necessary, succeed in explaining what the best business model looks like and provide a full and transparent plan with respect to the concrete actions that are required to succeed in the transformation. This book seeks to support readers along this business model transformation journey. First, the *BM typology* allows one to position the current business model, develop an attractive picture of the future business model and identify the gaps that need to be bridged. Second, the business model *crossings* provide insights into the required actions and allow one to check whether the organization actually fulfils the prerequisites for a successful transformation. Third, the subsequent chapters provide more in-depth examples of real-world transformation cases. Written by company and business leaders who had the experience of driving a business model transformation themselves, they may serve as best practice but also illustrate some of the perils that need to be overcome when moving toward a new business model.

PART THREE
Learning from successful transformational organizations

Case studies of companies radically shifting the level of inclusiveness

07

How Daimler is shaping the future of mobility: From car2go to moovel
Alexander Zimmermann, Günter Müller-Stewens and Christoph Färber

Over the past few years, we have seen a fundamental change in the mindsets of top managers in the automotive industry. Martin Winterkorn, Volkswagen Group's former CEO, for instance, surprised media and investors on 12 March 2015 when he said, 'We are driven by a fascinating vision – in the long term, we want to evolve from an automaker into a global mobility provider, the number one mobility enabler.'[1] One year earlier, Norbert Reithofer, the BMW Group's former CEO, said that 'Our vision for the year 2020 is to be the leading provider of premium products and premium services for individual mobility. Even today, we are much more than just a manufacturer. We are clearly moving toward being a provider of attractive mobility and connectivity services.'[2] Similarly, Dieter Zetsche, Daimler

AG's CEO, said in the same year: 'We regard ourselves not only as a vehicle manufacturer, but also as a provider of mobility solutions.'[3] This leads to the questions: What lies behind this fundamental shift in purpose from selling cars towards selling mobility? What does it mean for these companies' business models, and how will it be implemented? We take a close look at Daimler and its mobility services initiative in order to better understand the dynamics behind this business model transformation.

Daimler has had a long history since its founders, Gottlieb Daimler and Carl Benz, invented the automobile in 1886. At the time, the value proposition was a self-propelled vehicle (*voiture automobile*). In the subsequent years, the carriage shape was replaced by new chassis forms, and production has evolved from hand manufacturing to assembly belt production, which was introduced by Henry Ford in 1913 (the Model T). Daimler followed in 1935. Today, in its core vehicle business, Daimler is one of the key players in the premium passenger car segment and is the world's largest manufacturer of commercial vehicles. Besides these activities, Daimler has in the past repeatedly entered other market segments, industries and business models. In the mid-1990s, the then CEO, Edzard Reuter, wanted to turn Daimler into an integrated technology group, acquiring among others the aerospace firm Dornier and the electronics company AEG. However, this diversification failed, and Reuter's successor, Jürgen Schrempp, refocused the company on its profitable core vehicle business. In 1998, Schrempp launched his own diversification strategy by merging Daimler with the US mass-market car producer Chrysler and by acquiring stakes in Mitsubishi and Hyundai. This expansion also failed, leading to the break-up of Daimler and Chrysler nine years later. Since then, Daimler has followed a different path, focusing on profitable growth in the premium car business, complemented with innovative financial and mobility services. In the 2015 Daimler Directors' Dialogue, CEO Dieter Zetsche recalls that the firm has for some years been very busy optimizing and profitably growing its core business. While he sees this as critical, he also notes that the next task will be to build a broader foundation for the company's long-term future. This means facing digital challenges in all business areas and getting ready for fundamental changes.[4]

Business models and customer demands in the car industry have also been subject to constant changes. While, in the early days, customers bought cars as they did any other product, high cost prevented a large part of the population from owning a vehicle. To make cars more accessible, manufacturers joined forces with banks to offer customers financing solutions that allowed them to break down the substantial cost into monthly down-payments. Such financing solutions gained strong momentum and became an important competitive factor, as manufacturers began to strive for the best value-for-money offering. As a next step, leasing – originally developed for corporate clients – became increasingly relevant to private customers. In this business model, the car is owned by the lease provider (either a bank or a manufacturer's financial services division). The customer has access to the vehicle in return for a monthly fee. Insurance and maintenance costs are also covered by the leasing agreement. Technically, in this model, a customer only buys the right to use a car instead of buying the car itself, but still needs to choose a specific vehicle. As an alternative for those who require greater flexibility, car rental companies have long offered a broad range of vehicles that can be accessed at a daily rate.

In recent years, another business model has been added to this list of ever-evolving offerings. Car manufacturers such as Daimler and BMW, but also independent providers such as Mobility in Switzerland, Flinkster in Germany (owned by Deutsche Bahn) and Zipcar in the United States, began to offer car-sharing services. In this model, customers enjoy even greater flexibility than with car rentals, since they may pick up vehicles at a wide variety of places and only pay for their exact driving time. This service offering had its breakthrough as car manufacturers and start-ups began joining forces with the major car rental companies (eg Daimler and Europcar, BMW and Sixt, Zipcar and Avis). These possessed both the operational and the service competence to efficiently and effectively operate large fleets of vehicles and to manage contractual relationships with continuously changing drivers. Car sharing's relevance became apparent when the car rental company Avis paid US$500 million to take over Zipcar in 2013. While this valuation is still considerably lower than the €1.7 billion market capitalization of Europe's largest rental car firm, Europcar, it still shows that car sharing is catching up with established business models to become an important sector in the individual mobility industry. Recently, some new peer-to-peer platforms, such as Sharoo in Switzerland, have begun to make inroads into the car-sharing market, allowing individuals to offer their own cars to other users to rent. These offerings no longer provide vehicle fleets and services; they only link users and their cars.

In sum, from a customer perspective, using a car is evolving from a substantial long-term investment to a minute-by-minute service (ie pay per use). These new business models were accommodated by broader social changes, as the car is losing its role as status symbol. Instead, people's expectations and needs regarding cars and mobility changed as flexibility and environmental sustainability became increasingly important. As a result – not only in the automotive industry – ownership is increasingly losing its attraction and is increasingly being replaced by the desire to use cars or other goods flexibly, when needed (ie the sharing economy).

In parallel to these new models of interacting with customers, the competitive landscape in the industry is also changing dramatically. For a long time, the car business was largely predictable, with established players competing for a relatively stable market. As customer demand has shifted from owning a car towards mobility as a service, there are suddenly new or formerly unrelated players that have entered the arena. For instance, for a long time, public transport did not directly compete against the car business. Car owners were locked in by investments in their vehicles, which often made it financially less attractive to choose other means of transport. Since car sharing now charges customers for vehicle use on a minute-by-minute basis, the costs of getting from A to B are becoming more transparent and are becoming directly comparable to alternatives such as trains, buses and taxis. Early on, customers had the either-or decision to have a car and use it for most mobility needs or to rely on public transport and taxis. Today, thanks to increasing transparency, customers are able to flexibly combine multiple mobility services and means of transport and to pay for each use individually. In the future, we can expect that online platforms will serve as digital mobility assistants, making proactive suggestions concerning customers' needs, vehicles (both cars and public transport) will potentially drive autonomously and will automatically communicate with each other, and customers will buy mobility flat rates to use these services. The more flexible mobility solutions also require novel technologies and data management capacities.

Alternatively, pure platform players such as Uber, Lyft, MyTaxi or Didi Chuxing did not engage in vehicle development, but rather connect people who own a car to those seeking a means of transport. Based on a two-sided platform, they allow individuals to act as individual mobility service providers. As a result, you no longer have to produce cars to sell individual mobility. Compared to the traditional 'bricks-and-mortar' companies, these 'asset-poor' companies have a radically different conception of where and how value is created. It is like Facebook, the world's most popular media owner, which creates no content, or like Airbnb, the world's largest hotelier, which owns no real estate, or like Alibaba, the most valuable retailer, which has no inventory.[5]

A primary advantage of these platform business models is convenience: as Uber drivers pick you up and drive you wherever you want, customers no longer have to look for a pick-up station. These consumer platforms are direct competitors of taxi operators, which has already resulted in protests and even legal action to prevent Uber from operating. Despite these efforts to defend the status quo, changes in the business models and competition cannot be prevented. Currently, fast-moving start-ups are targeting novel business models. Uber recently launched a collaboration with the University of Arizona to develop advanced maps and optical sensors, as well as a partnership with the Robotic Lab at Carnegie Mellon University, a forerunner in autonomous driving. It is no secret that the company plans to launch driverless car services. There were rumours in the market in March 2016 that Uber had placed an order for at least 100,000 Mercedes S-Class self-driving cars – which are still not on the market. Uber would make huge savings on its biggest cost – drivers – if it were able to incorporate self-driving cars into its fleet. Some of the platform-based companies are also making efforts to go physical, to become direct competitors of car manufacturers.[6] For example, Lyft disclosed its cooperation with General Motors, one of its investors, to test a fleet of self-driving electric taxis in 2017.

Established vehicle manufacturers also see players from the information technology industry entering (or at least planning to enter) the car market from the other side, since they consider cars a platform to leverage their own business models. Recent examples include Google's parent company Alphabet's driverless car project and its cooperation with Fiat Chrysler to test 100 Chrysler minivans. Or take the serious rumours about Apple's ambition to enter the car industry with an 'iCar'. In May 2016 Apple invested US$1 billion in the Chinese ride-sharing company Didi Chuxing, a rival of Uber in China. Didi is owned by companies such as Alibaba Group Holding and Tencent Holdings, both of which are also investors in Lyft, Uber's biggest US rival, which last year took an investment from Didi. It is obvious that the battle is about more than ride sharing; it is about the questions: Which (type of) company will dominate the global mobility business in a situation where the industry's boundaries are disrupted and redefined? Who will control the direct interface to the customer? The power of companies like Google (with their Android system) or Apple comes from their smartphone-based continuous direct connection to the consumer, which does not stop at the doors of the car. These companies know much more about consumers' behaviour and preferences than any car producer.

The bottom line of these changes is that established companies must get ready to transform themselves radically, and sooner rather than later. For example, in a joint reaction, Audi, BMW and Daimler purchased Nokia's mapping service Here in 2015 for €2.8 billion – in competition with Uber and other bidders. The strategic reasoning was to prevent one tech company from monopolizing in-car mapping. High-precision digital maps, combined with real-time information from sensors on vehicles, are a critical component for self-driving vehicles, for the mobility of the future. It is an important basis for offering the customers new and more differentiated and brand-specific services.

But are the established car manufacturers able to move fast enough? For example, if we look at the executive or advisory boards of the German car industry, we still mostly see 'car guys', many of them still focused on economies of scale, quality, branding, fuel efficiency or the like, and not also on network effects, the role of information and data, new monetization mechanics and so on. Are they able to manage such a transformation? Are they able to develop and share a clear sense of the new rules of the game in the mobility market? Some are, but probably not all of them.

In reaction to these changing customer demands and the evolving competitive landscape, one of these established car producers, Daimler, has launched a new line of business. The Daimler Business Innovation Unit was created in 2007 to develop and implement new mobility business models. This unit initially formed part of Daimler's corporate strategy department. As one of its first businesses, it launched Daimler's car-sharing service car2go in 2008. Later, in July 2012, Daimler launched Daimler Mobility Services GmbH and its moovel mobility services platform.

The moovel platform represents for Daimler the entry into a radical new platform business model, compared to the established product business model of the Mercedes-Benz Cars. Some will see it as a radical business transformation that has happened only at moovel, with an evolution of the Daimler corporate business model into a mixed-model approach while the Mercedes Car Group remains focused on developing and selling premium vehicles in the traditional way. But it can also be seen in the long run as a fundamental change with an impact on the whole company if Daimler wants to stay ahead of the mobility competition and not be reduced to the role of an exchangeable hardware supplier to the mobility ecosystem. It will lead to a reinvention of the car as a connected mobile living space of the consumer.

car2go: From car ownership to flexible vehicle use

On 24 October 2008, the first car2go vehicles were available in the city of Ulm, one of Daimler's primary research locations. As CEO Dieter Zetsche pointed out, 'car2go is an intelligent and creative solution that provides a simple, flexible, and value-for-money approach to mobility with environmentally friendly vehicles'.[7] A fleet of 50 Smart fortwo cars was made available as a vehicle pool that could be accessed at any time. Following a one-off registration process, customers were able to hire the cars spontaneously in passing, or pre-book and use them for as long as desired. The service charged by the minute, with reduced hourly and daily rates. After usage, vehicles could be left at any public parking space within the city limits. Initially, car2go was available only to Daimler employees, but was soon rolled out to the broader public. In the years that followed, the business expanded quickly to more than 30 cities in Europe and North America. Operations in China started in 2015. The vehicle range has also been expanded, since car2go now offers Mercedes B-class vehicles in selected cities under the car2go Black brand.

In terms of the business transformation board (Figure II.1), the launch of car2go represents a transformation northwards, as the one-time decision to buy a car is replaced or complemented by a regular interaction with the customers whenever they rent a car. Daimler was in a particularly good position to develop a car-sharing service. This was emphasized by the former head of car2go:

> A corporation such as Daimler provides the ideal conditions for launching such a new service, since it can offer a broad variety of resources such as technical, managerial and legal know-how, but also marketing, communication and funding. It is in the very nature of such a large corporation that there are more formal overheads than for a start-up, but from my perspective this is overemphasized. Whoever has experienced how a Daimler business card opens doors around the world knows that formal overheads are a small price to pay compared to working on new ideas as a nobody outside of a global company ... I can say with total conviction that there is no other constellation that would have made it easier to become successful with car2go.[8]

In this context, it was particularly important to have managers who combined entrepreneurial spirit with the ability to deal with the political particularities of a large corporation. A senior manager explained:

> At car2go, we had and have a management that, on the one hand, has long-standing experience in the Daimler Group and knows where you need to be careful and how to deal with different types of senior managers on different hierarchical levels. On the other hand, they also have a strong independence from the established approaches and ways of thinking. They just decided that it was right to enter the market, look for partners, get the development resources and create the capabilities that are usually not around in such a corporation.[9]

Front end: Fostering customer interaction

To shift or expand the business model from selling a car to selling a car-sharing service, the customer interaction had to become more convenient and regular. For this purpose, Daimler, which had long focused on interacting with customers only in the firm's vehicle showrooms, needed to adopt novel means to communicate. A senior manager from mobility services notes: 'Think about what has made Mercedes successful. It was the fact that we could conceptualize, develop and produce wonderful cars. These cars were then handed over to the dealer – either one of our own dealers or independent ones. We always had difficulties with communication with end customers.'[10] When car2go started, vehicles could be located and booked via the internet or through a telephone hotline. The locations of pre-booked vehicles were then sent to the customers via text message. While this fairly complex process was sufficient for the first pilot test, car2go could only be successfully launched to the broader public thanks to the success and proliferation of smartphones, which strongly increased the opportunities to interact with customers and improved convenience for users. A senior manager noted: 'Without the launch of the first iPhone in 2007 and the rapid progress in app development, we would not have been able to launch car2go.'[11] Today, the car2go smartphone app allows one to locate all vehicles close to a customer, makes reservations easy, guides the customer to his or her car, provides vehicle-specific information such as fuel level, and suggests points of interest. In the most recent versions, customers can also decide to be actively reminded of and supported in using the service by receiving push messages if a car2go vehicle is parked near them. This again increases stickiness and frequency of use.

Besides these technical solutions, it was particularly important to learn from the customers and their experiences, as the head of car2go recalled:

> The enthusiasm of our customers has infused our team with energy and has helped us further develop our product. We have regularly invited customers for lunch or conducted workshops with them to ask what they did or did not like, what they noticed when using the vehicles, and what they would do differently. Our first customers have always enthusiastically supported us and were very forgiving when we made mistakes.[12]

Given the growing number of car-sharing service providers, it became increasingly important to bind the customer to car2go. One lock-in effect derives from the convenience argument. Since customers must register with their driving licence before being able to use the service, it is rare that they sign up for multiple services. However, this means that the early mover advantage is very important. Thus, car2go and its main German competitor, DriveNow (from rival BMW), have begun to launch their services in different cities across Germany and beyond. The firms recently also started competing in each other's markets. An example is car2go's launch in Munich, the home town and birthplace of DriveNow. In the Italian market, car2go was even faster than the local players, launching its first operations in Torino before its rival Fiat was able to establish its own Enjoy service together with the energy firm Eni.

Back end: Learning new skills

The back end also had to be transformed to successfully enter the new business model, as many supporting processes and technologies did not previously exist within Daimler. When the service was launched in 2008, the corporate controlling and accounting functions, as well as the legal and HR departments, were not able to deal with the particularities of the new business. Robert Henrich, the former head of car2go, remembered that he had to generate all customer invoices on his laptop and calculated all weekly statistics himself. The telematics system also had to be developed from scratch and was, at first, rather prone to failure. Since there was neither a dedicated call centre nor a customer service department, everyone in the team took to the streets between 5 and 8 am to fix cars. Over time, the processes and technologies were improved, and dedicated professional teams were established. Besides the substantial stretch, the former head of car2go sees this early phase as a critical success factor: 'As all employees, without exception, helped out everywhere whenever there was an immediate need, they all knew every little detail of the product by heart. This has made our management discussions very efficient.'[13]

To facilitate car2go's growth across Europe, Daimler decided to partner with one of its new competitors, car rental company Europcar. In 2011, the two firms announced a joint venture under the name car2go Europe GmbH. Europcar Group's CEO, Philippe Guillemot, noted:

> car2go sees us expanding our range of mobility services to include a highly innovative element. Europcar has been offering individual mobility solutions for more than eighty years and has always anticipated changes in mobility behaviour at an early stage. Now, together with Daimler, we are providing innovative urban mobility solutions to serve current and future needs and reach new categories of customers. The partnership generates synergies for both partners and offers a wide choice of mobility options for practically any occasion.[14]

The joint venture allows car2go to benefit from Europcar's expertise in fleet management and logistics. Furthermore, its extensive network of branches in 160 countries offers customers further places to register. Finally, the plan is for car2go's and Europcar's offerings to be increasingly integrated in the future. In Hamburg, car2go customers already get special terms when combining the car2go service with a Europcar rental and may drive to a Europcar rental station free of charge.

Monetization mechanics: Managing variable cost

Regarding the monetization mechanics, there was also a shift from upfront pricing (ie selling a car) to usage-based pricing (ie selling a drive from A to B). This required car2go to make a substantial upfront investment in vehicles and infrastructure. It also had to invest in winning customers. For this purpose, car2go initially offered a daily flat rate. This was used to the maximum by customers, which made it highly unprofitable. Furthermore, initially there were no fees for parking the car, resulting in additional costs. Today, with its established customer base, car2go only offers usage-based pricing and customary parking fees. With the current pricing scheme, the main revenue drivers are short-term rentals within the city limits (around seven to nine per day and car). Longer rental periods and distances are rather the exception. While some cities have already reached break-even, car2go as a whole was expected to generate positive cash flows from 2016 onwards.

Since car2go offers integrated point-to-point mobility, it covers all costs related to driving a car, such as investment in the vehicle, insurance, maintenance, parking and fuel. This is very different from the pure production cost in Daimler's established vehicle sales business. Given that the price per minute is largely defined by competition, the profitability of operations is primarily driven by managing these costs. Investments in vehicles may be optimized for instance by increasing vehicle usage. It is therefore important to put the right number of cars on the street, since too few cars will put off customers and too many cars will hurt profitability; car2go uses multiple statistical models to calculate vehicle supply. The starting point is the objective to always have a car within reach of a customer when he or she needs one. Based on socio-demographic data and comparisons across cities and regions, car2go first defines the business district within a city where it wants to offer its services. The size of this district, vehicle usage over time, and the required vehicle availability then define the fleet size.

There are other levers besides increasing vehicle usage. For instance, car2go has introduced the Eco Score functionality, which shows the driver how environmentally friendly his or her driving style is in real time. Three driving categories (acceleration, cruising and deceleration) are each represented by a tree. The better one drives, the more the trees grow and at some point even begin to host animals. At the end of the journey, drivers get an overall score. When driving is particularly poor, a warning message appears, asking the customer to drive more calmly. Eco Score represents a fun, playful approach to engage drivers in reducing CO_2 emissions and fuel consumption and potentially even limits the risk of accidents, thanks to more thoughtful driving. This not only has benefits for car2go's bottom line, but also contributes substantially to reducing its environmental footprint. These effects are currently being analysed by the Institute for Socio-Ecological Research (ISOE). The car2go platform has thus changed not only the monetization mechanics but also the mechanics behind driving the triple bottom line of people, planet and profit. While Daimler has always sought to come up with technological solutions to reduce its vehicles' fuel consumption, it now aims to change consumers' driving habits, which tend to have a much stronger impact on CO_2 emissions.

Despite these achievements, car2go alone did not seem to fully cover customers' evolving needs, as competitors such as Uber entered the arena, offering mobility solutions independently of whether a customer is willing or able to drive a car. It became clear that Daimler had to transform further, from a one-sided business model with car2go as an isolated offering to an open and more inclusive mobility platform business model with Daimler AG in its core. In reaction, in July 2012, Daimler launched its moovel mobility services platform. The value proposition is offering mobility as a service (instead of selling automobiles or their usage).

moovel: From vehicle use to mobility services

With moovel, Daimler moved even further northwards into a truly multisided platform business. In an interview, moovel's former CEO stated that the firm wants to be the 'Amazon of mobility': 'moovel's purpose is to provide people in cities with every possible mobility option. This will allow us to always offer the best way to get from A to B by using public transport, taxis, limousines, rental cars, rental bikes, car sharing, trains, long-distance buses or flights. We invite everyone who can contribute to this purpose to join us.'[15] Launched in 2012 as a pilot in two German cities (Hamburg und Stuttgart), moovel is currently acquiring a large number of partners for its platform in order to offer customers ever more flexible point-to-point mobility.

The long-term objective is to establish moovel as the leading and completely neutral platform for urban mobility. However, in a first stage, it strongly builds on car2go, which provides an excellent starting point for offering a broader range of mobility services – moovel can specially benefit from car2go's efforts and investments in establishing a large customer base. This is particularly valuable, since typical car2go customers already have a strong affinity to novel mobility approaches and are familiar with using a smartphone to plan and book individual trips. An additional advantage is that moovel can again build on Daimler's excellent reputation and other companies' trust in the firm. This has helped to open doors to many potential partners, such as public transport companies. Customers' trust is also key. A moovel IT expert asks, rhetorically: 'Who do you think users would rather entrust their sensitive mobility data to – firms that are always criticized for their lack of data security or us?'[16]

Front end: Creating scope

The idea of moovel is that customers register once and can then access the whole possible mobility services spectrum in an integrated way. Thereby, moovel aims to strongly increase the scope of services, flexibility and convenience. Customers may search for, compare and book point-to-point mobility without having to enter multiple apps or websites. In particular, the ability to compare different options concerning time, cost and – potentially – environmental footprint is a strong advantage of the platform. This for instance means you take a car-sharing vehicle to the nearest train station, take a train to the city centre and jump on your reserved rental bike to cover the last mile to your destination. The borders of the different modes of transport are blurring, getting closer to the vision of seamless mobility on a given route.[17]

Besides the broader offering, interactions with customers are also changing. This has fundamental implications for Daimler's own car2go service. The moovel team expects that the vast majority of car2go customers will, in the near future, book the service through a platform like moovel. The idea behind this is that customers interact with the firm whenever they have a mobility need and not just when they are looking for a car-sharing vehicle. Accordingly, the moovel platform's front end follows a very different logic from car2go's. It no longer focuses on the question of which vehicles are available near a customer's location. Instead, it focuses on the customer's complete mobility needs and, subsequently, the platform calculates duration and prices for multiple mobility options.

The ability to channel mobility demand allows Daimler to get to know customers much better. In turn, this provides important data to improve Daimler's own services, such as car2go. If for instance customers increasingly look for mobility in areas where there are few car2go vehicles, the firm can dispatch more cars to offer a cheaper alternative to taxis and limousines for customers who are willing to drive themselves. Additionally, Daimler's aim is to remain close to the customer, hoping that a positive connotation of its mobility brand may also trigger the decision to buy a Mercedes car, for example when customers move outside a city to an area where car2go is not present, or suddenly need to own a car because of changing personal circumstances (eg the birth of children).

Increased convenience is probably the most important customer retention factor. However, the competitive pressure is high. As moovel's former CEO suggests, 'It's no coincidence that there is one Google, one eBay, and one Amazon … It's a global market and in the end there will be a small number of possible winners.'[18] Unlike the case with car2go, using moovel does not necessarily require registration. For an offered route, customers still have the option to book directly through the partner in question (eg public transport providers). Accordingly, moovel needed to develop other means to lock in customers. One is to offer registered customers the opportunity not only to plan but also to book and pay for services from several partners (currently car2go, Deutsche Bahn, MyTaxi and several public transport providers) directly via the moovel app. This not only makes it easier for customers, who no longer have to share their payment information with many different firms, but also binds customers more closely. Besides the convenience of having a single point of contact for booking and paying for an inclusive range of services, there are also network effects in such a platform business model. As the user base grows, the routeing algorithms are automatically improved, securing even better service quality for loyal customers.

An additional factor that traditionally drives customer lock-in in the automotive industry is a manufacturer's brand. While the brand will still be important in the future, brand values will potentially change. As a senior manager at moovel argues:

> Firms such as Apple are not known for entering industries where brands do not play a role.
> However, the brand value and brand attributes will probably no longer be the same as the

ones we see today at premium car manufacturers ... For instance, the technological developments in terms of autonomous driving will probably redefine passive safety and will likely reduce the accident rate, as computers will take over more and more decisions on behalf of drivers. This will not only make it possible to build cars differently; it will also create new challenges for manufacturers whose brands are currently built around outstanding vehicle safety.[19]

To deal with the distinct properties of brand value in the new and traditional businesses, Daimler introduced a strict brand distinction. The premium car business remains under the Mercedes brand, while the new mobility services have their own brands. They do not even use Mercedes vehicles, but Smart cars. The Smart brand was first introduced in the 1990s in cooperation with the Swiss watch manufacturer Swatch. Initially, the ambition to create a new form of urban mobility, with a stronger focus on unique design than the most advanced technology, did not get the expected traction. However, today, this established brand, with its distinct positioning, is the ideal nucleus around which to build the new mobility services.

Back end: Joining forces

The back-end transformation is particularly driven by the inclusion of many different partners. The primary success factor in building and managing such a broad partner network is usually not the technology or the customer base alone, but the long-term strategy and a convincing story for the future. All the players know that the industry will change, but nobody really knows how, where and when. This uncertainty can help one to gain support. A senior manager notes:

> Every new strategy that is well thought through is taken very seriously. New partners are usually willing to collaborate, since they fear the risk of not being part of a platform that succeeds in the long run. Interestingly, it even helps us that multiple players in the market develop similar platforms (eg Deutsche Bahn with Qixxit or Moovit). This creates a herd instinct, where everybody wants to be part of everything.[20]

For partner management, moovel could benefit from experience gained during the rollout of car2go. On the supply side, car2go depended on city governments' willingness to grant it permission for its free-floating car-sharing service and to support it, for instance via access to public parking spaces. The moovel platform also depends on support from its partners, such as public transport providers. While the Daimler brand turned out to be very helpful with established organizations and public transport providers, it was not effective in the start-up community. To build a reputation among these small, innovative firms, it was important for Daimler to become an active member in the community. For this purpose, Daimler Mobility Services began actively acquiring other firms to complement its offering and strengthen its position in the mobility market. For example, in 2014, it bought MyTaxi and RideScout, two platforms that allow the locating and booking of driver services. Besides gaining access to the firms' competences and customers, these deals make it increasingly interesting for others (eg taxi providers) to join the platform. As moovel's former CEO explains:

> The acquisition of MyTaxi ... is by no means an attack on established taxi operators. Quite the opposite, we would like to invite the taxi operators to work in close partnership with moovel and MyTaxi to exploit the potentials and opportunities offered by mobile internet services. In this light, the coming months will see us concentrating intensely on close collaboration with the taxi operators.[21]

Additionally Daimler announced in July 2016 that it will merge MyTaxi with Hailo, another large taxi-app provider, based in London. Together they account for about 100,000 taxi drivers. This investment comes in addition to the €500 million that Daimler had already invested to build up its mobility platform.[22] These successful acquisitions allowed Daimler and all its mobility brands[23] to gain a stronger reputation in the start-up scene, which also facilitated access to other potential partners in the future.

New processes and capabilities were also necessary to launch moovel. For this purpose, it was important not only to gain new employees but also to change the ways competences are built. A senior manager notes:

> We have a marketing unit, which is particularly strong in online marketing. Our controlling department is highly engaged in developing new payment systems and, last but not least, we have a large IT development backbone that takes care of app development and IT innovation. Altogether, Daimler Mobility Services employs around 700 people, many of whom you would not expect to find in an automotive company such as Daimler ... In recruiting, we do not follow the classical industry approach of defining a position and hiring someone from the job market. Instead, we rely on our strong network in the start-up community and on the contacts of Daimler's IT development service providers. They suggest people to us, who start on one project, often outside Daimler, and are eventually taken on-board. It is more of a start-up recruitment model.[24]

Monetization mechanics: Getting a share of the pie

The revenue streams for moovel work very differently to those of car2go. While car sharing is related to high investments in vehicles and variable usage cost, moovel's primary investment goes into developing the platform and marketing

it to contributors and customers. Accordingly, moovel is free for mobility customers, and only charges partners a small agency fee for each service sold
through the platform. For the future, other revenue streams are also possible,
such as payment service fees for transactions made directly on the platform. In the more distant future, one could even think of more innovative revenue streams such as flat-rate mobility offerings in a certain area as already
internally tested with the mobility allowance for employees. Last but not least,
an online platform always offers opportunities to use it for customer-individual
advertising. This is particularly the case for mobility service platforms that
allow one to get to know and locate customers and thus to develop and display
commercials that are aligned with both customers' usage patterns and current
locations.[25]

Summary and outlook

In terms of the business transformation board (Figure II.1), Daimler has engaged
in a two-step transformation from south to north. In a first step, with the introduction of car2go, it has moved from stand-alone transactions (ie selling cars
to customers) towards a more comprehensive service with an ongoing customer relationship. Whenever customers need a car, they can locate and rent
the closest car2go vehicle. This initial service, however, also increased standardization. While, in the traditional model, customers could configure a vehicle
in every small detail and could thus choose from millions of possible combinations, car2go offers only one fully standardized model. This standardization
makes servicing and handling the vehicles much easier, but also means that the
two-seater vehicles are not necessarily suited for all mobility needs. In a second step, the introduction of moovel has moved Daimler further north, beyond
the BM equator. Since the service offering extends well beyond car sharing
and closely integrates public transport, limousines and other services, customers have many more potential occasions to engage with the company. This
transformation also allows for mass customization, since it allows customers to
choose between different means of transport to get from A to B (see Figure 7.1).

The transformation of Daimler and its mobility services is ongoing. One of the
biggest future success drivers for moovel, according to a senior Daimler manager,
is technological developments concerning autonomous driving. The vision is that,
in the future, car2go vehicles will be capable of and allowed to autonomously pick
up customers, who either drive or get driven to their destination and who can then
leave the car on the street, where it awaits its next client. This would substantially improve car2go's flexibility and would thus reduce moovel's dependence on
other – currently more flexible – service partners. One could imagine that this may
at some point drive a backwards transformation towards mobility as a product,

Figure 7.1 Daimler's business model transformation journey

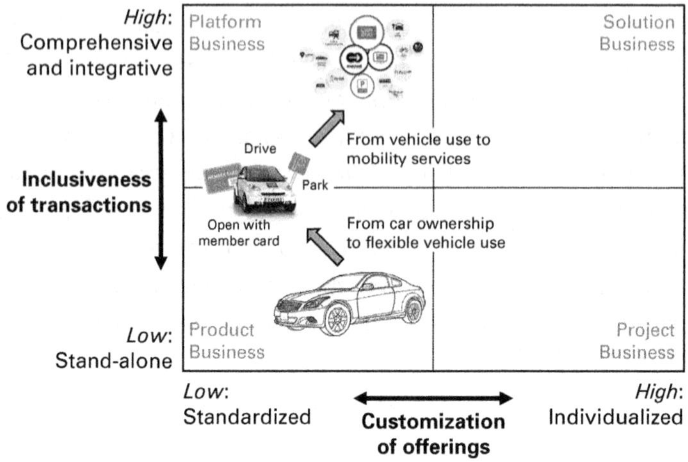

where a single service combines the convenience of a taxi or limousine with a car's flexibility at the price of public transport.

Interestingly, the novel approaches in the mobility services business are also impacting on the traditional car sales business. Here, Daimler has launched so-called Mercedes me Stores, which primarily seek to increase interactions with customers. As most people do not regularly buy premium vehicles, these stores attract potential customers by offering a bar area, a lounge and an innovative showroom where you can potentially design your virtual vehicle, while materials, colours and so on are within reach on large shelves along the walls. The show-room is thereby not the first priority. As Mercedes's head of brand strategy notes, 'Here, it's not primarily about selling cars ... The store is the best way to experi-ence what Mercedes is about without having to get into a car.'[26] The goal is to establish the store as a cool location where people want to hang out, so it regu-larly offers different events, from concerts to art exhibitions or discussion forums. While Mercedes plans 40 such stores around the world, this is only a first step to increase inclusiveness in the core business and to transform it further north-wards. As another initiative in this direction, the Mercedes me platform seeks to bundle an increasing number of services (in categories such as move me, connect me, assist me, finance me and inspire me) any time and everywhere. While there is still a long way to go, Daimler is on a clear path towards increasing inclusive-ness across its businesses. Clearly, the firm's transformation journey is far from over. In 2015 car2go was still running a three-digit loss, and it decided to withdraw from a number of cities.[27] But Daimler CEO Dieter Zetsche still believes in its sales target of €1 billion by 2020.[28]

Endnotes

1 See http://www.volkswagenag.com/content/vwcorp/info_center/en/talks_and_ presentations/2015/03/Part1.bin.html/binarystorageitem/file2/1+Rede+Winterkorn+en glisch+inkl+Verbrauch.pdf.

2 Said at the Analyst and Investor Conference, 20 March 2014.

3 Said at the annual shareholders' meeting, 4 April 2014.

4 Interview with Dieter Zetsche, The CEO Perspective, Daimler Directors' Dialogue 2015, Daimler AG Intranet.

5 For this, see a blog post of Tom Goodwin. See Hamish McRae (2015) Facebook, Airbnb, Uber, and the unstoppable rise of the content non-generators, *@TheIndyBusiness*, 5 May, http://www.independent.co.uk/news/business/comment/hamish-mcrae/facebook-airbnb-uber-and-the-unstoppable-rise-of-the-content-non-generators-10227207.html.

6 Fahrdienst-Vermittler: Uber setzt weiter auf das selbstfahrende Auto, *Spiegel Online*, 26 August 2015, http://www.spiegel.de/auto/aktuell/fahrdienst-vermittler-uber-setzt-auf-selbstfahrende-autos-a-1049884.html.

7 Daimler starts mobility concept for the city, 21 October 2008, www.media.daimler. com.

8 Interview with Robert Henrich, 5 Jahre car2go: Vom erfolgreichen Geschäftsmodell zum internationalen Service, 17 November 2013, http://blog.car2go.com/2013/11/17/5-jahre-car2go-vom-erfolgreichen-geschaftsmodell-zum-internationalen-service/.

9 Own interview.

10 Own interview.

11 Own interview.

12 Interview with Robert Henrich, 5 Jahre car2go: Der Start, 13 November 2013, http:// blog.car2go.com/2013/11/13/5-jahre-car2go-vom-start-des-pilotprojekts-zum-erfolgreichen-geschaftsmodell/.

13 Interview with Robert Henrich, 5 Jahre car2go: Der Start, 13 November 2013, http:// blog.car2go.com/2013/11/13/5-jahre-car2go-vom-start-des-pilotprojekts-zum-erfolgreichen-geschaftsmodell/.

14 Revolutionizing mobility: car2go and Europcar extend partnership Europe-wide, 21 October 2011, http://media.daimler.com/marsMediaSite/en/instance/ko/ Revolutionizing-Mobility-car2go-and-Europcar-extend-Partners.xhtml?oid=9915856.

15 Miriam Hecking (2012) Wir wollen das Amazon der Mobilität werden, Interview with Robert Henrich, *Manager Magazin*, 26 September.

16 Max Hägler (2014) Leichter ans Ziel – egal womit, *Süddeutsche Zeitung*, 13 June.

17 See http://www.smart-magazine.com/de/moovel-lab/; W Gruel and F Piller (2015) A new vision for personal transportation, *MIT Sloan Management Review*, **57**, December, pp 19–23.

18 Miriam Hecking (2012) Wir wollen das Amazon der Mobilität werden, Interview with Robert Henrich, *Manager Magazin*, 26 September.

19 Own interview.

20 Own interview.

21 moovel acquires mytaxi and ridescout, *Automotive World*, 3 September 2014, https://www.automotiveworld.com/news-releases/moovel-acquires-mytaxi-ridescout/.

22 Daimler bastelt weiter an seinem Mobilitätsangebot, 26 July 2016, http://www.handelsblatt.com/unternehmen/industrie/mytaxi-und-hailo-daimler-bastelt-weiter-an-seinem-mobilitaetsangebot/13926556.html.

23 For an overview of these services, see https://www.daimler.com/produkte/services/mobility-services/; moovel is one of these.

24 Own interview. The moovel Group GmbH employs 220 people in Germany and the United States.

25 See for example https://ideamensch.com/nir-erez/.

26 Jürgen Pander, 'Mercedes Me' in Hamburg: Autos raus und hoch die Tassen, *Spiegel Online*, 6 June 2014, http://www.spiegel.de/auto/aktuell/mercedes-me-store-premiere-fuer-ein-neues-verkaufskonzept-in-hamburg-a-973600.html.

27 *Manager Magazin*, 18 March 2015.

28 See http://www.wiwo.de/unternehmen/auto/daimler-zetsche-bestaetigt-milliarden-umsatzziel-von-car2go/13908452.html (22 August 2016).

LEGIC Identsystems Ltd: From selling ID cards to providing access to an ID network
Guido Baltes and Klaus U Klosa

LEGIC, a technology provider in the field of identification technology, has success-fully mastered a challenging transformation from being analogue-driven to be-coming a digitally driven business model. It began as a product business, which because of proprietary features had some stickiness. This, however, diminished and the product commoditized over the maturation of its market. Faced with this situation, LEGIC initiated a bold move to transform the business model from south to north, ie from a non-sticky product business to a platform business. Integrating its physical product offerings with software and service components, it managed to leverage its technology competences, an established partner network and brand assets into an innovative holistic offering. Not only has this been successfully launched in one of its key vertical markets, but it has also enabled LEGIC to suc-cessfully re-enter market segments it had lost during the maturation of its industry.

LEGIC and its roots in the ID technologies market

Since 1992, LEGIC has designed and provided contactless radio frequency iden-tification (RFID) technology for ID applications, ranging from access control and time and attendance to e-ticketing. The company was launched by Kaba AG, a Swiss-based, internationally leading provider of innovative access solutions for the security industry. LEGIC acts as a self-sustained company in the smartcard market, serving its partners, amongst them the Kaba Group.

RFID technologies are at the heart of what is frequently addressed as the 'Internet of Things' (IoT), and has revolutionized how we can identify objects and people. Such systems consist of one or more transponders, carrying identifying information, and a reader that accesses (ie 'reads') the identifying information stored on the transponders without line of sight. RFID applications span a large number of areas such as access control (eg automobile ignition keys) and ID management (RFID-enabled passports) or payment (eg proximity card features in credit cards). But it also deals with asset tracking (eg automated check-in and check-out of stock or cattle tracking) and activity monitoring (eg medication in-takes of elderly people).

The Internet of Things now aims to connect people and things any time, anywhere, for interacting, communicating and sensing purposes, based on exchanging data and information. Contactless identification is one of the core technologies that provides infrastructure for this seamless interconnection with a dynamic global network with self-configuring capabilities. Here, RFID seamlessly integrates people, physical 'things' and their personality into information networks. This 'personality' encompasses both physical and virtual attributes. Thereby, 'things' in the real world may 'sense' and react autonomously without human intervention.

At its kick-off, LEGIC was the first company to present a secure, contactless smartcard technology for access control and other identification applications at 13.56 MHz. Its direct customers are mainly implementers, ie system integrators that design, implement and maintain customer-specific solutions or products like ID terminals. More than 250 such partners are licensed to use the LEGIC ID intellectual property (IP) and technology for developing reliable ID systems for their end-user companies. Every day, more than 150 million people in more than 100,000 companies and institutions identify themselves with LEGIC ID technology. The origin of LEGIC's profitable and growing business fuelled its self-conception as an innovative pioneer in technology for access control.

At its core, LEGIC's technology traditionally materializes as a product-based, key-and-lock type of offering, with reader chips (part of the reader terminal identifying the respective smartcard) as the 'lock' at one end, and transponder chips (part of a smartcard) as the 'key' at the other. This product offering is complemented with a token-based control system (Master-Token System-Control) for convenient management of rights and applications at the end-user company. Designing these components in Switzerland, LEGIC traditionally operates as a fabless semiconductor company in the ID security domain.

LEGIC's product offerings, following a lock-and-key characteristic, show fundamentally different life cycles: the 'lock' parts, ie reader chips, are designed for stationary devices (eg door lock, point-of-sales terminal) and are built to last, not only in terms of durability but also with regard to forward compatibility. They are fairly complex, as their architecture anticipates compatibility with future technologies, and addresses LEGIC partners at the point of design-in decisions. Once designed into, for example, a partner's reader terminal product, subsequent design-out is unlikely, creating further demand along the life cycle of the product into which the reader chip has been designed. The 'key' parts, ie the transponder chips, are in contrast simpler, cheaper, consumable devices: in the US, per hotel lock, 100 key cards are consumed per year, while the lock itself (and the built-in chip) will typically last for about 10 years.

The complementing Master-Token System-Control has built LEGIC's reputation for enabling convenient handling of multi-applications, ie use cases where one smartcard serves various applications (eg a student ID card: to pay for meals, buy coffee, check out books, enter access-controlled laboratories, enter a car park). LEGIC's licensed partners profit from this by being able to provide top-class ID solutions to their end-users – without having to be experts in ID technology. In contrast, the partner's selling proposition is typically close to the end customer's use case (eg a hotel, a university).

LEGIC's product business model as a vendor of physical ID security

LEGIC's 'traditional' product business model is based on a physical offering that entails a proprietary key-and-lock characteristic: the design-in decision of a LEGIC partner not only binds the partner's product to the designed-in reader chip but also binds the partner's corporate end customers to LEGIC's matching transponders. Partners driving these design-in decisions thus represent LEGIC's strategic customer base.

For this reason, the reader-to-transponder ratio of numbers sold reflects the development of the market. In its early days at the end of the 1990s, this ratio was far above 100 for LEGIC. However, the market quickly adopted affordable, contactless access applications for low-cost environments such as ski ticketing. This, in part, was fuelled by reader-chip prices being cut in half from one generation to the next. Emerging low-security, contactless applications, together with technology advances, enforced commoditization of the market as a whole and of the low-end segment in particular. In order to cope with this market evolution, LEGIC strategically and gradually focused its product business towards more demanding, ie multi-application, scenarios, which in turn resulted in a significantly decreasing ratio of about 50 in the mid-2000s.

As a further effect of this market maturation, the product business model's inherent key-and-lock scheme lost its proprietary characteristic: LEGIC's reader chips now also worked with competitors' transponders, eg MIFARE® cards. While this improved competitiveness for the design-in decisions of partners, it caused an even further ratio drop, which caused the transponder part of the business to remain flat (in terms of numbers). The impact on revenue was even greater. Facing commoditization on the transponder side since the late 1990s, towards the mid-2000s growth in numbers sold no longer compensated for decreasing prices. The company, with its fabless value structure, was thus forced to revise its strategy.

Along the way, the management board of LEGIC found its long-standing product business model being put into question. Even though the market adoption of contactless applications was growing impressively, and though LEGIC's number of units sold was growing, LEGIC's revenue was expected to flatten out. This rendered future IP development, the core of LEGIC's brand and reputation, no longer affordable.

In anticipation of this, the company management board of LEGIC considered various scenarios for adapting the business model in order to create additional streams of revenue for sustainable growth. However, considering this, path dependencies occurred. Moving the established product business model further up the value chain into project or solution business may have seemed obvious. However, this vertical expansion would probably bring LEGIC into conflict with its partners and thus spoil the existing product business. Instead, a horizontal expansion was considered. By adding complementary software and service offerings to the existing product portfolio, a transformation northward into a platform business model was prioritized.

As a result, the inception of near-field communication (NFC), technology-wise in 2003, market-wise in 2004 (NFC Forum), to be featured in a mobile device in 2006 (Nokia), caught LEGIC's attention: it was one of the pioneers to experiment with this new technology. Integrating NFC into its technology roadmap, LEGIC began to ship NFC-enabled reader chips in 2007 and pioneered a card-in-card solution that ported on to an NFC-equipped Nokia mobile phone to work as a smart device. The same year, however, with Apple's iPhone, the smartphone paradigm hit the market, not only erasing NFC-supporting Nokia but also diverting attention to the app ecosystem – converting prospering NFC expectations into a sleeping beauty. This backlash of LEGIC's intended business model transformation was further amplified by the dramatic impact of the financial crisis.

While LEGIC was still recovering from the deep financial impact of the crisis, its blueprints for software and service expansion were reawakened in 2011 by hospitality customers pointing to a major US market companion, which showcased opening a hotel's door locks with a mobile phone. Profiting from the dozing assets of the past, LEGIC was prepared to jump aboard. It started exploring the mobile ID case with new enthusiasm, both on the technology and on the customer side. Based on positive results, a software and service project to showcase mobile ID as testimonial case for LEGIC's transformation towards a platform business model was kicked off. Confidence was regained and employees were informed of the strategic intent beginning in 2012.

Transformation: From a physical key-and-lock-type product business to a software and service platform offering

At this point, LEGIC's management board and CEO were clear in their intent to transform LEGIC northward from a product business model into a platform business driven by software and services. This was further amplified by significant changes in the market environment: LEGIC partners in the hospitality industry, eg system integrators and door lock providers, were pushed by their end customers, ie hotels, to provide a credible perspective that mobile ID technology and capabilities would be on their product roadmap in the near future. This suddenly turned mobile ID capability from a sleeping beauty into a prerequisite for remaining on a hotel chain's supplier list. It was to be expected that other vertical markets would follow this scheme.

This turned LEGIC's idea of software and service expansion into an opportunity at the core of its business, providing its partners with a convenient yet capable solution to offer mobile ID technology to their corporate end customers. Facing this, LEGIC pushed to develop a technical analogy for its physical ID architecture – a trusted service to manage credentials on mobile devices. This trusted service management (TSM) platform would be provided as a white-label service to LEGIC's partners, thereby enabling them to provide mobile ID solutions to their end customers. Such mobile ID solutions would allow end customers to run their ID infrastructure (door locks, terminals, etc) with credentials signalled via mobile networks to mobile devices of single users, as an alternative to the smartcard. With technology IP and experience available from the early attempts in 2007, building the technical core of the TSM proved to be a comparably easy task, as did using NFC alongside Bluetooth. However, despite early wins in the technology field, transforming the organization as a whole proved to be the true challenge.

The software and services project, initially intended as a horizontal business expansion, turned out to be a business model transformation, impacting the company as a whole. In this respect, an external expert was hired and installed as the entrepreneurial leader of the software and service team. He brought to the table his experience in the software industry and processes within diverse vertical smartcard markets. To strengthen that role and enable strategic autonomy of the team, he directly reported to the CEO and was appointed a member of the management board. His job was to implement the software and service project as an embedded entrepreneurial team, and to build up what was supposed to be the future competitive edge for LEGIC. Notably, he was appointed a member of the board without any operational responsibility other than for the software and service team, which was at the time a small project in its very early stages. However, the team was not only expected to harvest the new business opportunity laid out with a mobile ID solution but also strategically intended as the root for the transformation into a platform business that would not only affect LEGIC as a whole but also pave the way to digitized businesses for LEGIC's parent company, Kaba AG. The entrepreneurial spirit and leadership style of the hired and installed entrepreneurial leader motivated previously rather reluctant people to join the team and support the project: early movers now received recognition for pursuing new paths, for example agile developing and testing, which soon also resonated beyond the team.

Front-end transformation: Towards a holistic offering the LEGIC way

The software and service project was positively perceived on the market as a revival of LEGIC's front-running role in innovation. However, besides successfully tackling technology challenges, LEGIC still had to develop a comprehensive value proposition and monetization scheme to encourage the adoption of its service in its customer base.

The comprehensive value proposition would feature not only mobile-enabled reader chips and a TSM platform but also a software development kit (SDK) enabling LEGIC partners to create customer-specific mobile phone apps and a low-cost transponder as an offline back-up. LEGIC did not expect smartphones to render smartcards completely obsolete. Instead, smartcards were expected to play a role in most applications for the foreseeable future. Therefore, LEGIC synchronized development of a very low-cost transponder by backward-integrating and developing a proprietary physical chip design, whose cost price was to match the lowest end of the transponder market. This enabled the market readiness of LEGIC's comprehensive value proposition by the second half of 2014: the LEGIC way.

In addition, the newly developed LEGIC Connect services bundle packages tailored to different customer segments and use case complexity. As a part of that, onboarding services provide professional service that supports customers to conceptualize their use case, customize the relevant features and update their infrastructure. This onboarding is offered not only to LEGIC partners but also to the end customers of LEGIC's partners. The market, still in an early stage, results in end customers struggling with integrating mobile ID technology into their business processes and pricing. LEGIC aims at automating these services by way of standardized training, tutorials, webinars and the like. This, however, cannot be expected until sufficient saturation of use cases is reached.

This new, holistic offering, as well as the increased complexity in customer interaction, required new sales capabilities compatible with longer sales cycles and consultative support. For LEGIC, being a traditionally hardware-driven company at heart, this formed a tough challenge, for example regarding adoption of controlled market experiments as part of agile (software) development.

At the same time, the 'traditional' hardware business entered choppy waters, as the industry was still recovering from the impacts of the financial crisis. This caused a situation of continuous conflicts of interest. At the same time, there was a need for cost efficiency in the traditional business and for investment in an uncertain software and services opportunity. This was fuelled by a 'no loss-making unit' paradigm in the Kaba group. Therefore, it was discussed whether merging LEGIC's innovation capabilities with Kaba's R&D might provide a viable strategic option. At this point, however, the value of direct market access for the innovation team prevailed. Following this, sales personnel were asked to test the waters to seize market opportunities for the transformation into a platform business, and simultaneously urged to meet their counterparts in the product business. These inherent conflicts, as well as varying levels of acceptance and enthusiasm regarding the intended business model transformation, caused concerns to the extent that the management board began using change barometers to determine what was happening. These highlighted that the need for change was perceived as crucial and urgent, while the mid-term strategic targets seemed rather unclear.

While this signalled that the transformation had yet to gain momentum, the holistic offering enabled LEGIC to successfully re-enter market segments it had lost during the maturation of its industry. In particular in the hotel industry, the holistic offering, the convenience provided and the well-balanced security offered an attractive package that enabled LEGIC to get the Cromwell hotel in Las Vegas operational with the TSM-based mobile ID technology at the end of 2014. In the first quarter of 2015, four global hotel chains followed. Since then, more global hotel chains have become operational.

Back-end transformation: Towards an integrated architecture and agile software development

Traditionally following the 'failure is not an option' paradigm of the security industry, LEGIC had to adopt agile software development with customer-centric application prototyping and platform design in order to push the software and service business. In addition, for accelerating the ramp-up process, the software development was to a larger extent externalized. While this led to quick wins on the technology roadmap, the externalization of the newly established competences further increased agitation about the strategic reasoning.

Facing this situation, the CEO identified the need for entrepreneurial leadership and invited all employees to pose their questions to the company management in company public Q&A sessions. Answering those questions was not only found to support clarification of the strategic intent but also supported the management in identifying open issues on their side. The first Q&A session was opened by the CEO with a longer address on his entrepreneurial vision and anticipation of the future, naming mobile ID solutions as a tremendous opportunity as well as a serious threat – the business solution for the company thus being somewhat open, as it once again intends to pioneer the market.

After this opening address, numerous questions were posed by the people attending. The board members' answers were found convincing, and together with the opening address fueled acceptance of and curiosity about the software and service project among the attendees. On the other hand, this clarified the shift in paradigms for employees – raising questions as to whether they would feel confidently matched with the envisioned future – leading to a slightly increased personnel fluctuation. This, however, provided the opportunity to extend and renew LEGIC's competence base in anticipation of the challenges ahead.

To further fuel this renewal of the company's capabilities, the head of R&D, assigned to the 'traditional' R&D side, took the task of internalizing the experiential learning experiences from the software and service project. Thereby, LEGIC's R&D soon went into a learning loop for adopting agile methods on an even broader base. Alongside that, the software and service project team build up competences and resources that initially had been externalized stepwise during maturation of the prototype. These activities allowed for scaling the back end from agile prototyping to a reliably scaling operation of the system.

This back-end transformation was complemented by multisided efforts to leverage the established partner network into new strategic partnerships that would be crucial for the market adoption. Mobile network operators (MNOs) were attributed a key role in this partnership, as they provide access to SIM cards as a secure element and manage transfer and monitoring of credentials via their mobile network. LEGIC leveraged the ID Network, the legacy of LEGIC's long-standing and established professional management of its partner ecosystem, to offer MNOs a one-stop-shop access to 150 million people in more than 100,000 companies, served by hundreds of LEGIC partner companies.

Monetization transformation: Towards integrated pricing and recurring revenue schemes

On their way, LEGIC's software and service team tackled their challenges successfully, with one question remaining: what would be an acceptable pricing model for their customers?

The beauty of the key card business in this respect is striking: you sell a card, it will be replaced, and you sell it again. The monetization of the new model is far more complex: who is paying for what, in what fashion? A hotel, for example, is accustomed to paying for key cards as they are consumed over time. What would be the analogy for such a situation in the new model?

As those questions could only be answered by a customer, it was a key target to get a paying customer operational. Working together closely with a system integrator as a strategic partner, the Cromwell was first at the end of 2014, and four further hotel chains quickly followed. This provided valuable insights into accepted pricing models: while the smartcard pricing was based on consumption, mobile ID solutions are accepted as a subscription service for an installed base of reader terminals, ie door locks in the case of a hotel. This recurring part of the pricing model is covered by a per-lock-per-year subscription.

However, as adoption is in an early stage, this model may be considered to be in flux. Prices for such fees cover a broad range – reflecting a similar broad range of service levels offered. Based on a value pricing of what LEGIC has to offer, the price value in hospitality would be more than $100 per lock per year, while the services can be offered at a price of nearly half of that based on the LEGIC Connect services. With that, LEGIC is currently in a pioneer position to shape customers' expectations and their cognitive anchors.

Adding to this integrated, recurring revenue stream based on small amounts is the software development kit. This kit acts as part of the service bundle used by the customer to customize the solution and integrate it into the customer's value chain. Here, the pricing is based on a licensing model; that is, the customers will be charged for the number of smartphone apps being developed with the SDK.

As seen from the hotel cases, these apps seem to provide the highest, directly perceived value to the end customer: a hotel integrating mobile ID technology into its proprietary smartphone app can offer its hotel guests the possibility to skip the check-in procedure and head directly to their room. Such customers may have appreciated the hotel's app, leading to future direct bookings with that app, instead of any arbitrary, price-driven, travel agent e-booking. This would result in a double-digit margin improvement on the directly reserved room – which is a good reason for embracing the mobile ID solution from a hotel's perspective. And, in turn, it seems that the mobile-access-no-need-to-check-in feature of a hotel app is the feature most embraced by hotel customers: a win–win situation delivering a prosperous future for LEGIC's software and service endeavour.

Outlook

Looking back we can see that LEGIC was able to transform its business model several times (see Figure 7.2). Currently, it seems that LEGIC's business model is well set to survive a disruptive change of paradigms moving into the market. The company has not addressed it primarily as a technological challenge, but rather as a business model innovation. With that, it has put itself at the forefront of the developments and has used these as an opportunity rather than a threat. However, the situation is still quite dynamic, and the dominant paradigm of the future has yet to emerge.

Thus, the roles of partners in LEGIC's business ecosystem might change, as well as the pricing model currently in place. This can be expected to increasingly stabilize as LEGIC enters further vertical and regional markets to establish LEGIC's Connect services as the platform of choice in mobile ID solutions.

Figure 7.2 LEGIC's business model transformation journey

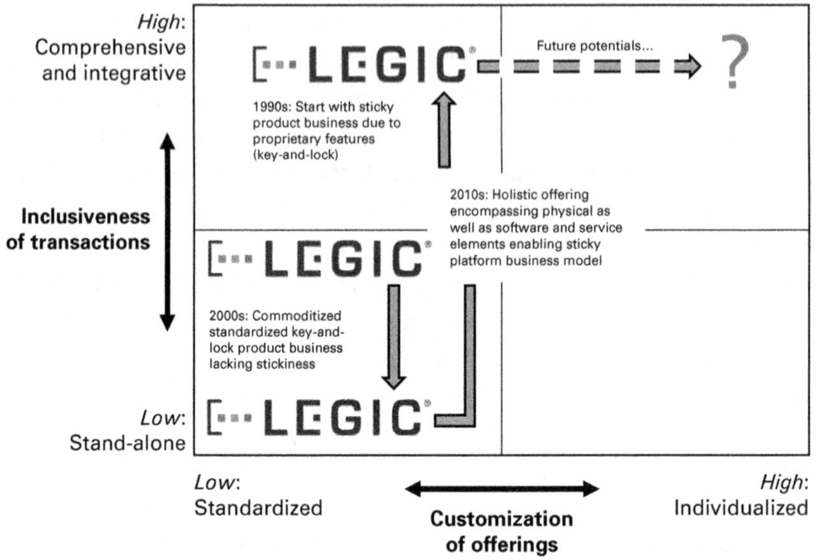

In its early days, LEGIC started with a product business that, owing to its proprietary key-and-lock characteristic, entailed some stickiness with retention-oriented customer relations. Market maturation however has affected this proprietary feature, and both the product price and stickiness have gradually decreased over time. This has been anticipated as a strategic threat, given the competence-based positioning of LEGIC within the market.

At this point, LEGIC's management boldly transformed the business model into a platform business that would still encompass its physical product offering (ID transponder and reader chips), but better leverage its technology competences, the established partner network (LEGIC's ID Network) and brand assets. With its holistic offering being positively received and the vertical launch in hospitality implemented, this transformation can be regarded as having been successfully mastered. There were some companies that did not master this challenge of transforming from an analogue to a digital business model.

Nevertheless, the road will probably not end here, as this transformation, now that it has gained momentum and harvested some initial successes, will further evolve. The initial experiences with customer cases seem to indicate that in the future, for example, onboarding services may emerge into more customized services as part of the holistic offering. Moreover, as further vertical markets are added to the portfolio, industry-specific solutions may emerge. Such service customization may entail augmentation of the initiated transformation eastward, toward a solution-oriented business model.

In addition to that, LEGIC's parent company, Kaba AG, has announced plans to merge with Germany's Dorma Holding to form a new market-leading group in building security and access products. This aims at addressing megatrends such as urbanization and digitalization. The merger thus may put LEGIC's software and service innovation into the strategic focus of the newly formed group. The aim of leveraging these assets within the new dorma+kaba Holding may motivate reconsideration of the merging of LEGIC's innovation capabilities with the new group's R&D, as now not only the technology but also the business model is successfully established.

SAP: From pioneer of standard enterprise software to leading digital company

Carsten Linz[1]

SAP's company evolution 1972–2009: The integrated suite as growth engine

Today, SAP is the world's leader in enterprise application software, with more than 300,000 customers in 190 countries and 77,000 employees in 130 countries.[2] Back in 1972 the company began as a start-up with the idea of developing and licensing standardized and integrated software packages as an extendable system. This approach stood in sharp contrast to the industry standard in those days, namely developing software for every customer individually on a project-by-project basis. It was June 1972 when in Mannheim, Germany five former IBM engineers – Dietmar Hopp, Klaus Tschira, Hans-Werner Hector, Hasso Plattner and Claus Wellenreuther – founded their company System Analyse und Programmentwicklung (System Analysis and Programme Development) as a private partnership.[3] The young company began its business with one customer, the German branch of Imperial Chemical Industries, a handful of employees and surprisingly enough no computer at all. Therefore, the first programmes for payroll and accounting were developed during night shifts on the mainframe computer of their very first customer. The software was developed on-site in tight collaboration with the customer, which allowed the young company to build truly business-relevant applications right from the start. In 1973 the first commercial product for financial accounting was launched, which later was named SAP R/1.

In 1976, SAP GmbH (Limited) was founded, and in the following year moved its headquarters to Walldorf, Germany. In 1982 the SAP R/2 era began. The new company was built on the dream of real-time computing, namely software that processes data when customers ask for it rather than processing it overnight in batches, which today is known as online transaction processing (OLTP). Following this ambition, the young team stored the data locally; hence there was no need to process the mechanical punch cards overnight. Consequently, they called their software a real-time system, leading to their product named SAP R/2 – R for real time, which was unique at that time. SAP's first flagship product truly packaged software application processes and integrated enterprise business functions in real time on a mainframe computer. As an example, an invoice from the billing transactions would pass through to accounting, where it would appear in accounts receivable and cost of goods sold. As an off-the-shelf standard software package, SAP R/2 could be offered to a broader market and started to broadly replace the project approach for customized software, because it could be installed more cheaply and quickly. The company kept growing and, 10 years later with the launch of SAP

R/3 in July 1992, the new client–server era started and SAP's real-time approach reached the desktop. SAP R/3 could automate all of an enterprise's business processes, from manufacturing to sales, services, distribution, finance and human resources, and efficiently allocate resources across complex enterprises. The SAP R/3 suite comprised various software modules, and its common architecture allowed for seamless integration amongst them. This major milestone made SAP the de facto standard in the so-called enterprise resource planning (ERP) market. Subsequently, SAP started to enhance its ERP offering by functional applications like customer relationship management, supply chain management and also industry solutions like utilities, consumer products, retail, oil and gas, and so on. SAP had a clear applications focus, and the company strategy was to be platform-agnostic; hence all SAP applications could be run on any database (DB) from every major vendor and on any server operating system, for example Unix, Linux, Solaris and Windows Server, which often was referred as an 'any-DB' strategy. This lowered the typical system entry barrier and made SAP software interesting for a broad set of customers. In the second half of the 1990s, the internet radically shifted the focus for business software from integration of processes within companies to integration between enterprises. Open protocols and web services were pushed as the 'holy grail' of software integration, with the promise that selecting and integrating the best product is preferable to selecting one large integrated solution from a single vendor. Start-ups began to offer these 'best-of-breed' solutions for a specific business function, which focused on a very limited set of business processes but with the promise of a lot of functional depth, for example Siebel for customer relationship management or i2 for supply chain management. At that time, there was a lot of debate about whether SAP could keep its leading market position, but over time it showed that customers looked for seamlessly integrated end-to-end processes across many functions. In consequence the advantage of SAP's suite approach with its wealth of integrated applications was generally favoured over the best-of-breed approach in which companies purchase software by application area from different vendors. Wikipedia puts it this way: '[SAP] had the advantage of being integrated with the rest of its ERP solution: in the domain of the large multinational clients, the twin arguments of total integration and single-vendor sourcing proved decisive.'[4] In 1998 two of SAP's co-founders, Dietmar Hopp and Klaus Tschira, announced their decision to resign from the company's executive board. Both made the transition to the SAP supervisory board, where Hopp took over as chairman. Meanwhile, the supervisory board named Henning Kagermann co-CEO of the company as the first non-founder – alongside Hasso Plattner. In May 1999 in the middle of the 'new economy', SAP co-CEO Hasso Plattner announced the new mySAP.com strategy, which completely realigned the company and its product portfolio. This new strategy combined e-commerce solutions with SAP's existing ERP applications on the basis of cutting-edge web technology. As a result, employees, customers, suppliers and other business partners could work together across company borders. In 2000, SAP entered the world of electronic marketplaces and corporate portals by outsourcing its corresponding areas to its SAP Markets and SAP Portals subsidiaries, respectively, and starting a partnership with Commerce One. In 2001 SAP acquired the Israeli company TopTier, at the time one of the leading corporate portal vendors.[5] As service-oriented architecture (SOA) standards led to a focus on easy exchange of data between systems and enterprises, SAP made the strategic decision to plan its future around this concept. In 2003, SAP revealed the SAP NetWeaver application and integration platform to reach interoperability and reusability both inside enterprise and across enterprise borders, and hence help companies bring together a wide variety of IT systems. It combined SAP's traditional proprietary APAP programming language with open web-based technologies, for example Sun's Java. The platform was also required to counter the platform offerings of competitors like Microsoft's .NET and IBM's WebSphere, which were aggressively pushed in the market. In 2003 Hasso Plattner resigned from the executive board and since then has been elected chairman of the supervisory board. Plattner is the final SAP co-founder to leave the company's management team, but remains with SAP in an advisory role. In 2007 CEO Henning Kagermann announced that all SAP business applications would be made service-based in the medium term to provide its customers with the utmost flexibility possible. In doing so, SAP set the standard for the rest of the enterprise market. Under Kagermann's leadership, quarterly revenue gains and a constantly increasing market share kept SAP on top of the competition in the rejuvenated IT market. *BusinessWeek* named Kagermann one of the 25 best business managers in Europe. Despite the 'new economy' bubble burst, which resulted in a sharp decline in IT investments, customer faith in SAP's solutions remained intact.

Under Kagermann's leadership, in 2007 SAP announced its intention to acquire Business Objects, a French company specializing in the fast-growing market for business intelligence applications, which was successfully completed for €6.78 billion in 2008. This move broke with SAP's traditional strategy of avoiding large company acquisitions and preferring to grow its business organically. During the global financial crisis SAP also faced difficult circumstances. Thanks to special customer programmes and personnel cutbacks, as well as other cost-saving measures, the company was even able to improve its operating margin.

SAP's years from 1972 until 2009 were an era of exponential growth. Licence revenue skyrocketed, and the number of employees tripled. With R/2 and R/3, SAP redefined the software market and became the new de facto standard. Customer-specific software development projects became a thing of the past. The new normal was the off-the-shelf standard software suite on any database, which architecturally integrates various software modules and functions as an extendable system. The acquisition of Business Objects further broadened SAP's portfolio and made SAP the market leader in business software, enterprise performance management and business intelligence. Given this track record, SAP's future strategy should not only continue this growth trajectory but additionally take the company to the next level of growth.

SAP's 2010 digital strategy: Heading platform and going cloud

The new growth programme: Doubling the addressable market

In February 2010, the supervisory board named Bill McDermott and Jim Hagemann Snabe co-CEOs of SAP. In April 2010 they jointly announced an aggressive company-wide growth programme with the goal of doubling the addressable market for SAP via a dedicated focus on platform development and transition into the cloud. The plan was to continue growing SAP's core business with enterprise applications and business analytics and additionally pursuing three disruptive technology markets, namely mobile, in-memory and then cloud computing. Based on this strategy, the following company objectives were set for 2015: €20 billion in revenue with a 35 per cent non-IFRS operating margin, 1 billion users of SAP software, a €2 billion cloud business, and to be the fastest-growing database company.

The key challenge in starting this massive transformation programme was that there was no evident need for it because SAP was already the market leader in both enterprise applications and business analytics; hence it was all about taking a healthy company to the next level of ambition. Jim Hagemann Snabe noted in this context:

> The hardest thing in business is to change a company that is not in a disastrous place. We did not have a sense of urgency because of the strength of our core products and our commitment to growing those segments. We had to inspire our teams with a new opportunity and not a threat.[6]

One of the first milestones of the new growth programme was SAP's announcement in May 2010 that it was purchasing the California-based company Sybase, the largest business software and service provider specializing in mobile, to produce solutions for 'wireless' companies. The acquisition was completed for $5.8 billion in July and not only made SAP a viable player in the mobile market but, owing to Sybase's ASE and IQ database business, also provided SAP with additional columnar database experts for its most strategic bet.

The in-memory revolution: HANA as new digital foundation

The true foundation for SAP's 2010 strategy was the revolutionary in-memory database SAP HANA.[7] The early beginnings of HANA were about TREX, which became a SAP component in 2000. The SAP NetWeaver BI Accelerator was first rolled out in 2005. In 2009, Hasso Plattner presented the results of two years of research at the SIGMOD database conference in Providence, Rhode Island. SAP HANA was then developed in close collaboration between SAP and the Hasso Plattner Institute (HPI) in Potsdam, near Berlin, which is the university institute and excellence centre for IT systems engineering founded by Hasso Plattner himself. Subsequently SAP started to develop a professional version of an in-memory database for transaction processing and analytical systems using a columnar in-memory database and called it SAP HANA. For developing and enforcing such a disruptive technology, the combination of the independent and physically separated university research, combined with SAP's vast business and IT experience, proved to be a key factor for success.

SAP HANA was launched in 2010, and the first customers started implementing the platform in the course of 2011. As the next logical step, in February 2013 SAP launched the open HANA Cloud Platform (HCP), which allows the leveraging of HANA functionality to build, extend and integrate applications in the cloud, which is also referred to as platform-as-a-service.[8] By 2015, SAP HANA had become a market-leading platform for real-time computing, underlying the technology for all major SAP applications. Hasso Plattner explained the market need for SAP's in-memory solution: '[All existing ERP systems] were based on the idea that we know exactly what the user wants to know. In order to answer their question in a reasonable timeframe, we maintained aggregated data in real time – meaning that whenever we recorded a business transaction we updated all impacted totals. Therefore the system was ready to give answers to any foreseeable question, thus labelled a real-time system.'[9] In contrast, the radical idea of SAP HANA is to completely drop derived data like aggregates, tables and database indices due to the fact that all data is kept in memory and can be calculated on demand with close-to-zero response time. The disparate worlds of business transactions and business analytics should come together to build entirely new enterprise applications allowing full insight-to-action processing. Technically speaking, the SAP HANA database runs both online transaction processing (OLTP) and online analytical processing (OLAP) on one single system. Not only is such a system much faster in reporting and analytics as a result of the in-memory advantage but also the business transaction processing runs approximately three to four times faster thanks to the removed redundancies. Eventually, this allowed a focusing on the business logic and delivery of a full real-time application system for the enterprise. The combination of free navigation in very large data sets, the ability to process structured and unstructured data like social media, and the power of mathematical libraries inside HANA allows the building of applications on top, which had just not been possible in the past. Examples include hurricane damage forecasting, genomics and proteomics applications, new innovative ways of carrying out cancer research, traffic optimization and so on.

The cloud as the new normal: SAP's transformation into a cloud provider

The availability of high-capacity networks, low-cost computers and storage and the widespread adoption of hardware virtualization, service-oriented architecture and utility computing led to a substantial growth in cloud computing. According to Gartner, the worldwide public cloud services market was projected to grow 17.2 per cent in 2016 to total $208 billion, up from $178 billion in 2015.[10] 'This strong growth continues to reflect a shift away from legacy IT services to cloud-based services, due to the increased trend of organizations pursuing a digital business strategy.'[11] Forrester sees comparable growth and projects that the public cloud market will reach $191 billion by 2020.[12] As yet, no shared definition for cloud computing exists, but there is general agreement on the central characteristics of the concept. Based on US National Institute of Standards and Technology (NIST) definitions,[13] we describe cloud computing as 'IT consumed as a service via the internet on the basis of shared, elastic third-party resources'. Generally speaking, cloud computing also implies a shift in IT buying from the CIO to the lines of business.

Key advantages of cloud computing include regular software updates with new innovative features and new security functionality, subscription-based payment schemes without upfront capital investments, and operational flexibility for businesses with growing or fluctuating bandwidth demands. There are also concerns: despite high security standards, firms find it risky to put their sensitive business data into a cloud-based solution, as they often do not have full transparency where it resides. With the automatic update process in the hands of the provider, the well-known user interface might be adjusted or new features introduced unnoticed. Cloud contracts can also be regarded as fairly rigid, with a certain level of vendor lock-in for the buyer; for example, many last for three years as a minimum.

Given the ambition of SAP's new growth programme, with its goal of €2 billion cloud revenues by 2015, the company invested substantially in R&D to develop standardized and scalable cloud solutions for lines of business like HR, procurement, CRM and finance. At the same time, pure-play cloud companies attacked SAP in specialized domains, for example Salesforce.com in salesforce automation, which is a part of CRM. Another pure-play cloud company is Workday, which competes in parts of the human capital management market. The situation was comparable to the on-premises best-of-breed competition that SAP had in the 1990s, but this time in the cloud context.

This made SAP's decision to acquire a series of subscription-based software companies in addition to its own software developments even more logical. In December 2011 SAP purchased SuccessFactors (the leader in cloud-based human capital management software) for $3.6 billion, and in May 2012 it purchased Ariba (the world's largest business-to-business commerce network, which has been going through an on-premises to cloud transformation itself) for $4.3 billion. Hybris – a leading e-commerce company – was acquired in June 2013 for an estimated $1.3 billion. Fieldglass – the number one vendor management service provider for contingent staffing – followed in March 2014 for $1.0 billion. In September 2014 Concur – the leader in cloud-based travel-and-expense management – was acquired for $8.3 billion. Today, SAP's Business Network Group comprises Ariba, Fieldglass and Concur, using an open platform to connect internal business processes to external stakeholders.[14] In total, SAP invested more than $18 billion in external growth to further extend its footprint in the cloud market and secure a critical mass of cloud DNA across the company.

SAP's transformation: front end, back end and monetization mechanics

In the following, SAP's business model transformation, from south to north in the logic of the business transformation board (Figure II.1), is described regarding the shifts in front end, back end and monetization mechanics.

Front-end transformation: From selling software products to providing integrated business processes powered by the SAP HANA platform

'We believe that there is a new opportunity for extending the reach of type of applications that we are known for', said Jim Hagemann Snabe, co-CEO and board member for development, in 2009 at the Influencer Summit. SAP is well known for its strength in end-to-end process integration across all 'modules' of its application portfolio based on a common architecture. The future path was also clearly laid out in the new growth programme, namely to build on its integration strength and drive with innovation the breadth and depth of the software portfolio to the next level. For this purpose, a differentiating platform foundation that offered shared functions and tools was needed. The programme to make all applications run on SAP HANA can be considered one of SAP's biggest strategic bets in the company's history.

The transformation programme's endeavour started with the question of whether the existing SAP Business Suite, with its 400 million lines of code, could be adapted to HANA in a reasonable amount of time. If not, the alternative meant building a successor for the Business Suite from scratch. It was clear that customers must be provided with a non-disruptive technical move from the existing Business Suite to the next Business Suite on HANA. To meet both the adoption and the non-disruption goals, the following staged plan was developed and ready for execution in March 2012:[15]

1 Migration of all existing Business Suite systems to HANA.

2 Optimization of the existing enterprise applications towards the HANA platform.

3 Simplification by rewriting all enterprise applications.

The first step of the plan was relatively easy, as – with a few adaptations – SAP's existing applications worked on HANA as on any other database, because there was no change in data structure. Hence the benefit was geared towards reduced data footprint and immediate acceleration of analytical queries. In January 2013 the new 'SAP Business Suite on HANA' was launched with over 1,100 HANA-optimized processes. General market availability followed in June 2013, and the first goal – the migration of the existing Business Suite to HANA – was met.

The second step of the plan was more challenging. The team started the in-memory optimization with the operational reporting function, which was embedded directly into the enterprise applications, and it worked. Transactions and analytics were brought into a single system, SAP HANA became the single source, and unnecessary data transfers, consistency checks and data reorganizations were immediately removed.

The plan's third step – applications running 'in' SAP HANA and using it natively – was the most challenging, because it aimed at a completely new architecture for enterprise applications through the replacement of aggregates with on-the-fly calculated views. SAP started to rewrite its enterprise applications in mid-2012, and SAP Simple Finance[16] was the first solution of the forthcoming suite generation. It was written completely from scratch for HANA, replaced SAP Financial Accounting and Controlling, and was released at the SAPPHIRE NOW conference in June 2014. A massive reduction in data footprint was achieved, both in a simplification to the infrastructure and in the system itself. More importantly, tangible business benefits could be realized in the first implementation, when SAP moved its own financial system over to the new SAP S/4HANA Finance in only five working days, allowing nearly instant book closing whenever needed and making SAP the fastest filer in the German DAX blue-chip index.[17]

In February 2015, SAP's CEO Bill McDermott officially launched the rewritten, fourth generation of SAP's flagship suite in New York, named SAP S/4HANA:

> Today SAP is redefining the concept of enterprise resource planning for the 21st century … When Hasso Plattner invented SAP HANA, we knew the day would come

for SAP Business Suite to be reinvented for the digital age ... This is an historic day and we believe it marks the beginning of the end for the 20th century IT stack and all the complexity that came with it.[18]

The S/4 HANA launch in New York was a key milestone in SAP's history, because it proved ultimately that a new full real-time application system for the enterprise can be built on top of the HANA platform with applications that had not been feasible in the past and modern design principles with the SAP Fiori user experience. In the meantime further end-to-end business processes were rewritten, for example SAP S/4HANA Sourcing and Procurement and SAP S/4HANA Supply Chain.

The new suite, SAP S/4HANA, is deployable in the cloud, on-premises, and allows hybrid scenarios – combining on-premises and cloud solutions. The SAP S/4HANA cloud edition was launched in May 2015 to significantly expand the business scope of SAP's cloud offering built on SAP HANA. In addition to the available business scenarios, customers will now also be able to run their entire enterprise in the cloud with a digital core comprising the most essential scenarios including finance, accounting, controlling, procurement, sales, manufacturing, plant maintenance, project system and product life cycle management.[19] Customers can adopt the cloud edition of SAP S/4HANA via a subscription model.

The next logical step of the transformation programme was aiming at native integration between SAP S/4HANA and other SAP cloud applications like SuccessFactors, Hybris, Ariba and Concur to drive end-to-end digitized processes such as order-to-cash, procure-to-pay, plan-to-produce, request-to-service and more finance capabilities.[20] The goal is to allow customers to adopt the cloud at their own pace while keeping all the integration and business benefits of their existing SAP solutions.

In addition to extending the value proposition, SAP's digital transformation constituted a shift in customer engagement and value delivery approaches towards digital-enabled and retention-oriented interactions. The ambition was high, namely to drive seamless digitization of the entire customer experience with SAP. This includes more than branding and web-based advertising and embraces scalable approaches for a unified customer experience across all channels ('omnichannel') and an exploitation of content business opportunities. In addition to its strong global customer organization, SAP already had a track record of leveraging insight sales as a low-touch scalable sales approach to complement the traditional high-touch customer engagement for global key accounts. In addition, online experience is vital, as internal analysis showed that 80 per cent of business-to-business sales start with online search, with four out of five prospects putting SAP on their consideration list based on what they discover online. The respective transformation programme consisted of the following work streams:

1 Deliver personalized experiences in context with each interaction.

2 Create a single, harmonized customer experience while reducing the workload on employees.

3 Orchestrate business processes across marketing, commerce, sales, service and billing.

To further advance digital business and processes, in November 2014 SAP appointed Jonathan Becher as the company's first chief digital officer. SAP's CEO Bill McDermott explained his mandate: 'Jonathan will not only be responsible for building a major new revenue stream for the company, he will also make Run Simple a reality for customers and consumers that engage with us digitally.'[21] At the same time, Maggie Chan Jones was appointed chief marketing officer, and brought extensive cloud experience to SAP through having navigated Microsoft's transition from on-premises to cloud business and having led the launch of Office 365. As a first step, SAP's online experience was streamlined, which resulted in an elimination of over 80 per cent of the existing websites, the localization of global online content to the local markets, and the acceleration of online developments at reduced cost.

A special focus of the company's digital activities was put on cloud buyers, as website and product are converging for this user group; hence providing a seamless journey for exploring, trying, buying and using solutions on the web needs to be achieved for the digital cloud buyer. Once this was achieved, the online information and online functionality were reworked to deliver an easy-to-grasp simplified view of the portfolio, clear and transparent pricing on the web, frictionless trial and subscription ('try and buy') directly online, and an experience that seamlessly connects solutions, support and community. For example, SAP S/4HANA free-of-charge trials are available for cloud and on-premises editions,[22] in which customers can discover the value of the new suite across concrete roles and predefined scenarios, such as project manager, cash manager, marketing expert, purchaser and sales representative.

As the next step in the transformation journey, SAP started to combine existing online stores into the new SAP Store, where buyers can discover, try, buy, download and upgrade its software, services, education and content offerings. In January 2015 the SAP Store became publicly available. On this foundation the vision of omnichannel commerce and bundled sales across all lines of business could be realized. The SAP Store sells business analytics, mobile apps, cloud and first content and data offerings, all priced for individual purchase at typically under €1,000 with one-click buying. Having purchased software, the customer can either directly access the cloud system with the help of the access credentials or download it with the help of the individual licence key to run it on-premises. After-sales product and customer support is provided via the website. The SAP Store is also open to partners, who can publish and monetize their offerings though this low-cost channel and participate in SAP's marketing campaigns. In 2015, the SAP Store was live in 32 countries, with about 10,000 online transactions and 1.4 million unique visitors.[23] Beyond the SAP Store, the SAP Digital team drives the digitalization of commerce processes for SAP overall – eg fully productive trials, transparent online pricing, one-click registration, credit card billing, in-app purchasing and product and support communities – and showcases how SAP leads its digital transformation to C-level customers.

Back-end transformation: From linear software development chain to ecosystem of complementors and integrated DevOps model

SAP decided strategically to go beyond a database approach and to adopt a full platform strategy by establishing a leading platform with an open architecture. The strategic goal is to turn SAP HANA into the digital platform not only for all SAP applications but also as a basis for external software innovation coming from third-party providers like system integrators (SIs), independent software vendors (ISV), start-ups and customers. SAP invested heavily in the HANA platform, which today combines database, data processing and application platform capabilities in-memory. By providing advanced capabilities like predictive text analysis, geospatial processing and data virtualization on a single architecture, the HANA platform further simplifies application development and processing across big data sources and structures. As a result, in 2016 the German IT magazine *Computerwoche* described this strategic move with the headline 'From an In-Memory Accelerator to a Digitization Platform'.[24]

SAP has a history of scaling its business through partners. Early in the company history, SAP decided to let independent SIs deliver implementation and customization projects for SAP's clients, and today SIs still dominate the IT project business and deliver the bulk of SAP projects.[25] With SAP HANA as open platform, SAP decided to take the partner approach to the next level and apply it to the developer ecosystem community. This requires that other firms, including competitors, are encouraged to build applications that run on SAP HANA. In order to grow the developer ecosystem, SAP established professional partner ecosystem management with dedicated programmes to win and retain complementors, foster cooperation with and among the partners (eg co-innovation) and establish a cooperative profit-sharing model.

To build gravity around the HANA platform, SAP launched various partner programmes over several years. The SAP Community Network (SCN) brings together and allows the engagement of nearly 2 million members in blogs, discussions and personal and topic spaces in order to solve problems, learn and invent new ways of doing business.[26] The SAP PartnerEdge programme addresses development partners and value-added resellers and offers leading development platforms that help partners address industry-specific needs.[27] They can publish their solutions on SAP HANA Marketplace to join the ecosystem, sell their innovations to SAP's global customer base and participate in SAP's marketing campaigns. The SAP Startup Focus programme is geared towards entrepreneurs and young companies that focus on big data, predictive or real-time analytics solutions and are interested in innovating on top of SAP HANA. They can join the 12-month global programme and get support from SAP in both developing new applications on SAP HANA and accelerating market traction. Additionally they are given the opportunity to pitch to the venture community via the HANA Real Time Fund and SAP Ventures. The SAP–Apple partnership was announced in May 2016, and Bill McDermott, SAP's CEO, stated: 'By combining the powerful capabilities of SAP HANA Cloud Platform and SAP S/4HANA, together with iOS – the leading and most secure mobile platform for enterprise – we will help deliver live data to people wherever and whenever they choose to work.'[28] A new iOS software development kit (SDK) and training academy were launched so that developers, partners and customers can easily share and learn how to build native iOS apps tailored to their business needs. Tim Cook, Apple's CEO, emphasized the value of this developer ecosystem: 'Through the new SDK, we're empowering SAP's more than 2.5 million developers.' With the approach for holistic horizontal partner management, SAP aims at building up an ecosystem that further enriches its offering portfolio, hence driving portfolio inclusiveness and scale by leveraging network effects. The key benefit for the development partners and complementors is that they can monetize their innovations by being part of this central partner hub and benefit from SAP's marketing programmes.

Beyond the platform and ecosystem transformation, SAP shifted towards a cross-functional and integrated DevOps model. As a cloud company, the provider takes over the contracting of the operations and responsibility for the process from the customer, who outsources it. Through the acquisition of cloud companies, SAP acquired not only a critical mass of cloud DNA but also a vast operations landscape, and hence data centres all over the world. This strategic step implied a radical shift from managing solely its own operations toward managing customers' operations on their behalf via a dedicated cloud delivery organization. Furthermore, SAP decided in 2014 also to offer a fully managed private cloud for mission-critical applications such as SAP Business Suite, which offers elasticity and flexibility with optional subscription-based pricing, named HANA Enterprise Cloud. As a consequence of these strategic moves, a network of data centres around the world needed to be managed, and new criteria like service avail- ability and disaster recovery became critical to success.[29] The German news- paper *Handelsblatt* commented on the shift: 'A new office building and computing centres are visible signs of the restructuring SAP is undergoing.'[30] The beauty of the cloud concept is that the provider can drive more frequent innovations in the offering and improve operations.[31] Agile approaches allow the release of new of- fering versions much more quickly than ever before by shortening learning cycles with iterative customer feedback. SAP started to implement lean development methodologies in 2009 and had moved the entire software development processes from a waterfall-like approach to agile methodologies by 2012. The 'Lean@SAP' transformation programme covered the entire product value chain, and Scrum was used as the new standard development approach on a team level. The change affected about 18,000 developers in 12 global locations.[32] Given SAP's journey into the cloud, the next step of the transformation was to shift SAP's organization to- wards a DevOps model, a compound of development and operations. SAP started to implement a DevOps model in 2014. This implied a cultural change emphasizing the collaboration between the software development and development-related teams like quality assurance on the one side and the cloud operations teams on the other side, while automating the process of software delivery and infrastruc- ture changes.[33] This also implied an organizational realignment bringing together the teams from the development and operations sides for a specific application group. The resulting benefit was the ability to deploy new features and patches on a daily basis, shorten the time to market and last but not least improve productivity and efficiency, as a software version can be 'shipped' into the landscape in a fully automated fashion.

Monetization mechanics: From perpetual-licence model to subscription and transactional models for value capture

SAP's business model transformation comes with a big shift in how the company ac- tually captures value, namely moving from the traditional perpetual-licence model for on-premises software to the subscription, pay-per-use or transactional-fee model for cloud computing. The transformation started with educating everyone in the company – from senior executives to employees – on the basics of the cloud monetization mechanics to mitigate the inherent risk of a drop in revenues, earnings and stock price. SAP's CFO, Luka Mucic, himself sent regular updates to all em- ployees worldwide explaining the reasoning and the impact of the shift in monetiza- tion model in an easily comprehensible manner. Additionally, controlling guidelines like 'Cloud Business Models and Key Performance Indicators' were made available by the newly founded Global Center of Excellence Cloud in the Corporate Controlling organization and rolled out to the entire organization.

The traditional *on-premises model* is also described as a capital expenditure model (CAPEX), in which the customer buys software licences as well as dedicated IT infrastructure and additionally pays annual support fees for regular software updates. The fees for implementation and configuration of the software are typically charged by the system integrators on a time and material basis. In the past, for SAP as software provider, this meant relying on two income streams: the licence revenue from the upfront payments for software transactions and the perpetual maintenance revenue from the annually recurring maintenance payments.[34] In contrast, the *cloud model* is an operational expense model (OPEX), as it is centred on the idea of using shared IT resources as a service in a pay-per-use or transactional-fee model. Compared to the on-premises option, the cloud model does not come with any upfront costs, ongoing support fees or related infrastructure investments for the customer. While the customer is evidently able to convert fixed cost into variable cost, SAP, like every cloud software provider, has only one bundled revenue stream for delivery in the cloud and carries all the costs for provisioning the IT services, for example investments for data centres and operations costs for IT management. Luka Mucic explained the cloud monetization mechanics and its potential as follows:

> In the long term, revenue and profitability potential is even higher in cloud projects than in on-premise projects. Cloud computing requires some initial investment. But once you recoup these initial costs, you can generate high margins in that market. We estimate that a cloud computing contract generates more revenue than a comparable on-premise contract after about four years, leading to comparable profitability after around five years.[35]

Based on this long-term ambition and guidance, SAP's finance and controlling teams produced detailed predictions of the shift in revenue streams and its impact on the top and bottom line. The key question regarding revenue was how the cloud revenue growth could compensate for the anticipated decline in maintenance fees.

To effectively drive top-line growth in the cloud business, a conscious decision needs to be taken regarding pricing strategy. Revenue is generally recognized rateably over the term of the cloud contract. On the one side, subscription or pay-per-use pricing schemes are applied to most of SAP's software-as-a-service cloud offerings, eg SuccessFactors or Cloud4Customer. For a subscription model, the price point – typically per user – needed to be set competitively. Hence a floor-price model was chosen over a traditional vendor-specific objective-evidence model, which SAP used in the past to determine a fair value for its cloud subscriptions. Since the acquisition of SuccessFactors, SAP has changed to the renewal-rate-estimated-stand-alone-selling-price approach, which means that the renewal rate must be higher than the price point where SAP, in the long run, would rather walk away from the deal than accept a price below this point. In other words, the floor price is a minimum price, which consists of all directly attributable costs and a reasonable margin. On the other side, transactional-fee models are more appropriate for business network cloud offerings, in which the network's value increases as more users join the network and the more transactions are performed per user. Therefore, SAP's portfolio comprises a set of offerings, eg Ariba, Fieldglass, Concur, the Hybris as a Service platform and SAP Exchange Media, which are monetized on a transaction-fee basis.

It is obvious how radical the shift in monetization mechanics actually is when studying the profit and loss statements of pure-play cloud start-ups. They only become profitable after they have reached a certain maturity level with a decent customer base and more contract renewals than net new customers (the 'plateau' effect). The reason is that cloud fees are generally smaller compared to the large one-off licence deals; hence – when ramping up a cloud business – they are not yet sufficient to cover the corresponding costs for cloud infrastructure operations and customer acquisition. In addition, both revenues and profits are deferred in a cloud model, as they are recognized as the service is delivered. This inherent delay is also the reason why in January 2015 SAP lowered its 2017 operating profit target from €7.0 billion to €6.3 billion. The transformation programme shifted management attention to achieving a critical mass of installed base clients opting for the cloud as well as its subscription. Driving renewals also became a top priority, as customer lifetime value is increasingly determined by recurring sales instead of one-time sales. On the bottom line, SAP started to proactively manage fixed costs even more tightly as a result of the scale economies of the cloud business. Measures included a restructuring programme for divisions with lower growth rates, bundling and renegotiation of contracts with cloud infrastructure suppliers, for example for servers, and leveraging third-party data centres for SAP customers through partnerships. In 2015 SAP provided the financial markets with a new, aggressive outlook and its 2020 goals, namely revenue of €26 billion to €28 billion, cloud subscriptions of €7.5 billion to €8 billion and adjusted operating profit of €8 billion to €9 billion.

The next transformation step aimed at establishing next-generation management reporting and steering systems to reflect the focus on building and sustaining the customer's loyalty, for example measuring and incentivizing growth in successfully engaged customers as compound growth rate. One of these is the SAP Digital Boardroom, which provides contextual, real-time information about the state of the business to company executives. The solution uses SAP HANA technology to cut through massive amounts of data, both historical and transactional. Unlike the situation in the past, when predefined reports and static information were used and prepared before the meeting, the SAP Digital Boardroom lets the board members analyse data live and in real time while they discuss the business. The information is immediately available on every level – from balance sheet and profit and loss statement to the granularity of a single pipeline entry in a specific sales region. Additionally, predicting changes to the business and their impact can be done in the same interactive fashion. The SAP Digital Boardroom has been used by the SAP executive board since the second quarter of 2015 and has already generated significant interest from customers.

Heading for the future

In 2010, SAP realized that being a business application leader was not going to suffice to keep it a business visionary in the 21st century.

SAP's transformation programme took hold as the digital economy picked up steam. In 2015 SAP had achieved its self-set transformation goals: the company had nearly doubled its revenue since 2010 and reached €20.8 billion in sales and at the same time had nearly tripled its customer base to 296,000 customers. Today SAP is the number one cloud company in the world by number of users with more than 85 million, has increased its cloud and database revenue 100-fold and has achieved a cloud business of €2.3 billion. In 2015 new cloud bookings increased by 23 per cent, while cloud subscriptions and support revenue soared by 33 per cent. SAP runs the largest business network, in which approximately 2 million connected companies trade over $740 billion of commerce.

SAP invented the HANA in-memory platform, which now has almost 10,000 HANA customers and is the market leader in enterprise applications with SAP S/4HANA, the fastest-selling product in SAP's history. More than 1,300 customers have already selected SAP S/4HANA as their digital core, and more than 100 are live. The company took its value proposition to the next level of breadth and depth and today provides innovative and fully integrated end-to-end processes on top of the HANA platform across cloud, on-premises and hybrid scenarios – from both SAP and its open ecosystem. Bill McDermott comments:

> We started a journey 5 years ago, building the agile platform and solution for the digital economy. This took over $30 billion in acquisitions and billions in R&D. The results speak for themselves – we are the only end-to-end solution to help CEOs solve their problems. At the core of it all is SAP HANA, the great simplifier... With SAP S/4HANA we reimagined and reinvented how business processes will work in real time with

simplicity and higher value. We understand the power of integrating the world. Nearly $1 trillion in commerce runs through our digital business networks. ... Plus, we are working daily with top customers in the world to simplify, innovate and digitize business.[36]

Figure 7.3 SAP's business model transformation

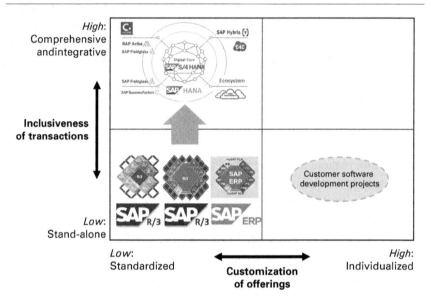

SAP's business model transformation required major change management for the entire company. New skills and competences were built up. SAP also shifted to new digital methods of customer engagement and value delivery like digital commerce, for example SAP Store, and towards a cross-functional and integrated DevOps model to drive simplicity and exponential growth.

Yet the transformation is not completed; it is a journey. Luka Mucic, CFO of SAP, provides the following outlook: 'We have transformed our company and made it leaner by shifting investments from non-core activities to strategic growth areas enabling us to capture the tremendous growth opportunities in the market. This puts us on a strong path for the future reflected in an increase of our 2017 ambition.'[37]

Endnotes

1 This is to acknowledge that this case study was reviewed by many SAP departments. Some individuals deserve a special mention for their feedback: Jonathan Becher, Claus von Riegen, Matthias Barth and Sven Meyers.

2 For SAP's corporate fact sheet, see https://go.sap.com/docs/download/investors/2016/sap-factsheet-apr2016-en.pdf.

3 For further details on SAP's company history, see http://go.sap.com/corporate/en/company/history.html.

4 Regarding i2's strategic competition from SAP, see https://en.wikipedia.org/wiki/I2_Technologies.

5 See http://www.globes.co.il/en/article-482115.

6 K R Lakhani, M Iansiti and N Fisher (2014) *SAP 2014: Reaching for the cloud*, Harvard Business School Case Study No 9-614-052, Harvard Business School, Boston, MA.

7 Initially referred to as High-performance ANalytic Appliance.

8 See http://www.informationweek.com/applications/sap-launches-cloud-platform-built-on-hana/d/d-id/1106889?.

9 H Plattner and B Leukert (2015) *The In-Memory Revolution: How SAP HANA enables business of the future*, Springer, New York, p 3.

10 See http://www.gartner.com/newsroom/id/3443517.

11 See http://www.gartner.com/newsroom/id/3188817.

12 See https://www.forrester.com/report/The+Public+Cloud+Market+Is+Now+In+Hyper growth/-/E-RES113365.

13 According to NIST, cloud computing is defined as 'a model for enabling ubiquitous, convenient, on-demand network access to a shared pool of configurable computing resources (eg networks, servers, storage, applications, and services) that can be rapidly provisioned and released with minimal management effort or service provider interaction'; see Peter Mell and Timothy Grance (2011) *The NIST Definition of Cloud Computing*, Special Publication No 800-145, http://nvlpubs.nist.gov/nistpubs/Legacy/SP/nistspecialpublication800-145.pdf.

14 See http://go.sap.com/solution/business-networks.html.

15 H Plattner and B Leukert (2015) *The In-Memory Revolution: How SAP HANA enables business of the future*, Springer, New York, pp 64–67.

16 With the launch of S/4 HANA, SAP Simple Finance was renamed S/4 HANA Finance.

17 With the shift from month-end to event-based automatic processing of accounting entries, efficiency savings of up to 20 per cent could be achieved. The financial close could also be completed 86 per cent faster as a result of real-time analytics, which made the closing of the books – including group consolidation – achievable in only 8.5 days.

18 See http://news.sap.com/sap-unveils-next-generation-enterprise-software-new-business-suite-sap-s4hana/.

19 See http://news.sap.com/sap-announces-sap-s4hana-cloud-edition/.

20 See http://news.sap.com/sap-s4hana-drive-your-digital-transformation-with-the-industrys-first-digital-core/.

21 See http://news.sap.com/jonathan-becher-chief-digital-officer-maggie-chan-jones-sap-chief-marketing-officer/.

22 For SAP S/4HANA trials, refer to www.sap.com/s4hana-trial.

23 See www.store.SAP.com.

24 Martin Bayer (2016) Platform as a Service: SAP will seine Cloud mit Service Marktplatz aufwerten, *Computerwoche* (Germany), 11 January.

25 SAP's own consulting division is focused on leading-edge customer projects, in which the latest SAP innovations get deployed in the first releases, and the feedback loop to the development teams is pivotal.

26 See http://scn.sap.com/.

27 See https://partneredge.sap.com/en/welcome.html.

28 See http://www.apple.com/pr/library/2016/05/05Apple-and-SAP-Partner-to-Revolutionize-Work-on-iPhone-and-iPad.html.

29 See http://www.sapdatacenter.com/.

30 Christof Kerkmann (2016) SAP im Bilanzcheck: Großbaustelle Walldorf, *Handelsblatt* (Germany), 21 April.

31 Provided the system governance lies with the cloud company and not the customer.

32 See http://link.springer.com/chapter/10.1007/978-3-642-23391-3_15#page-1.

33 See https://news.sap.com/cloud-daily-software-updates/.

34 Note that the customer does not buy the software, but licenses the intellectual property.

35 See http://www.sap-investor.com/en/2014/quarter-2/special-cloud/cebit-2014-join-the-team.html#sthash.c4y7g8hc.dpuf.

36 SAP (2015) SAP digital business white paper: Value creation in a digital economy: Adapt or die in a digital world where the consumer is in charge, p 2.

37 See http://news.sap.com/sap-announces-preliminary-fourth-quarter-and-full-year-2015-results-2/.

Netflix: The master of business model transformation[1]
Günter Müller-Stewens

In 1997, Reed Hastings was angry. He had to pay a US$40 fine for returning a rented video six weeks late to a Blockbuster store in California.[2] At that time, Blockbuster was the dominant player in the video rental business, but the largest part of the video market was fragmented into 'mom-and-pop' retail outlets. However, by building a strong brand and establishing operational efficiencies, Blockbuster was pushing mom-and-pop rental stores out of business. The firm already ran hundreds of rental shops across the United States. Customers had to go to one of these stores, find a video of their choice and then pay a rental fee for the temporary use of this video. Thereafter, customers had to return the video to the store within a given time to avoid paying a fine. This business model continued to be very successful, even when the market evolved from VHS (Video Home System) tapes to DVDs (digital video discs).

However, Hastings, a former computer scientist, was determined never to pay a fine again. There had to be a more customer-friendly way of meeting people's need for rented entertainment. This thought was the beginning of an amazing success story. That year, he and Marc Randolph founded Netflix. By 2016, Netflix was the world's leading internet television network, a provider of on-demand internet streaming media and flat-rate DVD by mail, with more than 57 million customers in nearly 50 countries, providing more than 2 billion hours of television shows and movies per month, including original series. In October 2016, the company's market capitalization was about $55 billion. Its path to success had not been easy: the competition had been very strong, and technology had to be drastically changed. For Netflix to survive, it had to fine-tune and reinvent its business model continuously – even radically at times. And this is still happening.

A *Forbes* article calls Hastings 'the master of adaptation'.[3] This capability was crucial, because Netflix followed its principle of 'Give people what they want, when they want it, in the form they want it' from the very beginning.

Start-up and first adoption of a subscription-based model

Netflix started by offering a video-direct-by-mail rental service in the United States. In April 1998, the company launched a website offering customers the opportunity to rent or purchase videos. Customers could select videos online, and Netflix would mail them for a seven-day, in-home rental. Netflix charged $4 per DVD rental plus $2 for postage. Customers had to return the DVDs in Netflix's pre-paid and pre-addressed envelopes. This allowed the company to raise additional advertising revenue from their envelopes. Despite Reed Hastings's dislike of fines, Netflix – like Blockbuster – charged late fees, but at least customers no longer had to visit a physical store. The transition from VHS to DVD videos supported this business model, because the cost of mailing decreased with the flatter and more durable DVD discs instead of bulky VHS tapes. Looking back on this early phase, Hastings said: 'The first big challenge was getting the profitability and stop consuming cash because you have to acquire markets and customers and you have to buy DVDs. Both pay back only over time. And we underestimated the logistical challenges.'[4]

Introducing the subscription-based business model in 1999

Nevertheless, this starting business model just did not gain enough traction, despite the convenience of mailbox delivery. Therefore, in October 1999, just two years after the company was founded, the first business model transformation occurred. The new business model was mainly built on three pillars:

1 *The flat-fee pricing model:* The subscription model meant that subscribers could create and manage a list of DVDs – called the *queue* – they would like to receive online. When a DVD was returned, Netflix would automatically mail the next DVD in the subscriber's queue; this was managed by the Netflix website. Customers could also pay a flat fee of $15.95 per month for unlimited DVD rentals (with four, later three, movies outstanding at a time), without incurring any late fees and with free delivery. All of this increased the service's convenience (no due dates, swift home delivery, pre-paid return envelope).

2 *Increased customer satisfaction and partnering:* Netflix discovered the strategic importance of having one of the largest movie libraries very early. At the beginning of 2001, Netflix offered its customer base (about 300,000 subscribers) about 7,000 titles. To extend the selection of titles continuously and swiftly enough, Netflix decided to form an affiliation with movie distributors such as Warner Home Videos, Columbia Tri-Star, DreamWorks and Artisan. Since 2000, Netflix's collaboration with these companies has been based on direct revenue-sharing agreements, but sometimes also on exclusivity, with some titles not available to its competitors. A new position, chief content officer, was created for the person who would manage the relationships with the studios and drive these initiatives.

   To gain more efficient access to new customers, Netflix engaged in clever contracts with DVD player manufacturers. Companies such as Sony and Panasonic included Netflix service offers when selling new DVD players. Netflix also formed an affiliation with computer manufacturers such as Apple, HP and Sony to incorporate DVD drives into their models. In 2001, it also introduced a co-branded version of an online DVD rental service with Best Buy: Best Buy promoted Netflix on its website and in its stores; in return, Netflix directed its customers wishing to buy DVD players to the Best Buy website.

To increase its website's stickiness, Netflix improved its site's search functions to allow for more informed selections and to provide its customers with increasingly personalized information. In 2000, the company launched its unique personalized movie recommendation system, Cinematch, which uses member ratings to predict choices for all Netflix members. This tool cross-references to customers with similar tastes and interests; for example, customers who had rented title A and also chose title B. Based on its increasing volume of customer behaviour data, the company provides its customers with advice on whether or not to select a specific movie. This generates a positive network effect. The more information a customer shares, the better Netflix can customize its offering. This personalization is something stores cannot do. The Cinematch system provided Netflix with very interesting information: many movies on its list of the top 100 had failed at the box office, but customers actually paid more attention to these lower-profile films. This meant that many small and independent film studios were benefiting. Further, this attention had positive side-effects regarding the cash spent to buy such DVDs. In addition, a filter, based on the inventory system, excludes movies from the recommendation system that are out of stock, thus preventing customer disappointment.

3 *Efficient processes:* To prevent customers from visiting a competitor's local video store because they had to wait too long for their ordered DVDs, Netflix built up a network of shipping centres to improve the delivery time to one business day. At the end of 2004, Netflix had 24 such centres. In 2007, the company delivered its one-billionth DVD from one of its (then) 44 centres and could provide 90 per cent of subscribers with next-day delivery. To keep this shipping and receiving process efficient, Netflix invested heavily in automation and software development. At the same time, it allowed its customers to manage their subscriptions in their own online accounts.

Raising capital by going public in 2002

Based on this new business model, and supported by the growing number of households with a DVD player, the number of subscribers almost doubled every year – 1999: 107,000; 2000: 292,000; 2001: 456,000; 2002: 857,000. In 2000, Netflix launched an initial public offering (IPO) to strengthen the thinly capitalized company. But, in the shadow of the bursting of the internet bubble, and owing to ongoing scepticism about the business model's growth potential, the company had to withdraw its plans. Nonetheless, the company continued to grow and was able to realize its first positive cash flow quarter in 2001. This encouraged Hastings and his team to launch a second IPO in 2002. This time, it worked out, and the company raised $82.5 million on the NASDAQ. Five and a half million shares were offered at $15 per share, and the share price increased 12 per cent on the first day. In 2002 the company also broke even for the first time in five years.

Growing competition: The battle with Blockbuster

This new business model challenged traditional store-based DVD rental companies such as Blockbuster Inc, at the time the world's largest video rental chain, and Hollywood Entertainment Corporation, the second-largest video chain in the United States. These companies competed mainly in terms of their stores (their costs, their locations, their pricing systems, the range of content, etc). Along with the success Netflix was enjoying despite its competitors, the question arose of how long it would take until the incumbents reacted or new entrants entered the online DVD rental market owing to the low entry barriers. According to the then current rumours, the deep-pocketed Blockbuster was set to react right after the IPO. This threat scared the Netflix team: would it survive such an attack? Hastings sought to motivate his people by pointing to the excitement of the potential victory. He stuck to a routine of 'business as usual' and pushed his team to make steady improvements and to fine-tune the business model.

However, instead of Blockbuster, retail giant Wal-Mart was the next to enter the online DVD rental business in 2002, with a subscription fee of $3, less than that of Netflix, but Wal-Mart could not really compete with Netflix's service offering and experience.

Luckily for Netflix, Blockbuster only entered the market quite late, in June 2004. It started with a subscription fee of $19.99, compared to Netflix's $21.99. Blockbuster was clearly the dominating competitor in this market at the time: a premium brand, a 45 per cent market share, almost 9,000 stores around the globe (65 per cent of which were in the United States) and a $594 million cash flow from operations. In 2003, Blockbuster's rental of VHS tapes, DVDs and video games had generated 77 per cent of its total revenues of $5.9 billion. In the same year, Netflix's revenues had been $270 million, and it had a gross margin of about 33 per cent.

Its strong brand, database, distribution network and investment capacity allowed Blockbuster to gain a market share very quickly. Blockbuster, supported by Accenture, more or less copied Netflix's homepage, but initially the processes behind it (the billing, logistics, etc) did not work very reliably. This surprised the public and led to Netflix employees becoming optimistic again: *Is Blockbuster the strong new competitor we expected?*

However, Blockbuster's disadvantage did not last very long. At the end of 2004, it was already running 23 distribution centres (compared to Netflix's 30). It leveraged its network of stores in different ways, for instance by giving online customers two coupons for in-store movie or game rentals per month.

The two companies started a vicious price battle. Netflix's subscription rate dropped from $21.99 to $17.99, with Blockbuster following directly with a decrease from $19.99 to $17.49. At the end of 2014, Blockbuster also abolished late fees. It was clear that Blockbuster wanted the dominant market position in online DVD subscriptions. All this made the two companies' investors nervous. Netflix's share price crashed to $10 from a peak of $39. But, despite Blockbuster's progress, growing demand increased Netflix's customer base from 1,487,000 to 2,610,000 in 2014. The more Blockbuster promoted online rental, the more they educated their customers, which also drove them to try Netflix.

This was not the end of the battle. In early 2005, Blockbuster announced another major price reduction from $17.49 to $14.99; this, and the elimination of late fees, had a strong impact on Blockbuster's profitability. The question facing the company was: *Could this reduction in profit be balanced by increased demand, or was it overpaying to acquire new customers?*

The short-term question for Netflix was: *Should we follow Blockbuster and decrease our subscription fees?* Finding an answer to this was complicated by Amazon entering the online UK DVD rental market as a test market in 2014. Further, the assumption was that it would only be a matter of time before Amazon entered the US market. With its very strong retail site, Amazon.com, its customer acquisition cost would be close to zero. The good news for Netflix was that Wal-Mart was beginning to withdraw from the business. In May 2005, Netflix closed a cross-promotional contract with Wal-Mart that would direct all its 1.5 million online DVD rental customers to Netflix. In return, Netflix would promote Wal-Mart's online DVD sales.

The mutually destructive competition between Netflix and Blockbuster heated up, and each lost money in the process of depriving the other of customers.

Moving from physical discs to video streaming

The classical linear television business model is based on the assumption that users need a television set, because television channels or stations deliver their mostly exclusive content to television sets. Such television stations present programmes on non-portable screens, operated by complicated remote controls, at set times. These stations obtain their content from content-producing companies. In 2005, analysts began to predict that video-on-demand (VOD) could pose a major threat to online DVD rental business in the future, that this would disrupt the then current business model, that internet television would replace linear television, that apps would replace television channels and that screens would proliferate. The reasoning was that internet television would over time replace linear television, because the internet was becoming faster, more reliable and more available. Moreover, far more television sets would also make use of Wi-Fi, network connectivity and apps, and viewing by means of tablets and smartphones would increase further.

Netflix's purpose, which was always independent of the way its content was delivered, was defined as allowing its customers the best home video viewing. Its purpose was not to provide DVD rentals through the post. 'It's why we named the business Netflix and not DVD by Mail', Hasting said.[5] Therefore, the core question for Netflix was not *if* it was the right time to move to digital distribution, but *when* to do so. Given the fast pace of technology improvements, when would it be more efficient for consumers to receive a movie via the internet? At the time, broadband penetration was low, the available content very small and a movie's delivery costs very high. Further, most customers could not watch a streamed movie on their television screen, because they lacked internet connection to the television or the connection of the television to an internet-connected computer. In 2010, Jeff Bewkes, the former CEO of Time Warner, had this to say about the push of Netflix toward licensed content: 'It's a little bit like, is the Albanian army going to take over the world? I don't think so.'[6]

To prepare for the time when these major hurdles would no longer exist, Netflix invested heavily in new technology: $10 million in 2006, $40 million in 2007 and so on. The management team analysed three options for an entry strategy: 1) outsourcing delivery to their competitors, the cable providers; 2) building a stand-alone VOD start-up, such as Movielink or Vongo; and 3) integrating a streaming online video feature into the core offering, which would require a service integration of both delivery types: the DVD rental business and the streaming service. Without this in place, Netflix would not be able to differentiate itself from the VOD start-ups.

Netflix decided on the third option. The assumption was that the emergence of internet television would enable new apps such as Netflix and YouTube to build large-scale, direct-to-consumer services that would be independent of the existing multichannel video programming distributors (MVPD) (pay television). As a first step, Netflix introduced streaming in 2007. Initially, this was a bonus for its subscribers, allowing them to watch television shows and movies online on their personal computers without having to wait for a DVD in the mail. Thereafter, step by step and in line with the technical developments, Netflix cooperated with consumer electronics companies to stream on the Xbox 360, Blu-ray disc players and television set-top boxes in 2008, expanding this to internet-connected televisions in 2009 and to internet-connected devices in 2010. After this distribution channel diversification, Netflix complemented its customer base growth strategy with geographical diversification, starting in Canada in 2010, although it had only been in the United States for 13 years. VOD facilitated this shift from being a domestic company to a global one, because Netflix did not have to deal with local post of-fice organizations. In 2011, Netflix was launched throughout Latin America and the Caribbean. In 2012, the UK, Ireland and the Nordic countries could access Netflix. It subsequently expanded to the Netherlands in 2013 and to Austria, Belgium, France, Germany, Luxembourg and Switzerland in 2014 – constituting 66 million additional broadband households.

However, the emergence of the internet also created new opportunities for linear television networks. Many television networks, such as HBO and the BBC, were already moving towards internet television. For instance, the BBC app in the UK provided an on-demand interface for a wide range of BBC programmes. The linear television networks that failed to develop first-class apps would probably lose viewers and revenue.

The other side of the coin was Blockbuster, which had started a VOD service very early, but ultimately failed when the costs became too high. The company filed for bankruptcy in 2010. One of the reasons for this failure was the power struggles between the chairman and CEO, John Antioco, the top management team and the activist investor Carl Icahn, which began in 2005. Icahn undertook a successful proxy fight to be appointed to the board. He accused Blockbuster of overpaying John Antioco, who received $51.6 million in compensation in 2004. Icahn also disagreed with Antioco on how to make Blockbuster profitable again. Antioco subsequently left with a $24.7 million severance package. The company appointed James Keyes as the new chairman and CEO. He introduced a new business strategy that included de-emphasizing the unprofitable online service in favour of an in-store, retail-oriented model.[7] But video store economics also collapsed, because a significant part of a single store's content delivers negative profit. Online stores can drive revenue from a much broader and more optimized set of products than bricks-and-mortar stores can normally do.

Front-end transformation: Enhancing the perceived membership value

Netflix's goal became to be a global internet television network offering legal access to a rich base of movies, documentaries and television series, without commercials, and with unlimited viewing on any internet-connected screen for a monthly fee ('all-you-can-eat subscription'). This means the company does not stream all video types. It is focused on movies and television series, and therefore does not compete with companies such as Amazon, Apple, Sony and Google on the entire spectrum of entertainment. Some of the content is exclusive – available only on Netflix. New and exclusive series are released as a full season, hooking Netflix customers.

The players in the field mainly compete on price, exclusivity, range of con-tent, user experience in terms of personalization, and compatibility with different devices. Netflix's international advantages are its superior app and service, its global technology investment, its process knowledge, its data from related markets and its globally known brand. From the customer perspective, the main differentiator is its website, which has the features consumers want.

Currently, Netflix competes very broadly for a share of members' time and spending against linear networks, pay-per-view content, DVD watching, other internet networks, video games, web browsing, magazine reading, video piracy and much more. Piracy and pay-per-view are the only two competitors that offer a nearly full set of television programmes and movie content. One of Netflix's toughest long-term competitors for content is probably the Time Warner-controlled television network HBO (Home Box Office), because HBO bids against Netflix for many original content projects, and has a global reach and a strong technology capacity. But there are many other competing cable and broadcast networks as well as new online players, such as Amazon Prime Instant Video, LoveFilm and Hulu. Many consumers will subscribe to multiple services if each has unique and compelling content. The continued success of Netflix will depend on its ability to grow, because larger revenues can be translated into more content to provide its members with a comprehensive and competitive offering, and also into sufficient tech and marketing expenditure. It is a virtuous cycle that must be managed in order to lead to further growth.

However, there is no binding contract with its members, who can leave at any time, which reduces entry barriers to the system. Consumer behaviour changes once they have paid the flat fee. Further, because there are no barriers to prevent members from leaving, the company must find other ways to create retention. First, owing to Netflix's strong focus on content, the quality of its offerings keeps its members in the system, but this too can always be improved. Second, the convenience of being a member and consuming content is decisive. The pleasure of using Netflix probably originates from the easy selection of a video, the user's total control over when to play, pause or resume a video, and content that suits the taste and mood of everyone in the household. Members can watch a video as often as they want, at any time, anywhere, on almost every internet-connected screen, without commercials or commitments. Netflix offers one of the widest supported device ranges, including game consoles, tablets, PCs and internet televisions.

To obtain sufficient content and the right content, Netflix spent almost $3 billion in 2014. Instead of trying to have everything, Netflix strives to have the best in each category. Typically, its bids are for exclusive access, which means Netflix requires excellent relationships with content producers and strong bargaining power, which the quantity and quality of its customer base usually provide. The licensing of content is generally time-based. At the time of renewal, Netflix evaluates how often a title is viewed and considers its members' rating feedback to determine how much it is willing to pay. Another consideration is how many titles of a similar nature it has.

Netflix's strategy is to expand internationally as quickly as possible, while remaining globally profitable, as long as there are compelling markets into which to expand. Its economic power comes from its market-specific scale. When Netflix enters a market, the company must win the bidding for a substantial content offering, and must then market itself effectively to initiate membership growth. Each national market has a mix of local and global content tastes. Netflix assesses these from a variety of information sources prior to entry. After its launch, the company learns more about what is most popular and what is not in that specific market. The company improves its content mix by wisely adding and renewing deals.

To increase its stickiness, Netflix created recurring traffic by enhancing perceived customer value in multiple ways. Customer visits teach the platform to provide a better mass-customized offer and additional services, information and entertainment. Netflix launched its personalized movie recommendation system, which uses Netflix members' ratings to accurately predict choices for all its members, in 2000. Analyses of the terabytes of data provided by each recent click, each view, each repeat view, early abandonment, all page views and all other data drive the content that Netflix features on a member's initial screen. In 2014, a team of around 300 experts worked on this, analysing more than 60 billion 'view events' per year. Netflix regards a member's opening screen as the personalized ranking of what it thinks will be the most relevant content – selected from a diverse catalogue of content – for that specific member. Netflix's aim is to keep inventing algorithms and tuning them to generate higher satisfaction, viewing and retention. But there are numerous other areas in which Netflix is improving to keep its members in the system, such as how smooth the user's iPad scrolling is, or how well the content for a user's children works on a PS4.

Last but not least, sufficient traffic and related revenues ensure funds and extend the data for better customer insights, which in turn develop the set of offerings, allow innovations in this regard and continuously improve the customer value.

Back-end transformation: Global partnerships to realize scale effects

The Netflix platform serves as an infrastructure that enables the company to interact with its customers by providing them with an attractive offer and by allowing them to consume the content they want. Unlike YouTube, which is a two-sided platform, Netflix controls the content it provides.

Netflix delivers its streamed media through Microsoft's Silverlight platform, which allows programmers to develop complex web applications. In 2010, Netflix switched to Amazon's cloud services and started using some of the HTML5 technology's features to extend the range of devices that could stream video through Netflix to numerous web browsers, consoles and other devices. The latter include tablets and iOS systems, which do not support Flash. Netflix is now one of the largest clients of Amazon's cloud business.

Netflix's customers want it to work flawlessly, to always be available, to avoid stream rebuffering and so on. Accordingly, the company invested more than $400 million in technology development in 2014 to improve its service and app – and thus to obtain operational excellence. It emphasized streaming delivery, signing up, billing and customer service across the more than 1,000 devices used. However, strong scale effects are necessary to gain a return on these investments. Netflix put important technological developments in place, such as the introduction in 2007 of streaming, which allows Netflix members to directly watch television shows and movies on their personal computers, and the 2010 extension of this service to the Apple iPad, iPhone and iPod Touch, the Nintendo Wii and other internet-connected devices.

Netflix had to swiftly build global partnerships with consumer electronics companies, internet service providers and multichannel video programming distributors, which enables it to deliver movies and television shows across a full range of devices and platforms to ensure the right growth rate. For instance, in 2008, Netflix partnered with consumer electronics companies to allow its content to stream on the Xbox 360, Blu-ray disc players and television set-top boxes. The devices capable of instantly streaming Netflix movies and television episodes directly to consumers' televisions continue to expand.

In 2014, Netflix further improved its game in the consumer electronics space. Television manufacturers and companies building companion boxes, such as Roku and Apple TV, have long regarded Netflix as a must-have app for their devices. Netflix engineers developed the open, multiscreen discovery protocol DIAL by cooperating with YouTube and others. Not only is DIAL one of the technical foundations of Google's Chromecast device, but other television and consumer electronics companies are also increasingly implementing it to allow television viewers to control these devices with their tablets and mobile phones for a second-screen experience.

But Netflix works even further ahead. The company has been engaged in direct talks with chipmakers and top consumer electronics manufacturers to motivate them to rethink televisions with online use in mind. Netflix wants companies to make better smart television user interfaces and is also interested in more fundamental changes, including the addition of low-power wireless networking standards and a true sleep mode, which would allow consumers to instantly resume an online video after turning a television off and back on, as you do with tablets and smartphones.[8]

The more successful Netflix becomes, the more important it becomes to internet service provider (ISP) subscribers. Given their joint interest in making broadband work well for people, Netflix needs productive relationships with ISPs. The Netflix Open Connect programme allows ISPs to interconnect gratis and directly to the Netflix network, which results in a better video quality and reduced buffering interruptions for their joint subscribers. The market worries whether one side will charge the other for the interconnection that both need. However, Netflix strongly supports net neutrality to prevent large ISPs from holding their joint customers hostage to poor performance in order to extract payments from internet content firms and others.

Monetization mechanics: Using scale effects to increase margin

Netflix introduced the monthly subscription concept in September 1999, when it launched its DVD-by-mail subscription offer. Customers had to pay a monthly flat fee to access the unlimited DVDs they could rent without due dates, late fees, shipping or handling fees or per-title rental fees. Subscribers did not have to pay a membership 'joining fee', and could leave when they wanted and return when they wanted. This is still the way the company creates its revenue stream. The company's major source of revenue is the subscription fee of \$7.99 per month for an unlimited number of television shows and movies streamed via the internet to subscribers' televisions, computers and mobile devices.

The business model is based on fixed costs and scale effects: the more members Netflix has, the less influence the fixed costs have in terms of buying content, and the better the company's bargaining power in terms of reducing these costs.

In the United States, Netflix's margin structure is mostly set top down. It estimates its revenue for any given future period and decides what it wants to spend and how much margin it wants in that period. Although competitive pressure could lead to overspending when bidding, Netflix would prefer slightly less content rather than overspending. The same is true in terms of the marketing budget, since the spending choices influence the output variable, which is membership growth.

The margin structure Netflix has chosen is to grow its content spending and to market at a slightly slower rate than its revenue growth rate. It seeks to grow its margins an average of 200 basis points per year in the following years. This increase gives it scope to increase its content spending as it grows and to be profitable.

The primary forces propelling growth are its service, content and marketing improvements, and the improvement of its internet networks and devices. Conversely, the primary forces impeding growth are market saturation and the broad set of competitors all improving their offerings.

Creating and selling own content

Having now been in the market for about 15 years, Netflix realized that it was paying large sums to license other people's content in order to present this content to its subscribers. This left Netflix very vulnerable to competition, since anyone willing to outbid it could be licenced to present the shows and movies it wanted to purchase.[9] Netflix's business model was therefore very risky, because it relied heavily on content providers, and content owners increased their prices when Netflix built tempting profit margins. To survive, to secure its customer base and to compete against benchmark companies such as HBO, Netflix had to invest in producing premium, original content programmes in-house. It needed to be regarded as equal to premium cable providers. However, to succeed in this endeavour, the company needed enough scale to cover the costs of such productions and to profit from them.

In this phase, the big challenge for Netflix was to launch and brand original content. Developing content means developing a much closer relationship with the content; with each production, you have to develop and manage a new brand. Another major challenge was to manage such a mixed-model approach, because the dominant model was still the platform BM; but now Netflix is complementing it with a product BM by producing its own content.

Front-end transition: Investing in premium original content

In January 2013, Netflix regarded itself as close to the point of being economically strong enough to create original content that would debut exclusively on Netflix. The headline of the *Huffington Post*'s article on the event was: 'With "House of Cards", Netflix begins the future of TV'. This series is a remake of a popular 1990s British drama, and Netflix, which competes with HBO, Showtime and AMC, invested about $100 million in two seasons, consisting of 26 episodes.[10] In February 2014, it ordered a third season. It was the first time that a VOD company such as Netflix had made such an investment.

The success of this courageous experiment depended very much on how well its members accepted *House of Cards*. It turned out to be very successful. The many awards the drama received confirmed the content's top quality. Netflix made history and challenged the television establishment on 22 September 2013, when *House of Cards* won three Emmy awards, thus becoming the first company to win awards for a show that could only be viewed online. In total, Netflix received 14 nominations for the original shows it had produced – nine of which were for *House of Cards*.[11] It also received nominations for the Critics' Choice Television Award and the TCA Award.

These awards were a revolution in the television video business. Following Netflix's principle of 'Give people what they want, when they want it, in the form they want it',[12] its customers can watch all the episodes of a *House of Cards* season in one or a few sittings if they want to. Their consumer behaviour is not steered in any way whatsoever.

Why is this step into the content business so promising for Netflix? First, it has the power of its large on-demand platform, from which it can extract an immense amount of data to discern exactly what people would like to see. Based on its data mining, Netflix can analyse even very narrow niche demands very precisely and thus identify in what types of content it should invest. *House of Cards* is successful because people like political dramas, as well as movies directed by David Fincher with actors such as Kevin Spacey. With its capability to personalize its promotion of the right content to the right subscribers, Netflix, more than other similar companies, has the opportunity to promote original content. Currently, long after the premiere of *House of Cards*, large numbers of new members are just starting to watch the series. The drama's improved economics after its season one and the improved storytelling – owing to its creators being given more scope – are huge advantages.

A next step was licensing its original content to other distribution channels. Many other television companies have bought the rights to broadcast the series. For example, in Germany, the pay television station Sky Atlantic and, in Switzerland, SRF1 started broadcasting the series in November 2013.

Back-end transformation: Attracting the right talent

Netflix produces its original content on the basis of its customer data. By analysing the behavioural propensities of its paying customers, Netflix determined that a political drama starring Kevin Spacey and produced by David Fincher would appeal to a large cross-section of its existing subscriber base, resulting in a highly successful production (awards and popularity).

Netflix will continue to grow its original content offering (eg *Orange is the New Black* and *Crouching Tiger Hidden Dragon II: The Green Destiny*) as it gains scale and confidence. This will give the company the opportunity to develop all the competences required in the content business, as well as to develop the competences that such content contributes to the business. With each original production, the company will learn more about what its subscribers want, about how to produce and promote effectively and about the impacts original productions have on the Netflix brand.

It is important to attract the right talent to create premium content. Producer and director David Fincher was attracted to the project because Netflix committed to purchasing 26 hours of original *House of Cards* content with very little if any artistic interference. This provided him, as a director, with a platform for creative storytelling: Based on the storyline, he could vary the run times per episode, there was no need for weekly recaps and there was no fixed notion of what constitutes a 'season'.[13]

Monetization mechanics: Mitigating investment risks by data mining

Each original content production is very cash-intensive in the short term, which makes it risky. Similarly to the Hollywood studios, Netflix finds it difficult to estimate the cost coverage of a production's life cycle, but the market insights Netflix gains through its rich customer data reduce these risks. Further, its strong and growing customer base increases the probability that a production will find enough direct customers to match the profit goals. Indirect new customers can also be attracted from licensing the original content to other distribution channels. To date, Netflix has made its investment pay off.

But one question remains: *Can Netflix gain enough revenue from customers alone to satisfy the need for new content for its service, or does the company need advertisements to earn more?*

Looking into the future

If we examine the development of media consumption in the United States since 2010, we find, on the one hand, a decrease in the print media (from 7.7 per cent to 3.5 per cent), in radio stations (from 14.9 per cent to 10.9 per cent) and in television stations (from 41 per cent to 36.5 per cent). Pay television channels such as HBO (Time Warner), Showtime and Starz are losing market share. On the other hand, we find a strong (up to 23.3 per cent) increase in internet media services, the majority of which comes from video streaming.[14]

It can be assumed that this trend will continue over the coming years. An increasing number of media consumers will no longer even have a television contract; they will only subscribe to legal video streaming services such as Netflix, Hulu Plus and Amazon Prime. The classic media companies' natural reaction will be to diversify into the internet. Publishers and television stations will produce new online offers. In some cases, their offerings will need to be combined with a television contract. However, companies such as HBO and Showtime (CBS) have already announced streaming services without a television contract. They might undercut Netflix's subscription price of $9 per month by excluding parts of their premium content. Media companies will probably need to make two major strategic decisions: 1) find the right balance between producing their own content and offering foreign content; 2) find the right monetization mechanics between a television contract-based business model and a subscription fee-based business model.

Netflix has already surpassed its closest rival, HBO, with its number of subscribers. It has survived and thrived, because it gave many customers a better video viewing service. To guarantee and improve on this service, Netflix has had to adapt its business model effectively and continuously, and twice even radically. Figure 7.4 is a simple depiction of Netflix's adaptation process. The first radical transformation happened in two steps. The first step was taken in 1999 with the introduction of the subscription-based business model, which increased the inclusiveness of the transaction significantly, and the second step in 2007 with the ability to distribute content through the internet, enabled by the new video streaming technology. The second radical transformation was the subsequent decision to invest in original content. By this move of backwards integration Netflix added to its dominant platform business model as a distributor a new product business model as a movie maker. It used the data it got from its distributor business model to invest in a well-targeted way in standardized entertainment products. These data can also help to adjust new products directly to the specific needs of local markets, but this is far from real customization. Since September 2014, Netflix has been active in France. In spring 2016 the company was able to launch very successfully the new soap *Marseille*, completely focused on the French market, with actors like Gérard Depardieu and Benoît Magimel.

Figure 7.4 Netflix's business model transformations

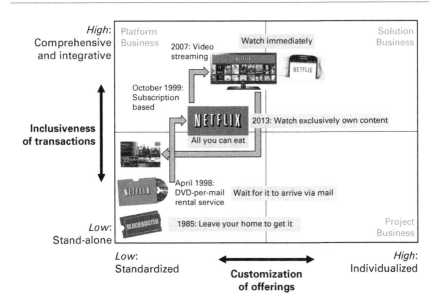

Netflix has had to take advantage of the swift pace of technological change to follow changing customer needs. It has had to go beyond its original capabilities and reinvent itself tirelessly. This challenge will remain, and new capabilities will be needed, such as the competence to market and brand its own content. In September 2014, Hastings was asked: 'What do you think is next for Netflix?' His answer was:

> Oh, there are a 100 things we would love to do! Streaming obviously has the future and will be relevant as long as the internet stays relevant ... So our challenge is to adapt to

new devices. We are always thinking about what the iPad is going to look like in ten years. How will mobile change? How can we produce more original content? How can we optimize for global distribution? You need to produce your own content so you are in control globally. We are now in 41 countries so we have 160 countries to go. So Asia is going to be a challenge, because it is such a different market. When I look at Netflix today, on a smart TV, I'm proud about what we achieved ... but I still consider it the Ford Model T. It is the first one to get mainstream, but we've got a long way to go. I see all the imperfections in Netflix. I see all the things that aren't working ... But as an entrepreneur that's how you have to look at your product. Compare yourself to what you want to be, what you will be, in five years, and that should be so much better than what you have today.[15]

In an internet-centric world of content consumption, Netflix must ensure that it can always create a great experience on an internet-connected screen.

Endnotes

1 The case is based on publicly available information. Some parts of the text are taken from the Netflix homepage (http://ir.netflix.com/long-term-view.cfm). Other parts refer to case studies: Netflix, Case E238, Stanford Graduate School of Business, 2007; The Price War: Netflix vs Blockbuster, IBS Research Center, 2009; Netflix: The US DVD rental company's competitive strategies, IBSCDC, 2005; Netflix, Harvard Business School, 2009.

2 Hereafter, all dollar amounts refer to US dollars, unless indicated otherwise. How Netflix got started, *CNN Money*, 28 January 2009.

3 P Cohan (2013) Netflix's Reed Hastings is the master of adaptation, *Forbes*, 22 October.

4 See https://www.youtube.com/watch?v=zCOOlNfs4oM.

5 See https://www.youtube.com/watch?v=zCOOlNfs4oM.

6 T Arango (2010) Time Warner views Netflix as a fading star, *New York Times*, 12 December.

7 See http://en.wikipedia.org/wiki/Blockbuster_LLC#Expansion_into_the_UK.

8 See https://gigaom.com/2013/08/09/netflix-chief-platform-partnership-officer-greg-peters.

9 Adam Sternbergh (2014) The post-hope politics of 'House of Cards', *New York Times*, 31 January.

10 D Grandoni (2013) With 'House of Cards', Netflix begins the future of TV, *Huffington Post*, 2 January.

11 See www.theverge.com/2013/9/22/4759754/netflix-challenges-the-tv-establishment-with-emmy-wins-for-house-of.

12 See www.theverge.com/2013/9/22/4759754/netflix-challenges-the-tv-establishment-with-emmy-wins-for-house-of.

13 Adam Sternbergh (2014) The post-hope politics of 'House of Cards', *New York Times*, 31 January.

14 S Schmid (2015) HBO und Showtime beugen sich Netflix-Druck, *Neue Zürcher Zeitung*, 3 January, p 29.

15 See http://thenextweb.com/entrepreneur/2013/09/12/inspiring-entrepreneurs-reed-hastings-netflix/.

Case studies of companies radically shifting the level of customization

08

Xerox: Transformation for the digital age
Jacqueline Fechner

Introduction: From a hardware company to a business process outsourcing provider

Xerox is a US-based global corporation that sells document services and document technology products. The company looks back on a history of more than 100 years. It was founded in 1906 in Rochester, NY as the Haloid Photographic Company, which originally manufactured photographic paper and equipment.

Xerography and the founding years

It all started when Chester Floyd Carlson, a young patent lawyer who worked for a local printer in the 1920s, got a small press on which he intended to print a magazine for amateur chemists. He started to think about an appropriate dupli-cating process.

After inventing the innovative xerography, Carlson was firmly convinced that it was of practical value to anyone. In 1947, Carlson entered into an agree-ment with the Haloid Photographic Company, which produced photographic paper. The agreement granted the company the right to construct a xerographic machine.

In 1948, 10 years after the first xerographic image, Haloid presented the Xerox Copier. After introducing the completely automated Copyflo with its innovative drum instead of a plate as photoconductive surface, the company renamed and became Haloid Xerox in 1958: xerographic products accounted for more than 40 per cent of the company's revenues.

In 1959, the legendary Xerox 914 entered the stage: the first automatic cop-ying machine for regular paper that went into serial and mass production. In 1963, 'Haloid' disappeared from the name, and the company continued to operate as Xerox.

In 1963, Xerox introduced the click price concept – a fixed price for a sheet of paper that is printed or copied. The concept aimed at optimizing the costs of printing and copying for customers. It included all costs connected with the printed or copied sheet such as repair, consumables and other services. With this, Xerox took the first step in a transition process that would gain additional traction decades later.

The invention of the copying machine allowed for a broad sharing of informa-tion. Moreover, it provided a simplified way to do so – an issue that has always been significant for Xerox. Xerox has always developed innovative solutions to improve how people work. The company calls it 'business engineering'. Xerox has around 140,000 employees, as well as offices in more than 180 countries.

Today, Xerox holds more than 12,000 active patents, and it invested more than US\$0.5 billion in research and development in 2014. The portfolio incorporates business services like document management and workplace optimization, as well as office equipment like printers, copiers, multifunction printers and supplies, and production equipment like digital presses, production printers and copiers, wide-format printers and workflow software.

Scalable document management during the age of business process outsourcing

Drivers of the first Xerox services were the customers' demand as well as the company's high level of innovation. It started with managed print services (MPS). The introduction of the click pricing concept had showed the company's innovative potential. The company could have been content with developing new machines and technologies with attractive pricing, assuming that customers simply want better and cheaper equipment and supplies. But instead, at the end of the 1990s, Xerox systematically worked on a document management concept that would allow an even stronger focus on customers' needs. The company started to look at the complete printing environment from a holistic perspective. The idea was to provide services that would guarantee control over all aspects of printing and additionally simplify the corresponding processes and management for the customer. The result was MPS, with the whole document output managed by Xerox, so the customer could concentrate on whatever its core business might be. MPS allows a customized outsourcing for the complete document output, including measuring and optimization, securing and integration, as well as automation and simplification.

Additionally, the customers can outsource and digitalize their complete printroom operations through centralized print services (CPS). This means that Xerox runs the complete end-to-end process and constantly optimizes it instead of only providing the production equipment.

An important driver of this development was customers' demands. On the occasion of a necessary hardware replacement, a big company asked Xerox not only to deliver new equipment but to operate the system too, because of its competences that would allow for optimizations. So Xerox for the first time delivered what became CPS and soon developed a comprehensive portfolio in this area.

However, services like MPS and CPS have become commoditized and subject to a price decrease. This shows the need to find new revenue streams in the services area to secure future business.

Market shift in the printing industry and key drivers for further transformation

The market conditions changed dramatically for the printing industry at the beginning of the new century, mainly characterized by a sharp drop in prices. The permanent development of innovative products meant that companies sticking to their traditional business models and portfolios faced an uncertain future. Printing experts like Xerox had to deal with a dramatic drop in volumes, which sooner or later would result in less revenue.

On the other hand, indicators of the future work environment were already visible. Companies had to cope with a growing number of complex processes, and integrated services continued to gain momentum over mainly product-bound services. This is why Xerox decided to take the next step and to target the next level of services – from *document management* to *process management* (see Figure 8.1). These advanced services aimed at the outsourcing of complete processes that go far beyond printing.

Figure 8.1 Xerox – from a hardware company to a business process outsourcing provider

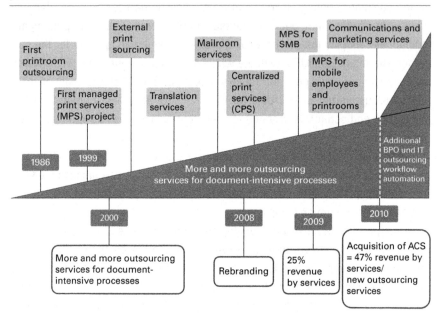

To compensate for shrinking product sales and to gain more profitability, the company started to develop services and solutions for document-intensive processes. Moreover, being an early adopter not only accelerates the transformation but confirms the market-leading position of Xerox.

Xerox implemented a new strategy: to enable more cost-efficient printing and furthermore an overall reduction in printed documents. The change *from a product-driven portfolio to a more and more service-oriented one where the product mostly functions as an enabler* was dynamically pushed forward. Multifunctional products served as a device to scan the particular context – and thereby accomplished their 'mission', because all further processing would be completely digitally. Digital alternatives, apps and solutions for workflow automation blazed the trail into a digital world.

There is one wish that all customers of printing companies have in common: cost reduction and significantly more transparency and control regarding document-intensive processes. In a digital environment, the printing of documents seems more and more obsolete – and there are enormous saving potentials regarding paper, toner and so on.

Business model transformation

Notwithstanding its successful development even in times of severe market crisis, Xerox faces the challenge of transforming its business model. The company is evolving from an already successful platform business model towards a more customer-individual offering. In this case study we concentrate on this transformation towards a solution business model.

To manage a change of this size and complexity means facing a lot of risks – and being prepared for large-scale investments. For example, the traditional, standardized, product-focused business line has to be not only continued but developed to secure its market share in this segment. On the other hand, a customer-individual solution business demands new structures and a completely different approach to engage with customers. This needs a cultural change across the whole company.

Xerox has to provide professional risk and change management as well as changing and rearranging structures in the three domains – the front end, with sales and portfolio, the supporting functions and delivery in the back end, and the monetization mechanics – to succeed as a provider and manager of complex projects, customized to each client's specific needs and to the end-to-end requirements.

Front-end transformation: From standardized product-centric to customized solutions

Business transformation requires changing the customer-facing front end and includes all activities the customer sees and experiences. In the case of Xerox's transformation from a platform business model to a solution business model, the changes at the front end consist of a development from standardized to single value propositions, which means integrated service-centric offerings. Solution-oriented process management requires the ability to adapt the offered solution to the customers' individual needs, as well as tight customer integration.

In its west–east crossing from standardized to customer-specified offerings, Xerox has already succeeded in completing most of the document outsourcing transformation processes. The company has already adjusted its portfolio, as well as the corresponding internal processes, which are described in the following paragraphs.

The transformation process does not affect just products and services. Other areas specific to the front end are involved too. Changing a product sales system to a solution sales system takes a lot of achieving. First, there's the customer contact: who is responsible for the purchase decision? Changing from selling products to complex solutions means that it's more and more the business value proposition that matters instead of just the technology value proposition. Where formerly procurement or facility management decided which printer should be purchased, now the IT department, other business areas and even the management are involved. This is for good reason: the added value of complex solutions lies in the field of costs and process streamlining, so the decision makers most probably belong to the C-suite.

Accordingly, the contact person at Xerox has to negotiate with the CIO, the CFO or another chief officer. He or she has to understand the business processes and should know the customer's industry very well to identify and promote the business value of the customer-specific solution. On the other hand, the contact person has to keep in mind that the decision maker on the customer side bears a considerable responsibility. Instead of paying a certain price for certain products, the decision maker has to decide to spend a considerable amount of money over a long time and to change internal processes, which makes the decision even more difficult.

In consequence, Xerox has changed its sales structure over the last few years, and is still in the process of transforming it. What are the changes in detail?

First of all, the required skills of the sales professionals have changed dramatically. Product-focused salespeople have to be educated to be able to sell complex solutions where the device is only the enabler. Xerox invested heavily in education for sales, for example training programmes that aimed to have salespeople acting more as consultants than product sellers and able to understand the customer's challenges and needs to design the right solution.

Not all sales personnel were able to adjust to these dramatic changes. On this journey roughly a third of salespeople failed, approximately a third became sales representatives with solid know-how, able to sell the new portfolio, and the remaining third took the opportunity to dramatically develop themselves and use it in their own careers.

Together with the change in sales representative education and know-how the organization changed. Before the transformation the sales function was organized by products and regions. After the transformation it adopted a strategic account organization. Xerox segmented the target accounts anew and focused its complex solution sales on the large enterprise segment. Standard services were sold via channel to the small and medium business market.

All in all, the Xerox portfolio is more and more directly associated with the customers' business processes. To cope with that, Xerox continuously has to increase its industry-specific competences regarding its internal organization. For example, workflow automation solutions require an industry-specific focus. Xerox is still in the process of transforming its sales organization by building up separate sales teams by industry, for example manufacturing, finance and public sector, to address this need. This transformation will continue over the coming years.

Looking to the solution once again, Xerox has to manage to deal with larger projects and with longer sales cycles. A cycle of around 6 to 18 months has to be considered. Therefore, internal sales management also has to be reworked. Long-term pipeline management and proactive demand management become more important, as well as short-term approaches like discounts to increase transactions. Xerox has also adjusted its sales channels to secure comprehensive, holistic key customer account management. Although the implementation of the new account sales organization is finished, in the long term the company still has to adjust and develop high performance skills in this area.

In 2008, new Xerox branding and the slogan 'Ready for real business' under-lined the transformation, making it clear that Xerox had changed.

Back-end transformation: Upgrading the back end from scalable production to flexible service structure

In order to realize complex, customized projects, Xerox had to substantially modify its operational back end. First of all, this meant providing more flexibility regarding customers' needs and improving the company's capabilities to process and implement their requirements.

New topics and processes like risk and SLA management

Bigger and more complex solutions also mean different challenges for the sales supporting functions. Xerox had to strengthen and expand functions like pricing, technical expertise and delivery.

In comparison to the situation in a product-focused environment, new topics and processes, especially in the field of pricing and legal matters, gained more and more importance for Xerox. The company established comprehensive risk management and a corresponding risk culture. Instead of fixing every single de-tail for itself, dealing with large projects meant specifying the technical and finan-cial targets and so getting a comprehensive view. Xerox is handling the transition from a current mode of operation (CMO) to a future mode of operation (FMO) as a long-term project. Once established, it has to be capable of reacting in a flexible way and managing every new and unexpected challenge that comes up – not least because of the contract-defined service level agreements (SLAs).

Adequate risk and change management is crucial regarding pricing and contracting. For the finance and legal departments, coming from the traditional product sales segment, this is fairly unfamiliar. Traditionally, the price had been calculated by adding a margin to the purchase price of the products. This calcu-lation is of course no longer valid for long-term projects. Today, a special Xerox pricing team has to develop a business case that includes complex solution elem-ents, including full-time equivalent (FTE) calculations, together with assumptions and risk options. It aligns the business case to the solution description and continuously adjusts through a bid process. Hence, the pricing team needs controlling skills as well as a deep understanding of businesses.

When it comes to contracting, customer-specific demands, SLAs and change management have to be considered. Xerox has to carefully customize every single contract. Therefore, the legal department has to provide a deep understanding of the solution business as well as certain negotiation skills.

Comprehensive bid teams with worldwide capacities

Bid management is affected by the change too. The bid team has to work on complex projects, and therefore roles and responsibilities have to be identified clearly within the team. Although it was possible to cover several salespeople with just one pre-sales specialist in the past, today a salesperson needs a bid team for every single offer – including a bid manager, a pricing manager, a contract manager, a solution architect, a technical architect, a transition and transformation manager, delivery specialists and so on. To make sure it can deliver these competences, Xerox created a special BidCenter in Germany. It is connected to the European and worldwide BidCenters and closely cooperates with the European and worldwide level when fixing a global deal.

To support these major changes, Xerox has introduced a consistent worldwide bid process – the bid management pursuit process (BMPP). It defines the operation as well as the corresponding roles and responsibilities during the bid process, which is critical for the coordinated team work of the rather complex bid team. The process precisely defines the tasks of the particular experts for legal matters, pricing and solutions and so secures maximum efficiency. It also specifies conditions for reviews and releases and so ensures adequate risk management.

Delivery platforms and shared service centres

The competence and capacity to deliver quality services on a global level are also of great importance, so Xerox invested considerably in the implementation of a coherent infrastructure. The company created globally active shared service centres that cooperate with the local service departments. The alignment of local and international capacities has been especially critical to the implementation profiting from local characteristics and conditions while providing a worldwide consistent delivery process.

The necessary global infrastructure for technical and back-office processes incorporates a uniform definition of services and competences, standardized invoicing, global delivery capabilities and the ability to use economy of scale.

What does this mean in detail? Xerox has used its own developed software to enable the delivery organizations to run the service for its customers globally with the same capabilities and quality. The same architecture is used, and the delivery processes are globally aligned. This enables Xerox to deliver worldwide to the same standards and SLAs, which becomes more and more important for internationally operating clients.

Monetization mechanics transformation: From cost-driven to demand-driven pricing

Regarding the monetization mechanics, changing the business model meant that Xerox had to move to a new pricing model. The new model reflects the customers' willingness to pay for customization in the context of a complex project. Primarily, this means a refocus from fixed costs to variable, engagement-related costs. Demand-driven rather than fixed prices for print and scan services imply that it is Xerox that now takes the risk.

Profit and loss hydraulics putting the focus on long-term revenues

The change from a product- to a service- and solution-focused approach has numerous implications for the P&L hydraulics of Xerox. The company had to completely restructure its balance sheet. Products produce revenues only at the time they are sold, together with annual revenues for the standard break-and-fix business. By moving into services and complex solutions, the long-time revenues increase. That makes a company more robust to overcome short-term economic periods of drought.

Another crucial point for Xerox is that changing the approach means facing the fact that the risks move from clients to company. Offerings like 'pay-per-use' or 'software as a service' as well as maximum flexibility in contracts forced Xerox into ensuring adequate risk management. Because of the lack of the usual guaranteed purchase price, Xerox developed payment models that covered the fixed costs but at the same time allowed for flexibility from the customer's side – with the effect that revenues could eventually appear in the profit and loss account more than a year later. Today, the most significant turnover in the profit and loss account is generated by services.

Outlook: Solutions for simpler work in a challenging environment

Xerox started its transformation journey a number of years ago and has made remarkable progress since (see Figure 8.2). Through an important acquisition in 2010 the company has the capability to generate business process outsourcing services. The provision of services has been very successful and caused significant improvements in business, competitiveness and growth. The company has grown from its origins of delivering on-site, small-scale contracts to being a professional shared service organization delivering substantial outsourcing contracts to its customers, underpinned by its own technology.

Figure 8.2 Xerox's business model transformations

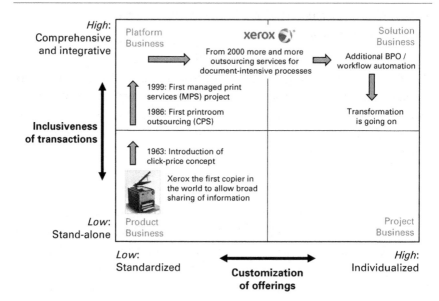

Such strategies allow for greater customer intimacy, including customer growth. Moreover, they ensure a reliable lock-out of the competition. By addressing enterprise challenges and meeting clients' end-to-end-requirements, Xerox consequently expands its market opportunities. The management of document-intensive business processes and information infrastructure allows customers to profit from numerous competitive advantages.

Integrated document management, business process outsourcing and IT outsourcing address a very big market. Significant synergy opportunities across the whole new portfolio tap an even bigger potential.

Finally, Xerox profits from smooth and steady revenue streams. All in all, there are three main points Xerox aims at: a complete service offer, expanded market opportunities and a secured global consistency.

The product/service mix of Xerox shows that over 50 per cent of deliveries today are services. As a service-driven and technology-enabled company, Xerox understands and redesigns the technology and thereby improves the efficiency and effectiveness of processes.

Looking to the future, there are several trends that deliver additional aspects and perspectives for the ongoing transition process. People are increasingly mobile, digitally literate – and green. This shapes how they will approach documents and print in the coming years and decades. Emerging technologies in which Xerox is involved can be used to help processes cross the 'paper–digital divide' that occurs and continues to grow. Constant changes in technology and work habits will bring new challenges for businesses. As a solution company, Xerox will constantly strive to make office work simpler, less tedious and even more productive in this context.

Infosys: Productization of a knowledge business – The transformation from project-based system integrator to digital service provider of productized and platform-based services
Matthias Barth and Carsten Linz

Infosys's company evolution: From start-up to global professional services firm

Today Infosys is a global leader providing professional services for consulting, technology and outsourcing as well as next-generation services. In 1981, seven engineers started Infosys Limited. From the beginning, the company was founded on the principle of building and implementing software applications that drive progress for clients and enhance lives through enterprise solutions.

In the 1980s, in the early days of personal computing, most IT services had been delivered on-site, with a dedicated focus on each individual customer. The delivery of such services is primarily based on direct involvement of project managers, consultants and IT experts. The focus for IT providers such as Infosys at that time was on a few large customers, with each and every project and service being designed and delivered individually on a custom basis. The upcoming client–server technologies at the end of the 1980s opened up new delivery models, resulting in new pricing and operations for IT service providers. Infosys took a revolutionary approach in designing, establishing and rolling out a global delivery model (GDM).[1] This allowed it to distribute application and business process life cycle activities across multiple locations, generating cost benefits by leveraging low-cost resources.

In particular, the years after Infosys's IPO in 1993 were a period of growth, taking the company from $5 million annual revenues in 1993 to $203 million in 2000 and reaching $1 billion in 2004. With more and more Indian providers looking for market share in the information technology outsourcing (ITO) and business process outsourcing (BPO) market, the pressure on revenues and utilization increased.

In 1993, Infosys's first product was the banking solution Banks2000, which was based on a custom development project and was rebranded as Finacle in July 2000. Starting with a focus on retail banks, Finacle proved a powerful choice for banks in the developing world. This product quickly gained market traction, and from 2001 to 2003 Finacle grew at rates of 50 per cent to nearly 100 per cent per year.[2]

In the late 2000s new delivery and service models – such as cloud – changed the entire business and ecosystem. New market entrants for cloud services such as Amazon or Google started gaining market share quickly. As a result of the cannibalization of classical IT outsourcing and margin pressure for projects delivered on an individual customer basis, Infosys put its focus on transforming its business model towards a product-centric business. Its goal was to build up a more margin-competitive portfolio of intellectual property (IP) assets.

Having set a standard with Finacle for the financial industry, Infosys quickly expanded and continued to invest in products. With the acquisition of EdgeVerve Systems in July 2014 it enhanced its portfolio with a second enterprise-scale product. It was incorporated to focus on building products on cloud, mobile and analytics. The EdgeVerve suite defines and develops products, helping its clients to transform to new technology for procurement, supply chain, marketing, e-learning, e-commerce and asset management. At the end of 2015, all Infosys products including Finacle became part of the wholly owned EdgeVerve subsidiary. Today the Infosys portfolio comprises products like Finacle, EdgeVerve, McCamish, BPO Forecasting and platforms such as the IIP analytics platform.

In 2015 Infosys revenues reached US$8.7 billion, with over 187,000 employees.[3] As of 31 December 2015, 96.8 per cent of the revenues came from existing clients ('renewed business').[4] Infosys's client base spreads across more than 50 countries. Infosys has its headquarters located in Bangalore and runs 85 sales and marketing offices plus 100 development centres globally. The traditional IT services with application development, testing, maintenance and so on in areas such as mobility, sustainability, big data and cloud computing remain the largest revenue contributor, with more than 60 per cent revenue share. This is followed by classical consulting, adding about one-third of corporate revenues. While products and platforms account for 5 per cent of its business, Infosys is looking to continuously enlarge this portfolio, including by acquiring firms that can add top-line growth. With CEO Vishal Sikka taking over in 2014, a Renew and New strategy was announced to enhance the competitiveness and productivity of current service lines by leveraging automation, innovation and artificial intelligence. In following this strategy, Infosys acquired Panaya, Inc, a leading provider of automation technology for large-scale enterprise software management. In addition Infosys announced the acquisition of Skava to help clients bring new digital experiences to their customers through IP-led technology offerings, new automation tools and expertise in these new emerging areas.

Managing Infosys's phased business model transformation

The following case illustrates Infosys's evolution from delivering custom projects to a product-focused service provider by describing its business model transformation. This is separated based on the two strategic paths Infosys pursued. The first is the change from project to product supplier, standardizing its offerings and productizing knowledge within the company. The second one is the transformation towards increased inclusiveness, specifically a more platform-based business resulting in improved customer retention, as well as an expanded ecosystem of partners offering services and solutions on these platforms.

Phase one: From individual customer project services to productized standard offerings

In the professional services industry, the classical business model has been constant for a long time, with a linear correlation of the number of professionals providing projects or services and associated revenues. In the past, firms grew by hiring more qualified employees, resulting in a proportional growth of their revenues. Revenue per employee and employee retention are the key performance indicators (KPIs) to measure for growth. It comes as no surprise that a lot of the larger Indian IT companies have more than 100,000 employees. In order to overcome this direct dependency and transform to a non-linear growth model, service providers need to invest in service delivery automation and IP-based assets that can be delivered in a repeatable way and include the companies' IP. These IP assets have to be designed independently of the people delivering them.[5] With Banks2000, later renamed Finacle, Infosys created its most successful product, driven by a separate business unit within the company. This can be seen as the first attempt to start transforming its business model to establish more sustainable, non-linear growth by long-term revenue streams. Multiple acquisitions over the last few years like Edge Systems, Panaya and Skava underline this strategy.

Front-end transformation: From custom projects to IP-based products

Traditionally, Infosys's core business has been centred on time- and material-based or fixed-price IT projects. These are mostly individual customer projects, with Infosys putting an emphasis on creating unique solutions based on clients' complex requirements. At the beginning of the 1990s, the Infosys leadership team experimented with creating reusable software products when they saw market opportunities.

In 1993, Indian banks were still state-owned. The business processes in banking were very similar. Infosys carried out a project for an Indian retail bank, from which it retained intellectual property and launched a standard product named Banks2000. This was a solution designed for branch banking, built using deep client relationships. By 1997 branch banking solutions were becoming a commodity, and in the light of globalization and expansion of private banking the Indian market was transforming. Infosys started to turn its key product into a centralized banking solution.[6] This allowed for a 360-degree view of end customers, enabling banks to better engage on the one hand and minimize their financial risks on the other. However, the new solution did not generate the desired growth rates. Competitors were ahead in terms of functionality as well as geographic presence. Infosys's banking unit management decided to transform its strategy by repositioning its solution, to establish a strong trusted brand by renaming Banks2000 as Finacle in July 2000. By doing so, Infosys repositioned Finacle's adaptability to existing client processes and systems.[7] This capability was essential to leading in a very dynamic and fast-changing banking market.

At the beginning, having dedicated sales teams was much too expensive for a single product. The strategy was to start leveraging multiple sales channels: using indirect sales models via local or regional IT service providers and using the top global hardware and software providers like IBM, HP and Microsoft. This measure proved to be effective, and the product quickly gained market traction. From 2001 to 2003, Finacle grew at rates of 50 per cent to nearly 100 per cent per year.[8]

Infosys had goals to further grow and expand on a global scale. In order to enter new markets and address new geographies, the firm needed to offer a superior value proposition to its prospects. With Infosys being a large global services company with a very good reputation, the banking unit started selling via the Infosys Services line of business, combining it with the business's strategy consulting and implementation services. In 2015 Infosys launched the AiKiDo services framework, including strategy consulting (Do), knowledge-based IT (Ki) and platforms (Ai). AiKiDo is leveraged to convey a compelling end-to-end message to existing and new clients.[9] This differentiated Infosys from its competitors, which were equal in product capabilities but smaller firms not able to leverage a large portfolio of in-house services in their sales process. Today Finacle is the market leader for centralized banking systems in Asia and Africa and looking to become a leader in the United States and Europe.[10] It is installed in 84 countries and used by 183 banks serving more than 16.5 per cent of the banked population.

Back-end transformation: From flexible customer project to scalable production

Infosys started productizing by converting the individual software developed for the first banking client into a more general and standardized solution that any bank could use. As the work of developing and understanding all aspects of a complex software product was quite different to running and executing projects, a separate organization was required that operated independently from the project services-led business. This banking product group introduced the role of product manager, which was filled by an industry expert in banking rather than a software engineer. A separate recruiting strategy was used: in contrast to project managers responsible for service business, industry experts with banking knowledge were hired. Infosys also required employees to stay longer in that product group in growing their seniority by acquiring and making use of their detailed product and industry knowledge.[11] The banking product group was also set up in such a way as to keep the employee base more stable; attrition was lower than in other business areas. With Finacle's annual revenues passing $247 million, the headcount of this organization increased to 5,350 in 2015.[12]

On the product side, Infosys's primary goal was to transform its intellectual property into a scalable product. Productivity increase became key for Infosys in improving its financial KPIs and mass-scaling its business. Several measures helped in achieving this:

- For more transparency Infosys introduced measures such as documenting its software engineering process, making it reusable.

- A new knowledge management system enabled developers searching for documentation and reusing code modules.

- An in-house solution called InFlux automated requirements management with customers, thereby accelerating product development and reducing gaps and errors at an early stage of the process.[13]

The software architects redesigned Finacle to increase the level of adaptability and scalability for deployment in a more industrialized way. Scalability was particularly important for addressing a client base of larger customers. Adaptability was key to position the product into landscapes of existing banking IT solutions, for example by addressing capabilities for handling multi-currency transactions.[14]

Over time market requirements grew into new areas, such as closer customer engagement and mobile banking services. Infosys again adapted its product strategy following an 'outside-in' approach to transform it into a standard banking solution. Reusing the experiences the banking product group had collected over several years, Finacle was enhanced with new product modules. Following a 'make or buy' strategy, customer relationship and treasury had been acquired and integrated, while Infosys self-developed the mobility functionality.

In 2015 the Finacle product covered various product modules such as e-banking, mobile banking, digital commerce and youth banking, and the digital marketing platform EdgeBrand had become a powerful banking offering, ranked 'Leader' by Forrester.[15]

Transformation of monetization mechanics: From individually priced projects to standardized price-list item

The transformation from custom projects to standardized product requires careful assessment and changes to the pricing, from individually priced projects to standardized, competitive pricing. When it first launched Banks2000 as a branch banking solution in the 1990s, Infosys focused primarily on the Indian market and was able to sell its solution at a premium price to Indian banks in the following years. With the liberalization of the Indian market and increasing globalization, banks started looking for central banking solutions. Decentralized branch banking solutions became a commodity, and competitors for banking solutions decreased prices for their products significantly. Infosys had to adjust the positioning and pricing of its prime product.[16] The new, redesigned centralized banking solution allowed Infosys to enter a new market for retail banks. As there were already two competitors of smaller size in this market, Infosys management decided to start positioning their software product into opportunities that would expand into more transformational deals, adding on top their higher-value services for strategy consulting, implementation and maintenance. Infosys started a dedicated Finacle practice supporting clients' implementation projects, also adding the credibility of a global presence to deal and sales cycles.[17] The combination of this brought Infosys into a position to keep its premium pricing. On the cost side, Infosys started to manage fixed costs by leveraging its global delivery model and increasing the rate of automation. Any tasks that did not have to be delivered on-site had been moved offshore to low-cost locations. At that time, the global delivery model allowed Infosys to leverage skilled resources in low-cost locations, giving it a cost advantage over competitors.

Being a classical IT consulting and systems integrator, Infosys offered a mix of time and material as well as fixed-price engagements in the 1990s and 2000s. In later years it also started offering outcome-based engagements, in which its revenue was based on realizing measurable business outcomes for clients. This had to be completely changed for the Finacle software product, which is offered on a price list on a per-user basis with an upfront licence metric.[18] With the acceleration of new deployment models, Infosys also started offering Finacle in the cloud in 2015. This required another complete redesign of the pricing, offering Finacle to clients in more flexible subscription-based pricing models.[19]

Finally the entire internal reporting on business success had to be transformed to a different set of key performance indicators. The goal for getting into the business of IP-based assets (such as software products) is to achieve non-linear growth by decoupling revenue growth from increase in headcount. Therefore, the key metrics, 'revenue by employee' or the Infosys PSPD (predictability of revenues, sustainability of such predictability, profitability of such realized revenues and de-risking) model of operation used for project services cannot be applied to a more long-term software product business.[20] On top of product revenue and margin KPIs, Infosys started measuring the percentage of revenues from its products on a corporate level.[21]

Phase two: From product company to an IP-powered platform service provider

In the years following the financial crisis in 2009, Infosys's revenue growth was under pressure as clients started transitioning from higher-value business transformation consulting for their own IT installations to infrastructure and BPO deals, which outsource parts of the IT landscapes. The results were declining key metrics such as 'utilization' and 'revenue per employee'. As a direct result, the push for more IP-based products increased even further.

Under the umbrella of its Infosys 3.0 strategy, the service provider focused on investing in platforms and products in 2013.[22] In concrete terms, Infosys created a separate entity, Products and Platform Solutions (PPS), increased spending for research and development and added intellectual property by mergers and acquisitions. Despite these investments, Infosys revenue growth fell short in that year, as client IT spend continued to transition from higher-value 'change the business' consulting to lower-margin 'run the business' infrastructure and BPO deals.

With Vishal Sikka taking over as Infosys CEO in 2014, the company's transformation was accelerating. Infosys continued to invest in platforms and software heads to establish sustainable, non-linear revenue streams and position for long-term revenue expansion.[23] Additional acquisitions came into consideration, with plans to add vertical-specific platforms and IP assets in industries such as healthcare, retail, manufacturing and financial services.

One of the vendor's key platforms is the Infosys Information Platform (IIP). IIP addresses enterprise big data analytics challenges such as inadequate accessibility to required tools; fragmented approach to data; and the lack of an industrialized version of a big data analytics solution. It is an open-source data analytics platform supporting the decision-making process by providing real-time analysis and forecasts.

Infosys leverages IIP to expand its product business by offering platform extensions. For Finacle banking customers the service provider enhances end-user experience by creating an ecosystem of extensions on top of IIP in key areas like big data, analytics, mobile banking and digital commerce.

Another example is in the sports industry. In 2015 Infosys engaged as global technology services partner with the Association of Tennis Professionals (ATP). The service provider operates the ATP Scores and Stats Center based on IIP. Sports fans can look at analytics and predictions for each tennis match on the ATP website in real time. Infosys offers a broad range of services in also managing the ATP IT infrastructure and connecting ATP players through ATP Player Zone, a mobile-based platform.

Front-end transformation: From single product offerings to integrated platforms open to clients and partners

With IIP, Infosys is addressing big data scenarios for which organizations are looking to quickly analyse large amounts of data and build reports across many different sources of structured and unstructured data.[24] Infosys combined and enhanced its classical offerings of consulting, application development and integration for analytical services to complete an offering or product that covers the end-to-end process around data acquisition, processing for analytical reporting, and forecasting for decision making.

In selecting their platform, clients today can either invest in vendor-proprietary software and hardware solutions or leverage open-source technology and tools. This creates challenges in two dimensions. On the platform-offering side, there is often a lock-in on vendor or technology.[25] In the open-source world, it is up to clients to pick the right toolsets, which also require the right skills. Clients must balance talent supply and demand, and have sufficient resources with the right skills for managing and operating them.

Infosys is looking to build its value proposition around these dimensions. While it built its own IP into IIP – by bringing in its own toolsets, algorithms, support packages, adapters and accelerators – it intentionally created it as an open, vendor-agnostic platform. There is no proprietary licence and vendor lock-in; that is, it is possible for clients to keep the deployments of IIP flexible and use pre-built components and packages from different partners.[26] An example of this openness is Infosys's collaboration with GE, an industrial company focusing on digital services, for offering an Internet of Things (IoT) platform that combines IIP with GE's Predix platform for data acquisition and processing.[27]

Back-end transformation: From a single product business to an enterprise analytics platform provider

Following the appointment of Vishal Sikka as CEO, the formerly independent Infosys Labs platform group was assigned to the delivery organization under the new leadership of Abdul Razack. Combining it with big data and analytics skills this group focused on the transformation towards platform and big data business and particularly had to look into ways for increasing platform adoption and streamlining operations of IIP.

The IIP platform is built on open-source components in three different layers, consisting of standard open-source components, Infosys and partner components, and additional custom services such as integration. This open and scalable architecture allows Infosys and partners to reuse widely available shared standard tools, yet add their own IP assets flexibly.[28] In 2016 IIP was made available on Amazon Web Services Marketplace to get new partners and customers quickly on-board.[29]

Infosys management also decided to focus on problem-solving techniques and automation. With the introduction of new problem-solving skills such as design thinking Infosys introduced a new methodology for its innovation process across the company. By collecting and consolidating reusable components across its customer projects, it built more automation solutions into its platform.

With the various open-source components and technologies changing frequently, Infosys also started offering tools to automate the set-up of IIP. There is scalability and elasticity on the hardware set-up, allowing for all sizes of deployment from small subsidiaries to large global firms. The built-in tools and accelerators also allow clients to deploy IIP in days or weeks rather than over several months or on a year-long project.[30]

In order to provide its clients with flexibility and speed, Infosys supports all current deployment models in public or private clouds as well as self-service deployments.

While platform-based offerings can be delivered with fewer low-cost, high-skilled employees, Infosys is focusing on adding high-value services through its data scientists and business analysts. As big data is an emerging trend, Infosys not only established a dedicated consulting practice but also started a strategic partnership with the widely recognized Institute for Computational and Mathematical Engineering (ICME) of Stanford University to carry out research on data science and establish solutions for industry verticals. Through this arrangement, Infosys will also gain access to talent at ICME to broaden its competence in this field.[31]

Transformation of monetization mechanics: From one-time upfront licence sales to long-term outcome-based business

Licensing costs for open-source platforms get increasingly commoditized. At the same time the trend towards digital transformation combined with limited customer understanding of the end results is creating an increased demand for long-term outcome-based engagements. Similarly to its competitors, Infosys decided not to use any fixed prices for selling its big data analytics platform. Instead it is pricing it on a combination of an outcome-based model based on business value delivered to its clients with a recurring subscription for maintenance. There are four different types of business outcomes for clients:

- business growth and innovation;
- operational efficiency;
- ensuring security and compliance;
- maintaining business continuity.

For example, clients in the banking industry can use IIP for predictive maintenance of their ATM machines. It is possible to predict which ATM is likely to fail in the next three weeks with a certain level of probability (eg 80 per cent). The business benefit for clients is to increase service availability for their ATMs by reducing outages, thereby increasing customer satisfaction and ultimately client retention. This incremental benefit for clients makes it attractive for Finacle customers, for instance, also to invest in IIP analytics services.

Impact of business model transformations and outlook

Based on its profound experiences from many projects across industries, Infosys understood that it had to continuously transform and adapt its business and service offerings to market requirements (see Figure 8.3). With the commoditization of classical IT outsourcing, resulting in pricing pressures and weak utilization, the vendor wants to establish itself as a trusted global provider of products and platforms. The first transformation, from east to west, was from projects to products, piloted with the Finacle product, and included the change from fully custom services and pricing towards offering and delivering productized services with standard pricing.

Figure 8.3 Infosys – from a project-based system integrator to a digital service provider of productized and platform-based services

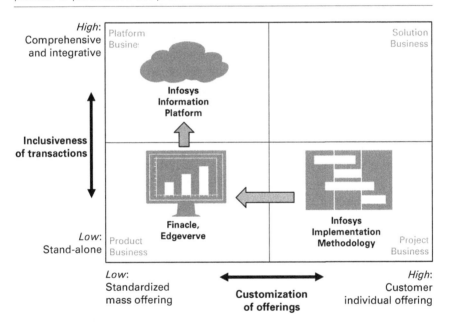

The second transformation, from south to north, was moving to a platform business with the goal of building more sustainable business models. By investing and launching its Infosys Information Platform IIP, Infosys has entered the market for higher-value IP assets, which secure its long-term margin competitiveness. In addition it combined those IP assets with classical IT services, for example the analytical services complementing Infosys's Finacle product based on the IIP platform.[32] This south–north crossing required opening up the platform offering for partners and complementors, and starting to rethink its pricing models from upfront licences to a combination of outcome-based licences and recurring sub-scriptions for maintenance.

A critical success factor for both transformations was to quickly achieve 'crit-ical mass' and scale for the products and platform offerings. Infosys managed these transformations successfully with products and platforms contributing an-nual revenue shares of 5 per cent of its overall business.[33] Finacle is installed by more than 180 customers,[34] and there are 200 engagements for IIP with 20 cus-tomers being productive across industries.[35] Finacle is ranked as 'Leader' in the Forrester Wave for omnichannel banking solutions: 'Infosys combines various elements of its portfolio into a leading solution … The omnichannel banking solu-tion leverages solid product architecture to provide a basis for flexible CX. Product strategy is well defined without any true gaps.'[36]

With its newly articulated strategy to evolve into next-generation service offerings based on combinations of products, platforms and services, Infosys is well positioned for a transformation into digital business. Analysts such as TBR believe Infosys is looking to build a platform portfolio capable of generating one-third of Infosys's total revenue in the long term: 'While Infosys will maintain its status as an IT services vendor, we anticipate the company – under the leadership of Sikka – will gain the image of a product and software provider, as the commoditization of IT services and adoption of cloud will compel it to expand its IP portfolio of vertical-specific offerings.'[37]

Says Vishal Sikka: 'The mission of our management team is to prepare the company to achieve an aspirational goal of US\$ 20 billion in revenue by calendar 2020 with at least 30% operating margin … New platforms and our Edge portfolio working on different revenue models will contribute disproportionally to our rev-enue per person.'[38]

Endnotes

1 P C Trimble (2008) Infosys: Maintaining an edge, Case No 2-0026, William F Achtmeyer Center for Global Leadership, Tuck School of Business at Dartmouth.

2 P C Trimble (2008) Infosys in a distinct business: Finacle, Case No 2-0025, William F Achtmeyer Center for Global Leadership, Tuck School of Business at Dartmouth.

3 Infosys (2015) *Infosys Annual Report 2014–15*, https://www.infosys.com/investors/reports-filings/annual-report/annual/Documents/infosys-AR-15.pdf.

4 Infosys (2016) Infosys factsheet, third quarter, fiscal 2016, https://www.infosys.com/investors/reports-filings/quarterly-results/2015-2016/q3/Documents/fact-sheet.pdf.

5 TBR (2015) TBR's Global Delivery Benchmark Research, 20 May.

6 P C Trimble (2008) Infosys in a distinct business: Finacle, Case No 2-0025, William F Achtmeyer Center for Global Leadership, Tuck School of Business at Dartmouth.

7   P C Trimble (2008) Infosys in a distinct business: Finacle, Case No 2-0025, William F Achtmeyer Center for Global Leadership, Tuck School of Business at Dartmouth.

8   P C Trimble (2008) Infosys in a distinct business: Finacle, Case No 2-0025, William F Achtmeyer Center for Global Leadership, Tuck School of Business at Dartmouth.

9   B Hristov (2015) Infosys promotes its business through its solution-led framework, AiKiDo, and invests in IoT capabilities to climb the value chain, *TBR*, http://tbri.com/analyst-perspectives/analyst-commentary/pgView.cfm?commentary=2590.

10 Infosys (2015) Infosys Finacle clients, https://www.edgeverve.com/finacle/customers.

11 P C Trimble (2008) Infosys in a distinct business: Finacle, Case No 2-0025, William F Achtmeyer Center for Global Leadership, Tuck School of Business at Dartmouth.

12 Infosys (nd) Infosys media FAQ, https://www.infosys.com/newsroom/journalist-resources/Pages/media-faq.aspx#projects.

13 P C Trimble (2008) Infosys: Maintaining an edge, Case No 2-0026, William F Achtmeyer Center for Global Leadership, Tuck School of Business at Dartmouth.

14 PC Trimble (2008) Infosys in a distinct business: Finacle, Case No 2-0025, William F Achtmeyer Center for Global Leadership, Tuck School of Business at Dartmouth.

15 Forrester (2015) The Forrester Wave: Omnichannel banking solutions, Q3 2015.

16 P C Trimble (2008) Infosys in a distinct business: Finacle, Case No 2-0025, William F Achtmeyer Center for Global Leadership, Tuck School of Business at Dartmouth.

17 P C Trimble (2008) Infosys in a distinct business: Finacle, Case No 2-0025, William F Achtmeyer Center for Global Leadership, Tuck School of Business at Dartmouth.

18 Capterra (nd) Reviews of Finacle, http://www.capterra.com/banking-systems-software/spotlight/59348/Finacle/Infosys%20Technologies.

19 Infosys (2015) Offering SaaS financial solution in the Verizon Cloud for U.S. banks, https://www.infosys.com/newsroom/press-releases/Pages/pay-as-you-go-financial-software-service.aspx.

20 V H Blogs (2011) Infosys founder retires, http://verneharnish.typepad.com/growthguy/2011/08/infosys-founder-retires-clever-kpi-mental-model-of-business.html#sthash.Jjp6a444.dpuf.

21 P C Trimble (2008) Infosys: Maintaining an edge, Case No 2-0026, William F Achtmeyer Center for Global Leadership, Tuck School of Business at Dartmouth.

22 Infosys, *TBR Professional Services Business Quarterly*, August 2012.

23 TBR (2013) Infosys will expand its global delivery reach and invest in platform solutions to achieve its 6% to 10% revenue growth guidance for FY14, http://tbri.com/analyst-perspectives/analyst-commentary/pgView.cfm?commentary=1865.

24 R Joshi (2015) Infosys shows discovery-to-decision platform innovation with IIP, HfS Research.

25   R Joshi (2015) Infosys shows discovery-to-decision platform innovation with IIP, HfS Research.

26   R Joshi (2015) Infosys shows discovery-to-decision platform innovation with IIP, HfS Research.

27   Infosys (2015) Infosys partners with GE to develop new solutions for the industrial internet of things, https://www.infosys.com/newsroom/press-releases/Pages/indus-trial-internet-things-solutions.aspx.

28   R Joshi (2015) Infosys shows discovery-to-decision platform innovation with IIP, HfS Research.

29   Infosys (2016) The Hershey Company partners with Infosys to build predictive analytics capability using open source information platform on Amazon Web Services, https://www.infosys.com/newsroom/press-releases/Pages/build-predictive-analytics-capability.aspx.

30   Infosys (2013) Infosys Information Platform – platform overview.

31   Infosys (2014) Infosys collaborates with Stanford University to accelerate education and research in data science and analytics, https://www.infosys.com/newsroom/press-releases/Pages/research-in-accelerate-education.aspx.

32   Infosys (2012) *TBR Professional Services Business Quarterly*, August.

33   Infosys (2016) Infosys factsheet, third quarter, fiscal 2016, https://www.infosys.com/investors/reports-filings/quarterly-results/2015-2016/q3/Documents/fact-sheet.pdf.

34   Infosys (2015) Infosys Finacle clients, https://www.edgeverve.com/finacle/customers.

35   Infosys (2016) Infosys earnings management commentary.

36   Forrester (2015) The Forrester Wave: Omnichannel banking solutions, Q3.

37   B Hristov (2015) Infosys promotes its business through its solution-led framework, AiKiDo, and invests in IoT capabilities to climb the value chain, *TBR*, http://tbri.com/analyst-perspectives/analyst-commentary/pgView.cfm?commentary=2590.

38   Infosys (2015) *Infosys Annual Report 2014–15*, https://www.infosys.com/investors/reports-filings/annual-report/annual/Documents/infosys-AR-15.pdf.

Transforming FUNDES's social business model: Becoming a customer-driven consulting firm to avoid mission drift in changing environments

Urs Jäger, Ulrich Frei and Silke Bucher

Introduction

Having launched its first office in Panama in 1984, FUNDES has become an influential consultancy provider in the field of economic development work, and has established offices in 12 Latin American countries. The non-profit's intent is to reduce poverty by integrating micro-, small- and medium-sized enterprises (MSMEs) into the value chains of large firms such as Nestlé, Wal-Mart, Holcim or Avon. FUNDES initially provided its services free of charge. At one point, however, the organization's main donor announced that it would be ceasing its annual donation; at the same time, FUNDES found itself confronted with an increasingly challenging Latin American business environment[1] and overall tightening economic situation. Thereupon, FUNDES shifted its business model from being a donation-driven, largely standardized service provider to MSMEs to offering customer-specific, market-driven projects to large multinational organizations and thus generating its own revenues. In terms of the business transformation board (Figure II.1), this represents a transformation of the business model to the east. The shift successfully preserved the organization's social mission and prevented a mission drift, while enabling FUNDES to become financially self-sustainable.

FUNDES's social mission meets a strong need in the region. Although Latin America enjoys relatively well-developed infrastructure and largely democratized governments, poverty remains a significant challenge, and the region still has the highest income inequality in the world.[2] The more than 18 million MSMEs, which account for 99 per cent of Latin America's private sector business population, play a crucial role in the region's socio-economic development. In 2010, these firms, including micro businesses with fewer than 10 employees, firms with 10–50 employees (small businesses) and firms with 50–150 employees (medium-sized businesses), contributed up to 50 per cent of the GDP of Latin American countries and created more than 60 per cent of the region's available jobs.[3]

The early 1980s marked the beginning of an increasing awareness in Latin America and other parts of the world that supporting the development of MSMEs is a powerful strategy for poverty alleviation. Leveraging this potential required overcoming a number of challenges that MSMEs and those wishing to start, sustain or grow a business were facing, among others relatively low levels of education, limited access to international markets and poor connections to large-firm supply chains. In order to confront these challenges and support the development of MSMEs, private and public organizations started offering so-called business development services (BDS). Funded with public resources from governments or local municipalities, private capital from philanthropy, or earned revenue generated by the providers themselves, BDS providers nowadays offer a wide range of services. This includes financial services, such as the provision of micro credits, credit guarantees, loans and other capital, and a diverse set of non-financial services such as training, consulting and advice, marketing assistance, access to information, and technology transfer among MSMEs.[4]

With an increasing number of business development service providers and a more challenging macroeconomic environment spurred by the global economic crisis of 2008, competition for funds and resources between these social actors has intensified. More recently, BDS providers have become interested in partnering with large firms. However, Dalberg, a global development adviser found that, in most of the cases, this interest has not become a reality yet, owing to 'the lack of familiarity between the sectors' and 'the challenges faced by NGOs in figuring out how to partner with businesses without compromising the integrity of their mission'.[5] Also, according to this study, the most common reason for business firms to partner with social actors is to receive support in implementing effective corporate social responsibility programmes. 'Advancing core business objectives' with the help of BDS providers played only a minor role for a long time. This motivation for cooperation is slowly gaining in importance, though. A new generation of business development services supports the inclusion of MSMEs in the value chains of large firms, addressing these firms' core business activities and at the same time better connecting MSMEs to national and international markets.

FUNDES is one of the few non-profits that took the opportunities related to the value chains of multinationals seriously. This required a strategic repositioning, together with profound changes in the monetization mechanics, and front end and back end of its business model. Despite challenges, FUNDES successfully transformed its business model from a non-profit organization that provided traditional, standardized MSME services into a mission-focused but also customer-driven, profit-oriented consulting firm that provides individual services to large multinational firms.

The transformation

In 1984, Swiss businessman and philanthropist Stephan Schmidheiny, together with the then Archbishop of Panama, created the non-profit organization Fundación para un Desarrollo Sostenible (Foundation for Sustainable Development, or FUNDES) as a response to the region's high poverty rates. FUNDES considered small businesses to be key to Latin America's development. Rather than focusing on individual actors, FUNDES approached MSMEs as a business sector and strived to resolve systemic problems rather than particular businesses' concerns.

Based on this philosophy, FUNDES developed and offered an increasing range of business development services over the following decades. This went along with frequent adjustments to its business model, always with the intent to adapt to a changing external environment and to ensure continued impact in resolving the most pressing obstacles to a more sustainable development of MSMEs in Latin America.

During FUNDES's first decade of operations, access to capital was its driving theme. At that time, the non-profit assumed that a lack of financial support was the main limiting factor for MSMEs' growth and success, particularly during their early stages of development. It therefore helped create a micro-financial sector by offering guarantees to creditors and also often provided micro loans directly to MSMEs.

By the mid-1990s, FUNDES had helped create a thriving micro-credit industry in many countries of the region. At the same time, the non-profit became aware of the fact that access to knowledge was at least equally important for MSMEs and that in fact, if there was a ranking regarding the importance of capital or knowledge, the latter should come first. In this vein, FUNDES began to undertake research on the most needed skills and based on this started to use standardized classroom-style lectures to educate entrepreneurs and employees of MSMEs on important aspects of running a business.

By 2004, FUNDES was undergoing another change, a gradual shift from a teaching institution towards a consulting service provider – put differently, it was adopting a more integral approach to training by installing best practices. With the generous support of philanthropic organizations such as the Avina Foundation and international development agencies such as the Inter-American Development Bank (IDB) and the Multilateral Investment Fund (MIF), FUNDES's new value proposition to the MSME sector was the delivery of high-quality but still standardized retail consulting. Since the majority of MSMEs were unable to afford the full price for such services, subsidies were still key.

By that time, FUNDES already had offices in 10 countries, and, although its overall service portfolio had changed over time, each of the country offices had developed its own focus in terms of services, some countries being stronger in training and others stronger in consulting, but all with an autonomous legal status. This product-like business model was however challenged a few years later.

In 2008, two new realities started to influence FUNDES. First, an increasingly severe financial and economic crisis in the United States of America was beginning to represent an international challenge and was quickly moving south. As a consequence, many industry sectors in Latin America began to suffer the consequences of rapidly falling demand – both locally and internationally. The uncertainties in turn significantly influenced the industry's investment decisions, and

FUNDES's donors and beneficiaries (MSMEs) began to reduce their investments in goods and services that were not considered absolute necessities – such as consulting services. Second, FUNDES's governing body decided to diversify its investment portfolio and informed FUNDES and some of its beneficiaries to start looking for alternative funding sources. It was deemed that a five-year transition period would be adequate for FUNDES to identify and activate such sources.

Confronted with these realities, FUNDES found itself with its back against the wall – it would need to reinvent itself once again, this time however with a dual purpose. First, it aimed to further increase its positive impact on MSMEs in the region: rather than reaching out to 3,000 to 5,000 MSMEs per year, the objective was now to support over 30,000 annually. Second, FUNDES needed to identify a business model that would allow it to fulfil this mission in a financially self-sustainable way. The solution consisted in transforming the organization's business model to the east (in the two-by-two matrix in Figure 8.4), from a product business focused on MSMEs and donors to a project business focused on large multinational firms and MSMEs.

Figure 8.4 Transformation from a product-based to a project-based business model (with the FUNDES logo also changing accordingly)

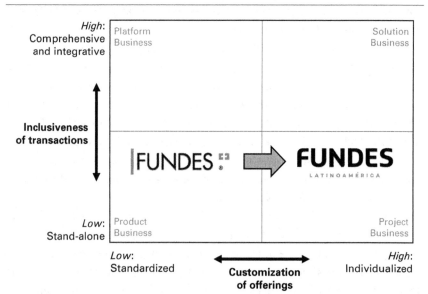

Monetization mechanics adaptation

Before the business model transformation, FUNDES received donations from the Avina Foundation and other donors. It did not generate any revenues, and thus pricing and margins were not an issue. When Avina announced a gradual reduction of its donation for the following years on an annual basis, FUNDES had to suddenly manage and reduce its costs at the same pace.

The first fundamental challenge was to find partners and customers that had the necessary resources to finance FUNDES's services. The weakness of its previous business model was its strong dependency on donors. Looking ahead, the FUNDES leadership saw a big opportunity to become more market- and customer-driven, by turning large firms with international value chains into buyers of FUNDES services. These 'anchor firms' would be interested in making such investments if FUNDES was capable of creating additional value for their businesses.

The FUNDES leadership thus developed a new business model based on the assumption that its organization would be able to create sufficient value for anchor firms. The FUNDES leadership saw opportunities in developing both large firms' upstream (supply) and downstream (distribution) value chains. Early in defining the new model, it became apparent that government agencies and international development organizations would also buy into this new approach by supporting it with additional funds, when needed.

The move towards individual services brought with it very fundamental changes. The original logic that a largely fixed amount of donations is available, which can be spent, had to change towards a thorough business plan. The focus on the specific needs of large multinationals meant that FUNDES had to base its calculation on the direct costs related to the human resources and materials required for providing these specific services. At the same time, FUNDES had to professionalize its pricing policy and adapt it to the standards in each market. Besides the reliance on variable cost, prices were also a function of the incremental value that FUNDES managed to create for its anchor firms in terms of risk reduction, cost savings, efficiency improvements and so on.

Front-end adaptation

As is common in critical business situations, it helped FUNDES to take a step back and evaluate the facts and challenges within a broader context. Realizing that MSMEs were not islands in the business world and that they depended, to an over-proportional degree, on the ecosystem surrounding them, FUNDES began to analyse the MSME world in a more holistic way, including all of the various players that influenced its chances of succeeding. What had been a weak point in FUNDES's previous front-end model – namely, the diversity of its offer from country to country – now became a decisive source of ideas for defining the new model.

In fact, the idea to support the inclusion of MSMEs into the value chains of large multinational firms was not completely new to FUNDES. Some of its country offices had already experimented with elements of this new type of service. This provided an opportunity to study these services in light of the new challenge to become financially self-sustaining. For example, in Bolivia, FUNDES had gained experiences with grouping together larger numbers of individual micro and small businesses with similar business characteristics into clusters and providing them with access to their three most urgent needs: capital, knowledge and markets. Market access was achieved by connecting the clusters either locally or abroad to large firms, ie their main buyers or suppliers.

After deciding on the new strategic direction, the FUNDES leadership considered early successes with the new 'FUNDES way' as very important in order to generate a list of convincing sales arguments for large firms as potential customers of the new model. A Brazilian steel producer with thousands of scrap metal collectors in its supply system became one of the early customers when it commissioned training and support in organizing its scrap metal suppliers. Whilst the customer (steel producer) benefited from the initiative because it ensured a constant and well-organized raw material supply, the beneficiaries (scrap metal collectors) were able to generate constantly growing volumes of business with a reliable partner and to increase their personal income. The most successful beneficiary in this project today manages a firm with dozens of primary scrap metal collectors under contract and pulls in annual revenues of approximately $400,000 – one of FUNDES's showcase projects to date.

Since then, similar project structures and content have been used in a variety of other countries and value chains, for example within the downstream value chain of a cement producer (customer) and hardware stores (beneficiaries), the upstream supply chain of a supermarket and a hotel group (customers) with its vegetable and fruit suppliers (beneficiaries), or the downstream distribution chain of a dairy product producer (customer) with hundreds of 'mom-and-pop' shops (beneficiaries). All of these initiatives constitute a response to the strategic challenge of FUNDES's customers to have well-functioning international value chains, while also allowing FUNDES to fulfil its social mission by strengthening MSMEs in their value chain.

The FUNDES leadership soon expanded the projects that were successful from the start related to the new 'FUNDES way' to a nationwide level, while a few painful failures helped to constantly improve the model. By 2012, year three of the implementation of the new business model, the number of customers and beneficiaries was still small. Regional expansion of at least one of the locally successful projects was urgent if FUNDES hoped to come close to the expected number of beneficiaries of 30,000 by 2014, year five of the implementation.

In January 2011, Michael Porter and Mark Kramer published their ground-breaking concept of 'the creation of shared value' (CSV) in the *Harvard Business Review*.[6] Their underlying statement was that any firm that aimed to be in business in the long run must not only create economic value for itself and for its stakeholders; it must simultaneously create value for the society in which it operates – not only to fulfil its social and environmental obligations but, more importantly, to gain a competitive edge. For FUNDES, this message fitted like a glove, and both authors of the CSV article began to support the organization in its endeavour in getting the message out to potential customers, mainly in the private sector. Large-scale marketing events were organized with the intent to raise awareness. In its sales efforts, the language of CSV also helped FUNDES to establish a close dialogue with its customers, focusing on the benefits of a long-term integration of MSMEs into the customer's value chain. This was new to the firm, as it had previously addressed MSMEs as a sector. Employees in FUNDES marketing and sales thus not only had to suddenly speak to different types of organizations; they also had to change from pushing their standardized offering into the market towards listening to the needs of large firms, in order to offer them a customer-oriented value proposition to their specific challenges in integrating the various actors along their value chains.

In 2013, FUNDES celebrated its first large-scale success. A leading international firm in the beverage industry commissioned the organization to strengthen its traditional channel of 'mom-and-pop' shops as a strategic countermeasure to the fast globalization and concentration process in the food retail business. Starting in one country and then gradually expanding to a regional scale, the initiative eventually reached over 40,000 small shops, and then proposed a further expansion to some 250,000 retail outlets in Latin America.

By 2014, further customers, for instance in the fast-moving consumer goods industry and in the credit card business, started to take their initiatives with FUNDES to a regional scale. With these success stories in its portfolio, FUNDES had the strong arguments it needed to successfully prospect for new clients and strengthen commercial activities. The groundwork was laid to carry the new model to a larger scale and create a back-end adaptation that would allow for a fast-track expansion strategy.

Back-end adaptation

Because FUNDES had operated as a non-profit service organization for 25 years, its biggest challenges under the new business model were related to prospecting and commercial activities. The most important common denominator with respect to FUNDES's staff had always been a strong focus on social and environmental skills. Commercial processes were never part of the job descriptions, either for the organization's management team or for its trainers and consultants. Now, the consulting teams needed to focus the content of their services on the particular customers' needs and adapt their services accordingly.

Every FUNDES executive will attest that the biggest challenges in the process of shifting the philanthropic non-profit towards an economically sustainable organization had to do with people. Of the organization's more than 200 original staff members, approximately 150 had to be let go in order to make room for 60 new employees who had the adequate profile to support FUNDES's new approach. In other words, 150 dedicated workers had to come to terms with the fact that they lacked the necessary skill set for the new 'FUNDES way' of supporting the MSMEs that they had served over the previous 25 years. The fact that they were excellent and committed professionals within their field of expertise did not make this step any easier. Incidentally, because of the personal consequences involved in this part of the change process, the most common complaint by industry experts was the time it took to transition the team.

Historically, FUNDES designed the country offices to implement initiatives that were typically financed by donations. The organizational and legal structures allowed the efficient and effective implementation of the philanthropic business model, in which the implementing country offices were treated as independent and autonomous legal structures (foundations). The central office, or headquarters, had the responsibility to financially support the country offices. Transferring resources from one country office to another was virtually impossible. Such structures became thus most incompatible with the needs of an internationally active, highly flexible and economically self-supporting organization, where the head office would predominantly act as a cost centre and would need to be financed through the repatriation of funds from its subsidiaries.

Consequently, in order to equip the new business model with an adequate legal framework, the individual country offices were gradually dismantled and replaced with a limited company (Ltd) structure. Service level contracts, signed between subsidiaries and the head office, allowed for the financing of head office activities. Changing the legal structure of the organization by no means implied a change to its mission. FUNDES had no intention of altering its original mission, and by improving its business model it actually aimed to reach a greater number of beneficiaries. See Figure 8.5 for a summary of this transformation.

Figure 8.5 Transformation of FUNDES's business model (dark grey: old model; light grey: new model)

Domain	Value drivers	West	East
Front end	Specification	Limited	Broad and flexible
	USP	Features	Adaptability
	Sales channel	Broad access	Focused dialogue
Back end	Production	Scalability	Flexibility
	Development	Standardized	Customer-driven
Monetization mechanics	Pricing	Competitive target	Willingness to pay
	Margin	Fixed-cost-driven	Variable-cost-driven

Lessons learned

Twenty-five years of experience working with MSMEs in Latin America was a solid basis for the identification and implementation of a business model that would allow FUNDES to focus even more strongly on its mission, while also having the potential to reach financial self-sufficiency within five years. A team of highly motivated professionals with substantial private sector experience were able to understand both the needs of the small business owners and the expectations of the stakeholders in the private sector. It was clear from the outset that whatever solution FUNDES would offer to its clients – the large firms – it would have to generate value (including economic value) for the paying customer. This was acceptable for the FUNDES board of directors as long as the creation of measurable and sustainable value for the beneficiaries (MSMEs) remained an integral part of the solution.

For FUNDES's leadership team, the steps in the process of such a substantial change in strategy were clear. In order to ensure strong alignment between the country organizations, every new process would need to be defined and documented in detail. This would allow for a simultaneous roll-out of the new 'FUNDES way' of doing business in the different countries. In this vein, manuals were written for each process, and teaching guidelines were established for the in-house trainers. A specialist was contracted from a leading global consulting firm to document all processes. Since regional scaling of the projects was one of the organization's early objectives, standardization was needed to ensure that the FUNDES solutions would be referred to as 'products' in the consulting world rather than individualized social services.

Under the guiding thought that 'structure follows strategy', the leadership team saw that FUNDES's previous structure of independent foundations in each of its countries would hinder the implementation of its new model. An offshore company was created as a ruling holding structure, and subsidiaries (Ltds) were established in each market. Timeliness was key to the smooth alignment of activities in all markets, as well as the resulting need to generate revenue and margins. FUNDES also needed to reduce costs, particularly at the head office level. The termination of some 150 staff member contracts was the most challenging element. Knowing that the organization needed people with a different skill set, FUNDES should have moved much faster in restructuring its team. Instead, employees were given a 'second chance' to adapt to the new way of doing business, even when it was apparent that terminations of contracts, in many cases, were the only viable solution. This created confusion on the human side.

When offering a 'nice to have' solution during economic (and often political) turbulence, there is an absolute need for watertight arguments of value generation. Social and environmental issues tend to be pushed to the back, while economics rule. FUNDES should have focused from the start on developing and communicating hard arguments as to why investments in MSMEs would be good for large firms' business, rather than confusing its early clients with a focus on socio-ecological value creation. The early customers did not understand why the non-economic values created by FUNDES would also improve their return on investment.

FUNDES's old model was built around strong-minded country managers who had distinct interpretations of the organization's mission. When making significant changes to implement any business model with regionally aligned processes, a strict and centralized operational structure facilitates implementation tremendously. It took FUNDES too much time to remove local particularities and interpretations, and FUNDES should have insisted from the outset on a single set of cohesive processes. In other words, the organization was too soft regarding the hard issues.

A focus on country organizations in a globalized business environment obstructs implementation significantly. Regional business units that included all countries, equipped with sufficient authority and responsibility for all of Latin America, should have been created earlier on, and country managers and their teams should have focused more on the implementation of the regional projects being sold by the regional business units.

Outlook

FUNDES focused in its transformation mainly 'eastwards', from a standardized offering to MSMEs towards an individualized service for multinationals. In the initial four years of its transformation (with more than 15,000 beneficiaries annually, more than 80 satisfied customers and a total revenue of $10 million to $15 million each year), FUNDES has only scratched the surface of the actual market potential size. The aggressive 2020 target to become one of Latin America's largest, highest-quality consulting firms, improving the performance of some 30,000 MSMEs annually and generating annual revenues of $30 million is ambitious, but achievable.

As the market potential of the niche that FUNDES has identified and begun to penetrate with its new model is vast, further investments are needed to strengthen the project business model. The new FUNDES model includes high upfront investments in customer-specific capabilities, and the capabilities to manage highly complex, customer-driven projects and volatile revenues, as it depends on the projects sold to customers. In particular further back-end adaptations are needed. FUNDES intends to implement strategic business units with regional responsibilities and authority, as well as to strengthen the business skills of its leadership team. Limited resources obviously slow down the change process, but also allow for constant adaptation and fine-tuning of activities before scaling takes place.

The MSME sector has always been and will always be the driving force of any national or regional economy in Latin America. By strengthening the performance of over 60,000 micro-, small- and medium-sized companies in the coming three years, FUNDES will continue to contribute to the socio-economic development of the region and make a decisive contribution towards a faster recovery from the current economic crisis.

Endnotes

1 U P Jäger and V Sathe (eds) (2014) *Strategy and Competitiveness in Latin American Markets: The sustainability frontier*, Edward Elgar, Cheltenham.

2 I Ortiz and M Cummins (2011) *Global Inequality: Beyond the bottom billion*, UNICEF, New York.

3 L Henríquez (2010) MIPYMES de América Latina: Tendencias y desafíos, Internal presentation, FUNDES International.

4 E Edgcomb and W Girardo (2012) *The State of Business Development Services*, Aspen Institute, Washington, DC.

5 Dalberg (2007) Business guide to partnering with NGOs and the United Nations, http://www.greenbiz.com/sites/default/files/document/CustomO16C45F85703.pdf.

6 M E Porter and M R Kramer (2011) Creating shared value, *Harvard Business Review*, January–February, pp 63–70.

Case studies of companies that sequence multiple radical shifts

09

Knorr-Bremse Rail Vehicle Systems: From brake control unit manufacturer to comprehensive rail systems provider
Bertram Langhanki, Rolf Haerdi and Carsten Linz

At the start of the 19th century, in the early days of vehicles operating on steel rails, train braking was carried out on a distributed basis, with so-called brakemen in each wagon using mechanical levers to apply the brake pads to the wheels. A combination of harsh conditions in the brakeman's cab and brakemen falling asleep because of the unchallenging nature of their work resulted in several severe crashes.

The revolutionary step taken by Knorr-Bremse in the 1920s was to replace this purely mechanical system – which was dependent for its operation on several individuals on each train – with a pneumatically operated system for the entire train, controlled by the train driver alone. The resulting improvement in safety and reliability meant that Knorr-Bremse brake systems quickly became standard equipment in many countries. They have remained unrivalled ever since and have exerted a significant influence on the formulation of European railway regulations.

Starting with brake control (ie pneumatic valves), the brake product portfolio was steadily extended to embrace air supply systems (ie compressors and related products) and brake mechanics (ie brake callipers and related products) as well as sophisticated electronic controls for wheel slide protection (ie an anti-skid system for trains), condition monitoring systems and many more.

Having set standards in the rail industry with its pneumatic braking technology, Knorr-Bremse expanded steadily, exploiting existing domains and also penetrating new markets outside Europe. Today, the Knorr-Bremse Rail Vehicle Systems portfolio includes doors, air-conditioning systems, high-voltage power switches, power resistors, auxiliary power converters, signalling and passenger information systems, train control management systems, energy metering and driver assistance devices, to name the most prominent.

Knorr-Bremse at a glance

The Knorr-Bremse Group is the world's leading supplier of braking systems for commercial and rail vehicles. Originally founded in Berlin by Georg Knorr in 1905, the company now has its headquarters in Munich and operates more than 100 sites in all continents of the world.

In 2015, the Knorr-Bremse Group's sales revenues exceeded €5.83 billion (2010: €3.7 billion), with an 11.1 per cent net return on sales. These revenues were generated by a workforce of approximately 25,000, with 43 per cent attributable to the truck and 57 per cent to the rail division. With continued long-term investment in modern facilities and engineering/production capabilities, and R&D expenditure of close to €347 million, the foundation has been laid for continued, innovation-driven growth.

While the product portfolio is being continuously enlarged, the traditional brake business remains the main revenue generator. Braking systems are, by definition, safety-critical products, and the utmost care has to be taken with engineering and production processes to avoid and/or detect errors and deliver on the company's zero-failure commitment. This approach can be found throughout the Knorr-Bremse Group and applies to all the company's product families.

Knorr-Bremse's year-on-year increase in sales revenues has been achieved by striving for excellence in four ways. The first is the development of an innovative and constantly expanding portfolio of products and services designed and engineered by the company itself and capable of being tailored to customer requirements. The second is a strong project and process orientation, anchored in two quality-driven business process concepts: Truck Excellence (TEX) and Rail Excellence (REX). The third is manufacture of products with a carefully defined degree of vertical integration, with a global network of production sites individually dedicated to machining, sub-assembly and final assembly. This allows the company to control most of the value chain and offer entire systems to customers. The fourth is a strong service orientation that underpins all the company's other activities. This service orientation provides reassurance to Knorr-Bremse's customers that they will be supported with parts and off- and on-site servicing throughout the vehicle's life cycle.

In what follows, the company's evolution from a product-focused company to a service-focused, solution-oriented market leader is illustrated by describing the sequential transformation of its business model. This will be separated into two phases. The first phase is the change from product to system supplier, resulting in improved 'stickiness' (customer retention). The second phase involves the transformation towards individual, customer-focused business with enhanced life cycle services.

Step-by-step business model transformation

The transformation of Knorr-Bremse happened in two phases. The first one was from a single product to a multi-system supplier; the second one was from a multi-system supplier to a full life cycle solution provider.

Phase one: From single product to multi-system supplier

During the first growth period up to the 1970s, the dominating value proposition was based on superior products that were engineered and produced in-house. Even though Knorr-Bremse managed to remain a tier-one supplier throughout this period, profitability was under threat from 1980 onwards. By this time, commoditization of the products in the market had grown, entrants from other industrial areas were tackling selected product families, and the premium levels of mechanical machining by Knorr-Bremse were being achieved by other contract manufacturers as well.

With the transfer of Knorr-Bremse ownership to Heinz Hermann Thiele in 1985, the first phase of business model transformation was initiated, with an approach proactively responding to these changing market conditions.

Front-end transformation: From product-centric to comprehensive multi-system value proposition

On the one hand, it had become evident that relying on superior products merely increased the risk of competitors also concentrating on individual products, attaining similar performance levels and stealing market share from Knorr-Bremse. On the other hand, rail vehicles were rapidly becoming increasingly complex. Knorr-Bremse responded actively to this trend by shifting its offering from a product to a system level. This development underlined the distinction between system suppliers like Knorr-Bremse and system integrators, ie the train builders.

As a consequence a value proposition based on premium products was enhanced by the capacity to develop and sell complete braking systems, from air supply and brake control right down to actual application of the braking force. Knorr-Bremse's advantage was that it already had all the products in-house that were required to design and supply a complete system from a single source. However, the company's primary achievement was to establish a standardized portfolio of products that could be combined to produce a braking system that was tailored to customers' specifications. This paradigm change was to shift complexity from product level to system level, developing the ability to provide systems for all kinds of rail vehicles ranging from freight cars, metros, trams and commuter trains to high-speed trains. The concept follows the idea of a core braking system representing the overarching architecture, enriched by modules represented by product groups with standardized interfaces and categorized functionalities.

This strategy succeeded and has enabled the company, for example, to gain a market share of more than 80 per cent in the Chinese metro sector since the start of the millennium – and more than 50 per cent of brake applications worldwide.

As an important side-effect, Knorr-Bremse's relationship with customers also changed. A strong relationship developed over years of cooperation was intensified even further by the greater complexity of the systems approach, which called for close collaboration between experts on both sides. The result was a high level of customer retention.

Following the success of this shift from products to systems, and with a view to growing the rail business further, the strategic decision was taken to diversify and move towards other systems related to rail vehicles. Through acquisitions Knorr-Bremse's portfolio was extended to include door systems, HVAC (heating, ventilation and air-conditioning) systems and many more, and still continues to expand. In the process, Knorr-Bremse managed to become one of the strongest partners for vehicle builders all over the world, supplying multiple safety-critical and comfort-relevant systems from a single source. In the meantime Knorr-Bremse's customer base, ie the train builders, had undergone dramatic change. Whereas during the first period of growth the market had been dominated by the 'big three' – Siemens, Bombardier and Alstom – many more had now appeared on the scene. These served particular regional sectors, especially in Asia (eg CNR, CSR, Rotem), and/or benefited from the expansion of railway networks driven by economic growth, population expansion and growing demand for rail vehicles, which allowed former niche players to flourish (eg Stadler, PESA).

Being able to put together systems to meet customers' requirements from a wide range of high-quality products enabled the company to supply systems for most types of rail vehicle in all countries via more than 20 different vehicle builders. This capability can be seen as one factor that has steadily driven the growth of Knorr-Bremse Rail Vehicle Systems' sales revenues from €86 million in 1985 to more than €3.3 billion in 2015.

Back-end transformation: From scalable mass production to systems engineering and flexible production

As the front-end focus changed to selling systems rather than products, an inter-face/integration unit became necessary in order to bundle products into systems. This department is referred to as 'systems engineering'. Its task is to analyse the specifications defined by the train builder for a given rail vehicle project, and choose from a standardized product portfolio in the engineering and production departments. The standardized product portfolio in turn was created by introducing a centre of competence (CoC) structure, with product responsibility clearly separated into air supply, brake control and bogie equipment. However, this change in organizational structure could have been carried out by any other company as well, since it was a logical consequence of the newly defined offering to the customer. Of much greater significance was the introduction of more intangible methods or tools, ie the Knorr Production System (KPS) and the REX process management system.

The REX system covers the entire process from product development to sales and after-sales service, dividing areas of activity into main and support processes, such as HR, FiCo and others. This management system is applied at all locations, starting with common international processes (CIP) for top-level process control, but also allowing local operating processes (LOP) in cases where adaptation to local requirements appears to be necessary. Introduction of this process management system was prioritized by top management and provided a basis for facilitating audits of all kinds, such as ISO, IRIS and many more.

The KPS was derived from the well-known Toyota Production System. Tools like poka yoke, Andon, worker guidance by PLC and one-piece flow were adapted to the characteristics of the Knorr-Bremse production process. In particular the adaptation of a system that had been optimized for high-volume production at Toyota to small-volume, project-oriented batch sizes provoked some mistrust, especially in an environment that had largely based its success on the long-term experience of production specialists. However, a smart combination of specialist experience with methods ensuring stability of production processes and hence consistent product quality appeared to be successful and has now been trans-ferred to production-related areas all over the world.

The introduction of both REX and KPS was actively managed as part of a top-level initiative under the supervision of a sponsor from the executive board. The change in both areas was realized by dedicated headquarter teams, who defined and rolled out standards and acted as consultants through workshops and regular site audits. Transparency is ensured by the use of appropriate, openly communi-cated key performance indicators specifically established for REX and KPS and applied worldwide.

Transformation of monetization mechanics: From itemized to system bundle

The change from a product to a systems offering, as described above, goes hand in hand with active adjustment of its monetization. With product-based sales it is natural to base the offer, delivery and payment on batches of products. The shift to a systems approach was accompanied by a bundling of project-related non-recurring and recurring costs on a complete systems basis, making a full price breakdown of the offer unnecessary.

However, this model, which concentrates pricing activities at department level, required close contact with the customer in order to derive the value of the sys-tems offering sought by the customer. In consequence, all departments contrib-uting to the system concerned have to fully focus on the cost aspect in order to allow the final offer to be profitable.

The rail industry is currently poised to evolve towards highly sophisticated concepts for ownership and servicing of rolling stock assets. These will involve physical assets being valued on the basis of their performance, and paid for over extended periods of time, rather than the current one-off payment system. As a result, the integration of sub-systems into a single solution will become essential for future market players and will require the development of complex systems for analysis and pricing of the offering.

Phase two: From multi-system supplier to full life cycle solution provider

For several decades up to the 1990s, growth was primarily driven by extending the systems and functionalities supplied by Knorr-Bremse. During this period, owners and operators of rail vehicles were predominantly state-controlled organizations that showed a tendency to concentrate on maximizing the number of vehicles that could be covered by the budget for a new vehicle project, with maintenance aspects regarded as secondary issues to be handled later by existing internal departments.

After the end of the last century, however, terms such as 'life cycle cost' (LCC) or 'reliability-centred maintenance' (RCM) became popular in the rail vehicle business – some 10–15 years behind other industries such as printing machines or elevators. At the same time a process of rail privatization began, with the UK going furthest in this respect and other countries following to a greater or lesser extent. The focus shifted from simply owning a rail vehicle to maximizing utilization of capital assets.

As a result, Knorr-Bremse's strategy was extended to include after-sales support services geared towards new critical success factors such as lead time, delivery performance, after-sales pricing models, long-term parts and service supply contracts, and expert teams to support the systems in use. Not only was this after-sales support called for by customers concerned to increase vehicle up-time rates, but it also became a crucial issue during negotiations for new vehicle systems in terms of total cost of ownership (TCO). This approach requires an in-depth understanding of the customer's specific business processes. Knorr-Bremse realized the need to change, and introduced RailServices as an independent business unit in 2003.

Front-end transformation: From braking system offerings to integrated vehicle solutions tailored to railway operators' needs

With the newly founded RailServices unit, Knorr-Bremse changed gear towards a broad, flexible and integrated service-centric offering by adding other service components such as analysis services, consultancy services, guarantees of systems reliability and responsiveness. By understanding maintenance processes in every detail, RailServices was able to provide in-house maintenance activities that had formerly been run by the railway companies themselves – or to perform them at the customers' premises ('shop-in-shop'). In order to accompany the vehicle operator during the vehicle's entire lifetime of up to 40 years, service contracts that could include experts on-site, continuous parts supply combined with inventory supervision, and fixed overhaul and upgrade schemes were drawn up and realized. What makes the Knorr-Bremse concept different is the fact that in-house rail experts can carry out an analysis of a given situation at the customer's site, and then develop the solution, incorporating feedback loops into product development and maintenance processes as well. A multinational service agreement, in addition to covering the life of a customer's fleet, can also apply to a regionally distributed fleet, which means that all vehicles receive full service coverage either for troubleshooting or for scheduled preventive maintenance wherever they are in the countries covered by the contract.

With increasing numbers of complete braking systems being installed in new vehicles, the demand for overhaul activities changed from single products to system service and maintenance. Knorr-Bremse's service contracts for systems allow both parties to optimize delivery performance and lead time based on preplanning carried out jointly by Knorr-Bremse and the customer. Preplanning of materials and utilization of experienced staff and testing equipment capacity is possible, as rail vehicles have to follow a relatively strict maintenance scheme. Both preplanning and the performance of Knorr-Bremse service centres enable customers to optimize their full vehicle maintenance and minimize vehicle downtimes. From 2010 onwards, initial indications suggested that the basic capacity created would be fully exploited in the near future, and so Knorr-Bremse started to explore the scope for further growth with an extension of its service offering. One important aspect for creating any new offerings was the integration of all Knorr-Bremse systems service activities into a single consolidated RailServices offering, which in the past had been strongly influenced by the inherent dominance of brakes. Thus strategy workshops included representatives from *all* Knorr-Bremse rail systems, ie brakes, doors, HVAC systems and more.

One workshop result was the emergence of a Knorr-Bremse total solution offering covering a system's entire life cycle. Special attention was paid to the final decade of the life cycle – with mid-life upgrades or vehicle modernization – as rail vehicle owners increasingly wanted to maximize the utilization of their capital expenditure. This enabled Knorr's customers to extend the life of their vehicles from 25–30 years to 40–45 years on average. To cover the needs of mature rail vehicles, an engineering department was established within RailServices that was fully dedicated to the modernization of mature systems. This department is capable of analysing a given vehicle's systems and coming up with solutions to improve time to life end, comfort and safety, including environmental aspects such as upgrades from lubricated to oil-free compressors. A second offering originating from the workshop was condition-based maintenance (CBM), which aims to exploit the market shift from purely time-based maintenance to maintenance on demand. This essentially identifies upcoming corrective requirements in order to avoid unpredicted downtimes for rail vehicles and move towards predictive maintenance. A dedicated team has developed a system called iCOM, which allows the customer to monitor the condition of all interconnected systems. This monitoring system can easily be introduced during modernization of a rail vehicle and can be combined with service contracts covering supply of parts, predefined repair and overhaul cycles and even expert staff for service activities on the train. The third extension of its offering – moving into the maintenance of entire rail vehicles – appeared to be a brave but logical step. It was only possible because of Knorr-Bremse's historically acquired expertise in delivering a large number of vehicle sub-systems, and its in-house expertise in design, production and services. Two companies were acquired in 2014 in highly liberalized markets – the UK and Sweden. All the offerings described above can be included in a vehicle maintenance or modernization contract.

Prior to the launch of the RailServices business unit in 2003, opportunities for servicing had to be identified and responded to by teams within original equipment

(OE) sales units. After establishing a RailServices headquarters team for sales and marketing, with a director reporting to the executive board, OE-independent RailServices sales teams were set up at each company site to serve all customers in the local market. It proved important to maintain a local presence, not only so as to be able to communicate in the customer's language, but also in order to understand developments in specific markets.

Back-end transformation: From a national, OE-related team to a worldwide RailServices organization

Parallel to the change towards local, independent RailServices sales teams at the front end, the service activities themselves were separated from OE production, and local service centres were set up in the back end. Given the amount of investment involved in setting up a service activity, it is essential to achieve a balance between the desired density of the service centre network in order to reduce transportation costs and times, and a cost structure that allows for competitive pricing. For those service centres carrying out the repair and overhaul of Knorr-Bremse products and systems, SAP-based service centre software has been created to cover all requirements such as material and capacity pre-planning, as well as order management from goods intake to goods delivery and invoicing.

The strategic expansion in 2013 was initiated and supported by a new executive board member dedicated mainly to RailServices, thus giving an even stronger management focus to the new initiative. In response to the growth of service activities, a new headquarters structure was introduced, consisting of a small RailServices governance team with leaders and teams dedicated to sales and marketing, engineering, supply chain and service operations. These functional teams promote cross-fertilization between product areas so as to achieve a unified service offering regardless of the particular product mix concerned.

By setting up its own engineering team with global coverage and acquiring two vehicle maintenance companies with a significant number of staff, RailServices not only increased its contribution to divisional turnover, but also strengthened its position within the organizational structure of the Knorr-Bremse Group.

Transformation of monetization mechanics: From ad hoc orders to multi-year framework contracts

With the move from single parts supply and single product repairs to delivery of original parts kits (OPK), parts supply and system service agreements, the nature of the contracts involved changed as well. Framework contracts covering several years, with price lists and a price escalation formula, became standard in addition to the unpredictable ad hoc business.

However, especially with the entry into CBM offerings, a complete rethink of monetization mechanics became necessary. Since the scope of supply could range from delivering diagnostic infrastructure to all-inclusive availability agreements, payment could either be related to hardware as in the past or be based on fulfilment of KPI-based service level agreements (SLA). The KPI most commonly used today are limited to reaction time, field technician availability, lead time for repair and overhaul, and failure rates within defined periods. Despite the current setting, the pace of the shift move towards more complex SLA contracts is constantly accelerating, and Knorr-Bremse is preparing for a move to payment by availability.

Impact of business model transformations and outlook

Starting with a pioneering invention by Georg Knorr a century ago, Knorr-Bremse has developed its current market and technological leadership by undergoing two evolutionary changes, one after the other. The first involved moving from being a product to a systems supplier and global technological leader. The second involved creating a total lifetime service support solution covering the entire range, from single product service to complete vehicle service. The combination of both changes has resulted in the company now offering full support for its products, systems and solutions from initial production to end of life (see Figure 9.1).

Figure 9.1 Two-step business model transformation of Knorr-Bremse – from brake products to systems to rail solutions

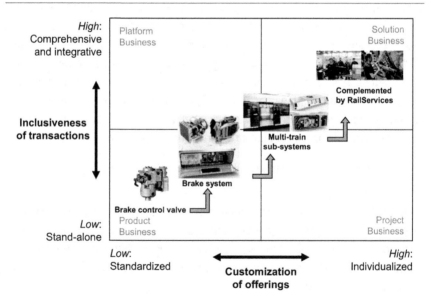

Both changes show an astonishing similarity in as much as in each case they involved a two-directional business model transformation. On the one hand there has been a northward transformation as the offering has developed from simple to complex, the back end from single location to network, and the revenue from an itemized to an integrated approach. On the other hand an eastward transformation has taken place, with the originally limited offering becoming highly flexible and based on demand-driven production capabilities and a clear orientation towards maximizing value for the money a customer is willing to pay.

Foundation of the RailServices unit in 2003 had a significant impact on the Knorr-Bremse Group's business. By 2007, RailServices accounted for 29 per cent of the €1,034 million sales revenues of the Rail Vehicle Systems division. From being an OE-oriented rail division for decades, nearly a third of the total revenue was now contributed by services. The performance of RailServices was also acknowledged by OE customers, and contributed to the further success of the OE business. Establishment of a stronger basis, combined with an increase in RailServices' offering, provided scope for further growth and resulted in more than doubled revenues by RailServices in 2014.

As well as payment mechanisms, the number and character of the players in the transportation business are changing. In the past, state operators managed all aspects of transportation, ranging across buying and owning train fleets (ie the assets), organizing all operations including drivers and other on-train personnel, owning and managing all spares, and last but not least operating their own facilities and personnel for carrying out all service activities from cleaning to heavy maintenance. Under the heading of 'privatization', new contracts for transportation are now put out to public tender, and there is a tendency to concentrate on core competencies. In more recent contracts the operators act as project managers. Whereas financial institutes own and lease the assets (ie trains) to the operator, the latter makes use of leased staff for running the trains and outsources maintenance of the assets to another party with its own or rented facilities and staff. Within this constellation, Knorr-Bremse is well prepared not only to take over system maintenance with SLAs but also to offer train maintenance.

With its global footprint, technological leadership and the solutions it already offers for the rail industry, Knorr-Bremse is clearly well positioned for continued success over the coming decades. In the light of recent acquisitions in the field of auxiliary power converters and train control management systems (TCMS) and the introduction of condition monitoring systems, there is a distinct trend towards upwards integration of the functions in a rail vehicle, and this will result in even more comprehensive and complex solutions for up-to-date rail transportation concepts.

Atlas Copco: From selling compressors to providing services
Ivanka Visnjic and Ronnie Leten

The Atlas Copco Group is a world leader when it comes to providing industrial productivity solutions. For over a century, the group has maintained its leadership position by designing and offering industrial tools and construction and mining equipment with a very high level of efficiency.

The origins of the Atlas Copco Group date back to 1873, when it started to manufacture and sell railway equipment. In the years that followed, it became the largest manufacturing company in Sweden. In the 1950s, Atlas Copco Group started to focus on compressed air and embarked on a journey toward global leadership in this area. The 1970s were a period of structural changes and rationalizations. A number of strategic company acquisitions paved the way for a broader product range and larger markets. In the 1990s, strategic acquisitions strengthened the position of the firm's industrial tools business in important markets. At the turn of the 21st century, the group consisted of three established business areas: compressor equipment, construction and mining, and industrial tools. All three units had an outstanding track record in product innovation, which resulted in market leadership in their respective areas.

While the tradition of product innovation dates back to the group's founding, the Atlas Copco Group has also applied innovation to a different context and evolved from a product to a solution business model. This case study discusses the process of how it transformed the business model of its largest unit – Atlas Copco Compressor Technique, an international leader in the manufacture of compressors and associated equipment – from selling compressors to providing services.

Motivation: The beginning of a transformational journey

A compressor is a device that converts power into potential energy by forcing air into a smaller volume and thus increasing pressure. The energy can be used for a variety of applications, such as textile production or plastic bottle manufacturing. The sizes and types of compressors may vary, but most variants represent complex pieces of machinery that a customer considers an investment good and uses for over five years. Investment in compressors is an important decision for at least two reasons: first, they are indispensable for the functioning of applications powered by compressed air and, second, they are highly energy-intensive, meaning they require a lot of electricity to produce compressed air. Owing to these intrinsic product characteristics and the critical role they play, compressors need ongoing care and servicing.

For a compressor manufacturing company that burnished its reputation and achieved success by maintaining an excellent product business model, a shift toward the provision of services may have seemed like an unnecessary risk back in the early 2000s. The growth opportunity from the emerging markets was promising, and the enduring focus on product innovation and efficiency was keeping the profit margins high. Why tamper with a system that worked so well?

At the same time, the economic environment was clearly changing. Global competition from the low-cost countries was starting to threaten a disruption of the competitive landscape in the form of commoditization and price declines. Some market segments, particularly those demanding smaller compressors, had already been feeling the heat. Product innovation and quality were still a strong source of differentiation, but the technology was fairly stable, and radical innovations in the near future were unlikely. The existing business model was likely to be under threat 10 or even 5 years down the road.

One way to protect the Atlas Copco Compressor Technique business (hereafter simply referred to as Atlas Copco) against such a potential strategic threat would have been to join the commodity players and low-cost entrants and focus on offering cheaper compressors. Another way was to create even greater value for the customers – beyond more innovative product features and functions. Because it was very important for customers to have a compressor that functions well throughout its use life, offering services that ensure such reliability was a way of providing superior value. For instance, estimates indicate that the initial purchase of the compressor is only a small amount (5 per cent) of the total life cycle cost, while servicing represents about 20 per cent and energy 75 per cent of the costs. Costs associated with potential production disruption are an additional expense. Offering services that help reduce energy cost and the threat of disruption creates a big potential for customer value creation.

Delivering superior value with a service offering was consistent with Atlas Copco's overarching strategy of differentiation. The move in the direction of services helped Atlas Copco complement its equipment sales with additional offerings and then, at a later stage, improve its approach to client-specific needs with a better-targeted solution. Thus, while the shift from a product to a solution business model may have been a radical change, it was consistent with the company's century-long strategic orientation. Atlas Copco decided to take that path.

Front-end adaptation: From selling equipment to taking over the compressor room

In terms of the business transformation board (Figure II.1), Atlas Copco first transformed northward from the product to the service platform business model. The one-off decision of buying a compressor was complemented by an inclusive range of services, resulting in a regular interaction with the customers. This was followed by a transformation westward from a platform to a solution business model, as more sophisticated services began to be added to the portfolio of service offerings in order to provide the customer with better and more customized utility.

At the time when Atlas Copco's service journey began, the business mantra was that equipment manufacturers would be more competitive if they focused on the production of equipment and left all their downstream activities, such as customer contact and service, to the distributors or retailers. However, Atlas Copco had decided to focus on good service and to interact with customers directly, instead of through the distributors. This meant establishing a network of direct salespeople and service technicians who operated through a global infrastructure of customer centres and gradually converting indirect channels into direct channels.

'We wanted to make sure that we own the relationship with the customers', emphasizes Ronnie Leten, the former president of the Compressor Division (Atlas Copco) and the current CEO of the Atlas Copco Group.

> So, while on the side of the supply chain we were relying substantially on the collaboration with our suppliers, our downstream business model was turning out to be quite vertically integrated with the customers. This close contact with the customers stands in stark contrast to [the approach of] our competitors, who have a less forward-integrated business model and operate through distribution channels.

Once the subsidiary infrastructure was there, service provision began through customer pull. Customers were demanding services, and Atlas Copco started by providing services on an ad hoc basis, at the client's request. On the basis of these service encounters, Atlas Copco started to accumulate the experience to deliver ad hoc services, which created the milestones for the service operations function. Gradually, customer conversations started to encompass service offerings too.

Initially the service portfolio was modest, and it consisted mostly of promoting spare parts and advocating regular check-ups and repairs. This portfolio was adequate, however, to create the first service relationship, and customers increasingly bought into buying services from Atlas Copco. Having a service provided professionally as opposed to being do-it-yourself ensured efficiency through economies of scale. Additionally, having a service provided professionally by the manufacturer of the compressor meant that the quality of the service was much higher.

Another part of the value captured for Atlas Copco and the customer was perhaps harder to quantify but is equally tangible. Having a closer relationship with the customer meant that Atlas Copco was continuously in step with customers' changing needs. Regular contact meant the company was the first to recognize that the customer might require additional products or services. This relationship also started to yield new insights into a diverse range of customer needs. Product and service innovations that address those needs started to emerge as well. Thus, customer knowledge and intimacy – combined with continuous innovation – meant that it was very hard for competitors to come in and take over the business.

As a result, the service range expanded and evolved. Ad hoc and reactive offerings, such as spare parts and ad hoc maintenance, gave way to more sophisticated and proactive service plans where Atlas Copco focused on preventing problems rather than having to solve an existing problem. The shift toward prevention means that customers no longer had to face expensive costs when a compressor breaks and has also decreased the risk of having a costly disruption of their own production process when a compressor breaks. Furthermore, Atlas Copco started focusing on the monitoring and optimization of the compressor functioning (eg optimization of the air flow), as well as guaranteeing the price and quality of its service.

Back-end transformation: From a product-centric structure to an integrated activity system

While creating value for the customer and capturing part of that value through successful service innovation, the real art of the business model transformation lies in designing and operating an activity system that delivers the desired services. Indeed, behind this value there is substantial foresight, investment and effort in execution. As it did with the transformation on the front end, Atlas Copco also gradually transformed its back end.

As the services evolved from the subsidiaries on the front end, the first back-office changes were implemented within the subsidiaries as well. Atlas Copco subsidiaries, headed by the general manager, who acted as a CEO of the company, increasingly started to appoint service business line managers to head the service activities. The first focus of the service managers was the quality of the service delivery. Hiring qualified technical teams and training them was the first milestone. It made no sense to have the business evolve toward more sophisticated services if it was not possible to maintain a broad, good-quality basic service presence. For example, interviews with customers in the shipping business suggest that one of the main reasons they would contract Atlas Copco equipment and services is because they are sure that at every port they can rely on a skilled Atlas Copco technician.

Once confident in their ability to achieve a basic service presence, subsidiary management started to focus their attention on developing and selling more sophisticated services or on moving up the service ladder. A dedicated service sales force was instrumental in achieving this goal. Having service salespeople sell services was important for the design of appropriate customer incentives as well as for customers' education about the intangible but substantial benefits of servicing. Subsequently, as the volume of service jobs started to grow, the operational efficiency became more important. The previous focus on marketing was becoming balanced with a focus on standardization of service processes, an increase in the use of performance measurement, and ERP systems that supported and quantified the processes. As Ronnie Leten pointed out, 'When you make the decision to be vertically integrated toward the customers, efficiency is very important. That means IT systems and big data capabilities.'

As the service business model transformation made progress at the level of individual subsidiaries, the global headquarters were observing the shift. Headquarters designated service vice-presidents (VPs) and service product managers who had the responsibility to oversee the development of the service business, exchange best practices, benchmark the performance levels across the subsidiaries and provide guidance to the service managers at the subsidiaries. Their main objective was to make the services professional and create a business out of what had traditionally been regarded as a support function.

This stage saw the first efforts to formulate a service strategy. The global headquarters started promoting the importance of achieving a high service presence, measured by the aspirational one-to-one ratio of compressors and service contracts. Furthermore, the concept of the 'service ladder' was developed to capture the progression from the basic service offering (eg spare parts) to more sophisticated services (total responsibility service plans). The VPs used all these concepts, which were grounded in experiences from the best-performing subsidiaries, to promote service best practices across all the subsidiaries.

While their efforts and successes were notable, the reporting structure within the headquarters created some limitations for the development of the business model. Having service VPs report to the product presidents sent a strong signal that services were still a support function and an add-on to products. This reporting structure in the headquarters also had implications for the subsidiaries. For example, the attention that services received from a subsidiary general manager, as well as the status and power dynamics between a product and a service manager, was likely to be directed toward products.

The lack of equality between products and services was creating several limitations. First, by lacking visibility and status, the service business struggled to attract top talent and investments. As products and services were subject to synergies (eg service success made customers more likely to repurchase products), this also had a long-term negative feedback on products. Second, if product and service organizations experienced conflicts (eg a dilemma to service the old compressor or sell a new one), the lack of equality would mean that products were more likely to win the argument. This was seen as unfair and created some resentment in the service organization. In the long run this product-centric thinking was often not in the best interest of the organization as a whole. Instead, it would have been better to make decisions with the customer's interest in mind.

Leten was fully conscious that giving more power to services was necessary if Atlas Copco wanted to seize the opportunity. However, Atlas Copco's excellent performance again presented itself as an impediment to making a change. Furthermore, in the mid-2000s, there was very modest understanding of such service business models, and the academic literature contained little information about best practices, strengths and weaknesses, which added to the challenge.

Leten remembers:

> We prepared thoroughly. We started by engaging a doctoral candidate from KU
> Leuven to better understand the role that services play in driving our performance and
> best practices that our subsidiaries developed in transforming their business models
> toward services. The results of the study represented an input into how we decided to
> transform our business model globally and gave me the confidence to move forward. It
> was a very well-thought-through process. We innovated our business model, though
> we may not have realized it at the time. We were ahead; that's why we are where we
> are today.

Thus, despite the inert forces and the uncertainty that were favouring the status quo, Leten decided to make a bold move by creating a separate division to host services on the headquarters level. The service division – labelled Compressor Technique Services (CTS) – was to take charge of the service performance across the entire Atlas Copco Group and had the freedom to raise resources and invest them in service development. Having a division, responsibility and resources signalled the importance of services for Atlas Copco.

With this signal in place, Leten managed to attract one of Atlas Copco's top experienced professionals – Nico Delvaux – to head the CTS division. Building on the milestones that the service VPs had set up, Delvaux formulated a compelling service strategy and assembled a strong team to help him execute it. The successes that followed bear witness to the effectiveness of the decisions taken. Service performance across the subsidiaries continued to rise. Emphasis on measuring market success was coupled with attempts to track customer satisfaction. CTS developed several new service products (eg connectivity, remote monitoring and optimization) and introduced service process innovations (eg service sales force training, service plan price calculator, 'Formula 1 technician training').

'It all starts from the fundamentals – recognizing that service is a business. Anybody can perform the service, the technical part, but they cannot make a business out of services', says Ronnie Leten. 'You have to measure, follow up and attract the top people. To ensure this, we created a separate division, because there is a big difference in how you get business and operational excellence in a product and a service environment. Nowadays at Atlas Copco, professional service is fully expected. Totally different league', he adds with pride.

Monetization mechanics: From product margins to customer value

The gradual shift from a product to a platform business model starts by creating customer value and continues by sharing this value between the customer and the service provider. The key to gaining a bigger share of the customer's pocket is first to make those pockets deeper by creating more customer value. As the previous sections suggest, Atlas Copco grew its offering by keeping customer value in mind. Moreover, by capitalizing on the economies of scale obtained through a large installed base of compressors, it performed services more efficiently than an individual customer, which resulted in good margins. Beyond the cost savings, the knowledge of compressor technology meant that Atlas Copco could perform services better than both the customer and a specialized service provider. As Ronnie Leten puts it, 'Let's imagine that the customer can service her machine for €100 an hour. With our economies of scale and expertise, we can do it better and faster – probably for about €60 an hour. We will then share this gain with the customer.'

By bundling together products and services, Atlas Copco also offered convenience and a one-stop-shopping facility to the customer, reduced the time it takes to sign the contract and allowed customers to focus on their own core business. Through the process of shifting toward total responsibility, the interests of Atlas Copco and its customers to keep the product safe and the service efficiently performed were much better aligned. Some of the more advanced contracts – dubbed 'air per cubic metre' – also allowed customers to shift additional risk to Atlas Copco. This 'peace of mind' value was something that a lot of customers were interested in.

The value-creating and value-capturing potential of these sophisticated services was even higher than the aforementioned efficiency gains reached through the shift toward professionalization of services that was achieved at the outset. There are several reasons for this. Compressors tend to be mission-critical pieces of equipment, and prevention of breakdowns means avoiding (very expensive) disruptions of operation. Furthermore, regular servicing ensures that the electrical energy needed to power the compressors is used as efficiently as possible. This means that – thanks to the service – energy savings are made, and customers' energy bills are reduced. 'For example, an unnecessary pressure drop of 1 bar reduces energy efficiency by 7 per cent. Pressure drops can be caused by clogged filters, for example. Therefore, performing timely maintenance and installation monitoring (eg for potential leak detections) is crucial for energy efficiency', said

Pieter Colen, a process development manager. These more individualized solutions resulted in an increase in the value per customer and allowed for higher margins and willingness to pay, as well as higher customer loyalty.

Finally, offering services brought financial stability for Atlas Copco. As with all durable goods businesses, the compressor business is highly susceptible to the ups and downs of the business cycle. More specifically, customers buy compressors either to develop the additional production capacity or to renew existing production capacity (by replacing the old compressors). During a downturn, customers will hold off on investments to increase their production capacity and postpone renewing the existing equipment. However, the servicing of existing capacity will remain almost intact. While customers can reduce the ad hoc services somewhat, they cannot avoid them completely. They are equally unlikely to terminate long-term contracts and face penalties. Moreover, a decision to postpone the renewal of the existing equipment may even mean more servicing of the old equipment.

Lessons learned and outlook: Products and services as equal partners to deliver the best customer solution

The emphasis on the 'downstream business' and growing the subsidiary network represented the first milestones in the transformation of a traditional product company business into a service platform business model. Later on, the creation of the service division helped to establish a power balance between the product and service businesses (see Figure 9.2).

Figure 9.2 Atlas Copco's transformation paths

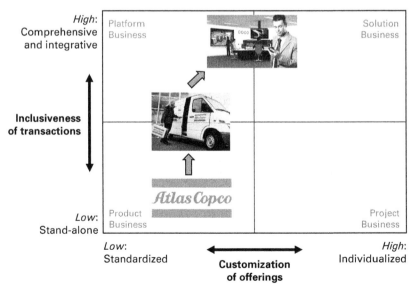

Once this equilibrium was established, the key objective became to maintain a strong and positive relationship between the products and services and turn points of tension to synergies. It turned out that juggling products and services is a challenging job. Subsidiary managers have to play a very active role in this process and engage in resolving conflicts and finding potential collaboration opportunities on a daily basis.

While challenging, the task of combining products and services and generally transitioning toward a solution business model generates substantial synergies. On a day-to-day basis, combining product and service portfolios allows Atlas Copco to propose well-targeted, customized solutions to the client's needs. In the long run, products and services allow for a substantial innovation potential. Having been actively involved in servicing, Atlas Copco focuses on designing compressors that are easier to service. Moreover, insights from the service delivery sector can be used to design better compressors, particularly by leveraging big data from sensors and other data collection tools.

Inspired by the vision to be 'First in Mind – First in Choice'® of their customers and powered by continuous innovation in their wide range of products and services, Atlas Copco Group has had many successes. For instance, it sells to customers in 180 country markets, aims for 8 per cent annual growth and ranks 23rd among the 100 most sustainable enterprises. Last but not least, Atlas Copco Group has managed to translate its successes into shareholder value: the company's A shares have produced an annual total return of 22 per cent over the past 10 years.

When asked about the future pathway for the company, Leten emphasizes:

At the end of the day, we should move toward that which is best for our customer – whether it is a product or a service. This is the most logical way to resolve the product versus service organizational paradox and also a sound long-term strategy. The general manager of every subsidiary is there to assure that we apply this principle in the field. On the headquarters level, we make sure that we continue investing in product innovation while professionalizing and improving our services. And these must go together; we must be brutally efficient and provide the best service experience to our customers and at the same time have the latest, most innovative products to offer them. You always have to do both; otherwise it is not sustainable.

Brose: From components delivery to global systems supplier
Günter Müller-Stewens

Founded in 1908, Brose is one of the top automotive suppliers in the world. It remains family-owned. Until the end of the 1990s, Brose was running a product business model, based on developing and producing components. Owing to the structural changes in the automotive industry, the company was facing the danger of becoming one of hundreds of second-tier and third-tier suppliers that has no direct contact with the large automotive producers – original equipment manufacturers (OEMs) – and is dependent on its first-tier suppliers' management decisions. To avoid this, Brose's board decided to transform the company in the direction of a solution business model.

The company: A family business for more than 100 years

Brose is a highly specialized engineering company in Germany. It can look back on more than 100 years of successful family business. In 1908, Max Brose founded a trading company for automotive parts and, in 1920, Metallwerk Max Brose & Co. Max Brose was the grandfather of Michael Stoschek, the Brose Group's major shareholder and chairman. Today, Brose is one of the top 40 automotive suppliers in the world, as well as the fifth-largest family-owned company in the industry.

Brose's customers are mainly large and global manufacturers in the automobile industry, which manage around 80 car brands, but also suppliers with a global reach. With nearly 24,000 employees at 57 locations in 24 countries, the company generated a turnover of about €6.1 billion in 2015 (compared to €2 billion in 2004) and invested €360 million (5.9 per cent). Most of its growth was organic. The company has made only two major acquisitions: the closure systems business of Bosch (in 2002) and the electric motors segment from Siemens VDO and Continental (in 2008).

Over the decades, Brose gained outstanding expertise in mechanics, electrics and electronics. These competencies are used in different combinations in the business units for vehicle door systems (51 per cent of total sales), seat systems (23 per cent) and drives (for electric motors) (26 per cent). The management board consists of nine executives: the CEO, the head of commercial administration, the head of production, the head of purchasing, the three business unit heads and two regional presidents (Asia and North America).[1]

The industry: Increasing pressure on automotive suppliers

The market of automotive suppliers is a very competitive one, and most suppliers want to be a first-tier supplier to the OEMs rather than only a supplier to another supplier. Owing to the tough competition, and the price pressure coming from the OEMs, the market is undergoing a process of consolidation. The suppliers want to improve their cost positions by realizing economies of scale.

The 10 largest suppliers worldwide account for sales to the automotive industry of about \$300 billion, which is about 60 per cent of the total market: 1) Continental (2013 sales to the automotive industry: €33 billion); 2) Robert Bosch (€31 billion); 3) Denso (€28 billion); 4) Magna (€25 billion); 5) Bridgestone/Firestone (€25 billion); 6) Hyundai Mobis (€23 billion); 7) Johnson Controls (€21 billion); 8) Michelin (€20 billion); 9) Aisin Seiki (€19 billion) and 10) Faureci (€18 billion). On average, they can realize an earnings before interest and tax (EBIT) margin of a little more than 5 per cent, or a return on capital employed (ROCE) margin of about 12 per cent.

Automotive suppliers must deal with several challenges. The consolidation of OEMs leads to increasing bargaining power. For instance, Mercedes bundles its orders of door systems across different vehicle classes, to realize higher economies of scale and to decrease costs by using the same components across different classes. Such activities are part of large purchasing cost reduction programmes to keep an attractive margin and to fulfil shareholders' return expectations. This results in increasing price sensitivity. To additionally reduce complexity of its supplier management, the OEMs have defined so-called 'system suppliers'. As a first-tier supplier, a system supplier is responsible for a complex integrative sub-system of a car and must manage all second-tier and third-tier suppliers that deliver components to the system.

At the same time, suppliers face increasing pressure to innovate for their customers. For instance, owing to increasing environmental awareness in the markets, OEMs put pressure on suppliers to produce 'green' innovations. Tight collaboration with customers is required, because innovations must occur faster and in more focused, more perceivable ways for end-users. Final solutions are often co-innovated.

Beyond customer pressure, the automotive industry is currently characterized by megatrends such as fuel consumption savings through increases in efficiency, lightweight designs, and electrification of both automobiles and motorcycles. Suppliers such as Brose must think about what substantial contributions they can make towards saving resources and sustainability with their present and future mechatronic systems, for instance through intelligent, lightweight design and functional integration.

Global production in the automotive industry moves towards new markets. The classical triad markets (Europe, the United States, Japan) are rapidly losing market share, and new markets are emerging (China, India, etc). The suppliers must follow the globalization of their customer bases. Global car platforms must be supported by local units of supplier systems, and a supplier must guarantee to its customers that it is able to globally fulfil their requirements. Furthermore, suppliers must show more flexibility, to react in shorter product life cycles. New car types must be served with customized systems based on standard building blocks and platforms. The big challenge is to be present at the large global platforms.

Owing to these major challenges, Brose's management decided to transform the company's purpose, followed by a radical change of the business model.

The transformation: Becoming a strategic partner

The decision to transfer Brose into a global systems supplier and strategic partner of selected customers in the international automobile industry had major impacts on the front end, back end and monetization mechanics of the business model. As a first-tier supplier, Brose was confronted with much more complex and customer-specific demands from its customers. Needless to say, a supplier still wants to sell as many parts of a system (eg a seat system) as possible in order to realize economies of scale. But now the perspective changes: the supplier must modify its products and processes, because each customer system looks different, adjusted to its specific needs, and the supplier wants to sell the benefits from a larger project to the OEM. Therefore, the supplier often plans and develops it in close collaboration with a customer, and produces and delivers it completely aligned to the customer's assembly line. This means that the product's hardware is combined with a large amount of services. To guarantee this, the supplier must make significant customer-specific investments, including the development of the additional capabilities that are needed.

While this creates dependencies on both sides, a family-owned company might have some advantages owing to its long-term perspective. For instance, the long-standing partnership between the Brose Group and Mercedes has been in place for about 80 years. Such lock-ins are driving Brose in the direction of a solution business model because they increase the stickiness between the customer and the Brose systems platform. The duration of a contract between Brose and Mercedes is usually six to seven years, because the door system is not design-relevant for the car. This gives Brose some long-term stability. But, because Mercedes also does not want to be too dependent on Brose as a supplier, the contract is based on multiple conditions (eg competitiveness, quality, reasonable pricing, etc). If these are not fulfilled, the contract can be cancelled, and it might take the OEM about one to two years to switch to another supplier. However, this does not happen very often, because of all the other components of stickiness. To reduce dependency on its supplier, Mercedes owns its product-specific tool. It can simply take the tools if it needs to switch suppliers. In such a case, the supplier has the role of mounting a set of components on a chassis produced by the customer.

Front-end transformation

Taking the role of a first-tier systems supplier needs decisions on the revenue structure. First, the company must focus on very few yet profitable and growing systems offerings (see Figure 9.3). A system should be as broad as possible an offering, including services. Second, to be profitable, the company must be able to have a leading position in this segment in the world market, as well as a significant share in the value creation and profit pool of a system. Third, to mitigate the risk of such a focused offering, the company must globally diversify its customer portfolio.

Figure 9.3 Mechatronic systems and electric motors

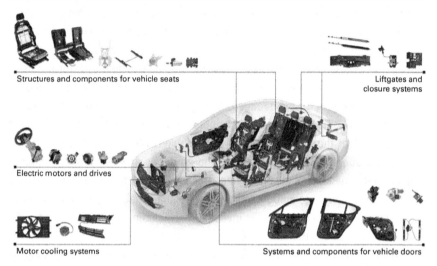

Structures and components for vehicle seats

Liftgates and closure systems

Electric motors and drives

Motor cooling systems

Systems and components for vehicle doors

SOURCE: Brose

Brose decided to focus on two systems: door modules (subcomponents) and seat structures (see Figure 9.4), because they fit the company's expertise in mechanics, electrics and electronics very well. Today, almost 80 per cent of Brose's sales are generated with these systems. Inside each system, the company is able to deliver thousands of different variants, following the complexity of the OEM's offering.

In 1987, Brose produced the first door module for Audi's 1987 Coupé model and delivered more than 40 million units. The company is seen as the inventor of the modular door system for cars, by dividing the door into wet and dry areas. The relevant functions are integrated in a module mounting: the closing system, the window regulators, the wiring harness, the interior door panels, the crash sensor system, the speakers and so on. By using new materials such as glass cloth-reinforced polypropylene, Brose contributes to the OEM's goal of weight reduction.

Figure 9.4  A door system and a seat system, both by Brose

SOURCE: Brose

As a systems integrator – and not only a seller of components – Brose can improve and optimize the quality of a whole system, for instance by ensuring the electromagnetic compatibility of the often more than 40 electric motors in a car.

In 2008, Brose acquired the electric motors section from Siemens VDO and Continental. At this time, Brose was the company's biggest client. The strategic rationale for the deal was: to increase its own value creation in the door system by vertical integration of a relevant supplier, which helps optimize its quality; to build up and strengthen competences in electric motors; to expand in new markets and products (CFM1, ABS, steering, etc); and to secure innovation (CO_2 discussion, weight reduction, electrification of the drivetrain).

But Brose does not only produce door systems; the company is a full service supplier. To earn the role of a first-tier supplier, Brose had to demonstrate that it has the technological and process competences to deliver and manage such a sub-system as a project. So Brose takes full accountability for all the suppliers that supply to it, even including the suppliers that are predefined by an OEM. Brose controls its suppliers mainly in the same way Brose is controlled by its clients: certifications, auditing tools, an enterprise resource planning system and so on.

Service cooperation begins when planning and developing the door system in an innovative way with the client. If a new model in a vehicle class has to be developed, there are usually almost no synergies from the old to the new door systems, because material and technical innovations have taken place in the interim. For instance, Brose must think about what substantial and innovative contribution it can make towards saving resources and sustainability with its present and future mechatronic systems, for instance through intelligent, lightweight designs and functional integration, as implemented in the window regulators. To cover the 'last leg' between provider and consumer, the customer can be enabled – eg via tools – to co-create larger parts of an offering on its own (prosumer), for instance when customers compose their own software by using business process management tools from model to code to take full accountability for the customer's business processes embodied in a service level agreement.

The door is produced synchronically with the pulsing of the customer's car production assembly line. The production of the door system starts with the receipt of an order by Brose. After production, the door system is previewed for the client and is now ready to be combined with the car body shell of the door and to be installed at the client's assembly line. All the Brose production sites deliver their systems based on a zero-failure rate, using just-in-time and just-in-sequence, directly to the OEM's assembly line, to avoid interim storage at the client site.[2] Just-in-sequence reduces costs for the customer, because the delivery happens four to five hours after an OEM places an order. This is only possible if the Brose production site is very close to the customer's assembly line or at the customer's site. This saves logistics costs, and fast quality loop reactions become possible. An early example is the opening of the production site in Meerane (Germany) in 1997 very close to Volkswagen Mosel. Another example is Brose Tuscaloosa, Inc (United States), which has been producing door systems for DaimlerChrysler's M-class and R-class models since the end of 2004. Brose products, featuring up to 247 variants, are supplied in line with the customer's own vehicle production schedule to the Mercedes plant 1 kilometre away. Logistics and IT competencies are also decisive for a customer project's success.

Another future possibility is that Brose employees mount door systems into car bodies directly at the assembly line. Another, less radical option, but one that decreases sequential costs for the OEM, is locating the Brose production site inside the customer's production site. These two options can also be combined.

To improve the customer orientation of the door and seat systems, Brose has reorganized the company by defining the abovementioned business units as 'door systems' and 'seat systems'. The multidisciplinary project teams of both units can be restaffed according to the specific expert knowledge needs. Brose has established focused, direct dialogue with each customer.

The interface with Mercedes in Germany is the central purchasing department at Mercedes. Only in the case of technical changes is there interaction with the development department of Mercedes. For instance, the C-class is developed at one site and produced at four sites. Mercedes has only one contact person at Brose; the contact coordinates and optimizes all interactions between Brose and Mercedes.

Back-end transformation

Brose's customers expected more flexibility and adaptability to changing demands. The module-based door system concept has helped address the increasing variant diversity of each new car product line. And Brose's global presence, built up over the years in the most relevant automotive markets, with development and production sites, enables it to react swiftly and to make local adjustments to changing customer needs.

Another challenge was to keep the cost structure under control in a customer-driven business model so as to be able to realize an attractive margin. This is not easy, because procurement savings targets of suppliers such as Brose are often primarily defined by a demand for decreasing prices by OEMs. It starts with taking care of lean overhead structures. Brose also wanted to ensure that the Brose system is not only tailor-made for its customers' needs, but also competitive concerning pricing. A Brose solution is based on standardized components and interfaces between sub-assemblies. Thus, in spite of individualized solutions, economies of scale can be realized for single components that are independent of any OEM or any product line. Brose's process excellence is often reflected if there are innovative ways to improve its efficiency. Finally, an executive board member has established a strong, global purchasing function with clear responsibilities.

To make all these changes happen, Brose has to retain and attract excellent people. Personnel are guided by Brose's corporate values (tradition and openness to change, internationality and regional commitment, success orientation and willingness to perform, commitment and responsibility, reliability and honesty) and corporate objectives (market leadership, growth profitability, quality and speed).

Transformation of monetization mechanics

Pricing is driven by customers' willingness to pay, which in turn is driven by the price segment in which an OEM's product line is positioned, because its target price for a new car model is broken down into the different systems and components. The question is always to what extent the customer is ready to pay for the increasing number of service activities added to the product it is buying.

It was always Brose's ambition to be part of the large global platforms. To get an order, pricing is initially sometimes below cost, and the calculation is to realize the target margin along a system's total life cycle. Yet, if Brose gets the order, significant customer-specific investments in the development of a new system must be made by Brose, usually without financial support from the client. This means a high financial burden and risks for Brose. Research and development costs are regulated by committed target costs and a specific development contract. In 2015 Brose invested €470 million into R&D.

The pricing and calculation of a door system, for instance, is based on a new model's expected production volume – sometimes even bundled across different vehicle classes – but there is no guarantee that this volume will be reached, because market developments can change in either direction. Here, OEMs expect high flexibility from their suppliers.

However, financial sustainability depends not only on the margin but also on optimized working capital management, efficient asset management and adequate leverage of the available equity.

The future: Challenges from a changing automotive industry

The sustainability of the solution business model of Brose will depend on the capability of the company to help the OEMs to cope with the huge challenges they face, which can even change the essence or soul of the car, as a vehicle to provide autonomy and a sense of self-directed freedom to its owners[3]: the rising global competitive intensity, the technological advances (interactive safety systems, vehicle connectivity, self-driving cars, etc), new regulatory priorities (eg vehicle use restrictions) and the digitization of the value chain (communicating robots at the assembly line, connected cars, etc). All these developments will also demand new expertise from suppliers; they must be the main source of the necessary complex innovations and uniqueness.

The pressure to innovate and to reduce costs will even increase for system suppliers like Brose. The digitization of the business models will offer new possibilities here. In spite of the uniqueness of Brose's solutions for each product line of its customers, it has to realize more cross-customer synergies with its systems to meet the cost targets of the OEMs.

In Figure 9.5 we summarize the transformation of Brose from a pure product business model to a solutions provider.

Acknowledgements

Our thanks to Michael Reiff (Manager Procurement and Supplier Quality, Mercedes-Benz) for his feedback, which allowed us to get a better understanding of the industry.

Figure 9.5 The business model transformation of Brose

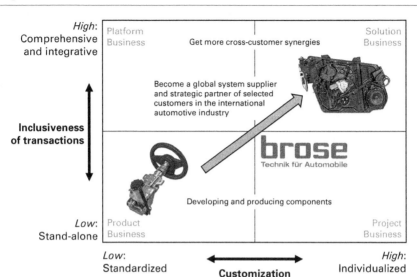

SOURCE OF PICTURES: Brose

Endnotes

1 See http://de.wikipedia.org/wiki/Brose_Fahrzeugteile; www.brose.com.

2 With the less demanding concept of *just-in-time* production, it is/was still possible to plan about two weeks ahead, to produce larger lot sizes and to be further away from the customer's production site.

3 P Gao, R Hensley and A Zielke (2014) A road map to the future for the auto industry, *McKinsey Quarterly*, October.

University of St Gallen: From education as a product to integrated education solutions
Markus Frank and Andreas Löhmer

The origins of executive education at the University of St Gallen date to the middle of the 20th century. As is the case at other business schools, this university's alumni wanted to have a continuous dialogue with the faculty and be up to date on the key topics of management, finance and business law.

For the faculty, staying in touch with the alumni network enabled them to develop research topics based on the needs of management practice, test new methods and tools, reflect on recent research findings, improve teaching skills and, last but not least, generate additional revenues that they would subsequently be able to reinvest in research and faculty development. To that end, the university's institutes developed various formats of open enrolment programmes in which executives from different firms and organizations came together to gain new insights into the latest business knowledge and to share experiences with each other.

A trend that had already emerged in the late 1990s quickly accelerated in the early years of the new millennium, as large companies and organizations began developing their own in-house executive education programmes. Firms wanted a curriculum that was fully aligned with their leadership development needs and the companies' business contexts. Furthermore, to some extent as a result of the events following 9/11, large companies and organizations also sought to reduce risks and travel costs for their executives in the area of leadership development. This objective resulted in programmes at business schools whose faculty delivered courses as part of the firms' own executive development activities, focused on the companies' business context, and often organized under the aegis of corporate universities or academies. In many cases, such programmes helped participants to get a step up on the rungs of their career ladder.

The University of St Gallen's institutes and departments seized the opportunity to develop the first custom programmes for their corporate network partners. The course content and teaching methodology were largely transferred from existing open enrolment programmes, and generic cases were used. The degree of customization was still very limited: primarily, corporate clients could choose from a relatively standardized portfolio of course modules to design a curriculum that suited their needs, and they were able to specify the location. The main selling proposition was the quality of the teaching content. Moreover, speakers from the clients' management team often delivered the company-specific content.

The same salespeople who were in charge of open programmes dealt with requests from corporate clients for customized programmes on the university's behalf. Conversely, on the client side, the organization's human resources (HR) people usually played a more limited role. Often being only remotely linked with the real business in the different business units, they refrained from any heavy involvement in the designing of custom programmes. For the most part, this activity was taken over by the business schools in order to be closer to reality when delivering their courses.

Open enrolment programmes were often used to cross-sell customized programmes. The administration, organization, briefing of lecturers, organization of social events, and accounting functions were also centralized in order to generate scale across open and custom programmes. Pricing was very similar to the fees of open programmes, only including a small customization fee. The main cost elements of the pricing logic were the honorarium for lecturers, and the rent of locations.

These early custom programmes focused on the core topics of the faculty, delivered in the proven, well-established format of in-class settings, with few pre- and post-teaching elements. The selection of participants and the transfer of learning to the workplace were tasks assigned to the client organization. The integration of the programme in HR and learning and development (L+D) processes was not actively supported. Owing to their standardization, these rudimentary custom programmes were repeatable and easily adaptable to different management levels. Customer relations were highly transactional, as the procurement of such a programme was based on well-defined requirements and a standardized brief. Experienced and renowned faculty, as well as proven formats and methods (cases, mini-surveys, etc), dominated the learning architecture. Accordingly, the management of relations with the core faculty and their institutes was crucial for the custom programmes' success. Costs had to be covered in the short term, as the activities were a simple extension of the open executive education programme activities, and there was little lock-in for the clients. Pricing was relatively cost-transparent, as clients usually assumed that the faculty's honorarium constituted the main cost component.

In 2006 the Executive School of Management, Technology and Law (ES-HSG) started its activities. Previously, the university's institutes had managed all executive education in a decentralized way. However, this approach created some redundancies, as programmes overlapped in part, and several programme managers often approached the same HR managers. Additionally, the lack of coordination hindered the inclusion of executive education activities in the increasingly relevant international rankings. The clients, however, demanded better coordination and service, and they increasingly referred to rankings when deciding on their in-house education service provider. In reaction to these pressures, the ES-HSG was established with the intention of having it serve two goals: first, to improve the appeal for potential customers by means of a more integrated executive education portfolio and a stronger position in the Financial Times (FT) European Business School Rankings (the objective was to reach the top ten by 2014); and, second, to contribute substantially to the funding of the university as a whole.

In operational terms, these two goals basically meant that it was necessary to develop new open and custom programmes from an outside-in logic, take customer needs and competition criteria as the starting point and invert the predominant inside-out logic of pushing existing content and methodology into the customized executive education market. The quality of the university's executive education activities would no longer be assessed against internal goals but based on the market instead, as reflected by customer satisfaction and the FT ranking methodology,[1] which sheds external light on the ES-HSG's performance through a rigorous process. The other fundamental change was the introduction of a centralized marketing approach to improve the visibility and comprehensiveness of the executive education activities. This approach included a central internet portal, a complete, up-to-date programme of all offerings, and information support for all requests regarding executive education.

The field of truly customized programmes for corporate clients showed very promising market potential in terms of both developing new content and formats and creating substantial new revenues. The ES-HSG approached this market in 2006. The key act was to engage dedicated business developers who had experience as executives on the board level as well as deep knowledge of the university's strengths and features in terms of research fields, content and faculty.

Putting the client in the lead: From standardization to true customization

While the early years of the ES-HSG still had rather a high degree of standardized content delivered in corporate programmes at the clients' end, a shift toward more individualized and customer-need-driven executive education approaches was being pursued by the end of the decade.

Front end: From standard lectures to tailored learning

It was obvious that clients in various (usually multinational) corporations were becoming increasingly demanding with respect to executive education programmes, because more transparency evolved through the web, especially as far as potential suppliers in the market and their 'solution' packages were concerned. Therefore, in addition to more specifics and flexibility with regard to content and methodology or didactics, there had to be a better understanding of the clients' needs. This requirement inevitably led to an offer of consulting services for learning and development architectures, the design and delivery of programmes, modules and learning interventions, and the full administration of programmes and academies. For the Executive School, it meant a search for a whole new set of client management skills on the school's own premises: a new kind of 'learning architect' had to be found. With former consultants, business leaders and training and development experts, the ES-HSG ramped up its skills in the field of customization regarding executive education for corporate clients. The architects had to be carefully recruited, as the criteria for selection were manifold: they had to be of an age that showed seniority in the customer relationship; in order to understand the client and the client's needs adequately, work experience in any organization was a must; and, finally, experience in the executive education and organizational development field was clearly demanded, as learning architectures that would be complex but understandable needed to be built.

The result of this thorough recruiting and on-boarding process of new hires led to a design competence of learning architectures that largely mirrored the clients' demands, while at the same time it offered enough flexibility to react to the resource constraints. The custom programme was no longer a teaching approach aimed at transferring knowledge but a learning journey that built and developed individual skills and organizational competence. Technology also played an important role on this journey, as it enabled the Executive School to do a better job of translating customer needs in learning with regard to flexibility, productivity and effectiveness, including own-branding. Whereas the 2010–2011 period introduced learning platforms and some e-learning modules into the customized learning process, the following years saw the advent of new solutions such as Virtual Launch, a web-based virtual classroom with breakout possibilities (Illustra TV) and the creation of a co-branded knowledge portal, 1place2learn.

For all relevant management and leadership topics, a matrix of learning methodologies (lecture, video, cases, simulation, experiential learning, coaching, etc) and learning modes had been established and was ready for use. Even though the solution's flexibility and the process's smoothness were at the top of the agenda for the team members, reality showed that bending the branch too quickly can sometimes make it flip back with a jolt. Trying to convince customers with flashy presentations that introduce new approaches or confronting them with different technologies for a pitch or within a specific programme delivery did not receive the expected welcome at all, because the client might not have been on the same level of sophistication as the Executive School. Thus, the new approach in the direction of the customer had to be implemented thoroughly and with patience.

Selling the customized solutions was a challenge in the highly fragmented and competitive market of executive education. Traditionally, these programmes have been designed in response to requests for proposals (RFPs) or direct customer requests. These were still seen as a very promising channel, including to broaden an international footprint in the segment, but the custom programme department was also trying to address potential clients proactively by expanding research into how the different industries behaved and how some particularly interesting firms were developing. The concept of a 'distinguished wish-partnership' was created by the custom programme team.

Back end: From scalable standard content to customized insights

Within a couple of months, the custom programme team reacted to the clients' changing environment. Where possible, it adapted the designs of the learning architectures and other customized education solutions to the organizations' needs. Even the customers with highly mature and sophisticated experience in the executive education field should not perceive any standardization in the pro-gramme architecture and teaching content. However, this customization also im-plied substantial changes for those tasked with delivering the solutions, namely the faculty members.

The faculty's strong research base was no longer the sole driver of the cus-tomized executive education approach, as the latter required faculty members to take a careful look at the customers' demands and tailor the content accord-ingly. Although most of the professors were joining the so-called 'in-group' and were happy to adapt their standard content to what the clients' HR departments or the businesses had foreseen for their senior management, there was also an 'out-group' of lecturers who were reluctant to tailor their content. The main reasons were different priorities and limited time, as the faculty had to address numerous demands, including graduate and postgraduate teaching, fundamental research and publishing, as well as project work (consulting and/or education) to finance their institutes. Additionally, the room for granting financial incentives was limited and thus did not necessarily help the custom programme team win over the faculty. In order to handle the faculty conscientiously, the team members – at least at the directors' level – had to be senior in rank. Despite all these challenges, the custom programme department showed great enthusiasm in doing things dif-ferently for the customer. The proposals delivered and the discussions held with the different parties at the customer's end unambiguously showed a substantial shift toward more tailoring and greater adaptability on the organization's learning journey.

As the development of programmes became more customer-driven, it also re-quired a stronger buy-in and joint design work (co-creation) from the client. The phase of conceptualizing an organizational development or executive education measure could take more time and required a clear commitment from the client's side. Faculty members were strongly looking into the possibilities of having the participants answer department-relevant surveys and/or having them describe their own leadership cases. Moreover, the custom programme team pushed strongly for closer co-design procedures with the clients in order to tie in all the relevant information from the business case and make sure the teaching content had an impact.

Monetization mechanics: Pricing remains under pressure

Pricing continued to be a great challenge, as the clients (for the most part) remained price-sensitive – all the more so because business schools in Switzerland have tended to have a different and slightly higher price point than those in the Eurozone. The services offered therefore had to remain competitive, albeit much more tailored. In other words, there had to be a greater focus on the importance of design and concept-work costs, while the pressure on expenses for the delivery continued to be high.

Clients and their programmes at the Executive School have shown different profitability ratios. Depending on the degree of the clients' sophistication and maturity level in executive education processes and their willingness to shoulder a large part of the responsibility for the programme design, some were seeking more help than others. Initially, however, clients had not been paying for this kind of services and support. This had to be priced in and monitored very closely in order to ensure profitability.

Executive education as an integrated solution: Developing impact-driven customization

Because its customers were exposed to more volatility in the markets as a result of the rapid acceleration in digital offerings and solutions, among other factors, these disruptions affected the business school at a similar pace. For the custom programme department, this meant yet another transformation of its business model and greater emphasis on the impact it could generate for the client on various levels. It seemed that pure education – with respect to residential and/or virtual teaching and learning as the golden way to enhance individual competencies, as well as organizational capabilities, no matter how tailored they were – was coming to an end.

Beyond increasing price competition and some clients' demands to outsource learning on the executive level, leadership and organizational development also grew more global and complex, as the L+D role within the organizations was under increasing pressure to deliver a real impact for the businesses by joining forces with hand-picked business schools. More and more management boards were asking for clear deliverables to connect the programme's learning objectives with the business results that were expected as an outcome. Generally speaking, the return on learning investment (ROLI) was given a time horizon of no more than two years, and expectations were rising. There was a strong tendency for the L+D function to become considerably more professional, acting as a real business partner, but also as a business school partner. In order to ensure impact and thus serve as a preferred education supplier, the ES-HSG faced pressure to expand its service portfolio. Teaching remained the focal offering, but other services had to be added, including transfer support and individual coaching. However, it was important not only to provide these services but also to integrate them closely with the teaching programmes in order to arrange for all services to follow a clear and consistent common thread.

Front end: From teaching to business impact

The services that the custom programme department was offering to its clients were increasingly tailored to a specific current or future business challenge. The school would no longer exclusively execute the design and delivery of executive education programmes or learning journeys at a given time in a more or less residential format. Instead, it would support the client and the client's target population – depending on where the emphasis was: organizational capabilities, individual competencies or both – with a newly developed architecture on up to three different levels: the delivery of content, the transfer of content to the client's business (with regard to subjects) and the sparring to address and solve individual management and change challenges (with regard to personalities). Therefore, a considerable amount of time was spent in gaining a profound understanding of the customer's demands. The offering's success was measured in terms of the direct business or individual impact that could be observed and quantified, and for which the business school could ultimately be held accountable.

While some early tries with the newly designed business approach ended in 'one-shots', others could be turned into ongoing solutions. The latter were important, as they showed – by means of participant sign-in and footprint in the relevant markets – that impact could be generated. If impact-driven customization was to be the answer to the business challenges the clients were confronting, only mid-term to long-term relationships with the customer could prove that outcomes from the development and training programmes had been implemented and the impact had been achieved. This approach demanded an interaction based on trust between the responsible players at the client's end and at the Executive School. Nevertheless, 'one-shots' were never to be disregarded, as the market also showed some demand for lean programmes.

There is no doubt that key account management and a close customer relationship became more and more important and ultimately even a game-changer (once the decision for a partner had been made). By being more of a sparring partner for the client – a sounding board for any organizational development or executive education query there might be – the custom programme team had a relationship that became more and more retention-oriented. Examples with clients have shown that, even during the acquisition phase of a project, proximity to the client and the client's potential or explicit business challenges could be crucial. Discussions on the phone, via Skype or FaceTime, or through face-to-face interactions or written exchanges gave the customer the impression that the team was going the extra mile, even before participation in the pitch has been announced or the contract signed.

Back end: From selected expert lecturers to networks for the unforeseeable future

The skills needed as part of the programme management environment were further improved and required a great deal more knowledge to deal with customers' multiple demands. Skills such as conversation techniques (listening and asking the right questions), knowledge of the industry, and innovative and proactive suggestions for how to design a programme or a development measure to address the client's challenges were no longer sufficient in the 'new world'. Here, a new skill set had to be installed, and it had to match the new, integrated demands from the business world convincingly: overall organizational development and alignment as mantra and toolbox for HR professionals; integrative strategy development for boards and executive committees in a lean yet effective way; innovation and business model transformation for those seeking new impulses for saturated markets; managing disruptions in order to challenge oneself; and digitization as the new buzzword in organizations.

Because of this complex set of skills and expertise that was necessary to meet client demands, the importance of networks rose sharply. The need for highly differentiated skills that far exceeded the pure education topics made a proactive knitting of relations to internal institutes on the one hand and to external third-party think tanks on the other hand unavoidable or – even better – an undeniable premise. As the Executive School had already been working with numerous external providers in its previous and existing programmes, the in-depth usage and extension of the knowledge hub could be handled easily and made the University of St Gallen an even stronger partner. To this end, another skill within the team was required, namely network communication. The network was set up and used in a way that made it flexible enough to respond efficiently to the clients' requests and to last-minute changes. Whether specialists in the university's institutes, professionals from third parties, or expert agencies, they were all tied together in a grid of potential contributors to create an impact for the customer.

Since 2013, the Executive School has tackled an increasing number of projects in which clients ask it to take on the role of 'general contractor', by integrating and aligning the other partners according to the project's demands or liaising with associate schools representing additional expertise and/or geographical proximity. Sometimes this is a challenging task, as the partners in the executive education market are larger and have a strong reputation. In order to have them agree to the client's wish to subcontract to a potential competitor, the assigned programme directors and key account manager have to build trust and acceptance amongst their counterparts. Building on diplomacy and intelligent network communication, projects could, for example, be delivered successfully with the support of Hult Ashridge Executive Education (UK), Columbia Business School (US) or ESSEC (France). This sort of inclusion saw the ES-HSG move into a position where its existing and potential clients considered it an exclusive and sophisticated solutions provider.

In the end, flexibility in dealing with third parties with the aim of addressing the customers' demands has been and will be a strong driver and can become an important asset for business schools in the future if they are to survive.

Monetization mechanics

Having transformed into an impact-driven customizing business school with retention-oriented customer relations does not necessarily imply a steady stream of revenue from the clients' side. Every year, despite the quality of the results and their subsequent impact, some clients renegotiate prices from scratch and revise their leadership development portfolio.

Cost coverage in an impact-driven customization process or delivery remains a challenge. Only a small number of deep client commitments for long-term measures could be reached and other smaller ones initiated. True impact-driven customization initiatives, however, can only be profitable in the long term, owing to the high upfront investment on the part of the school and its faculty. Accordingly, customers need to be identified that seek a longitudinal relationship and collaboration with a specific business school.

Even those clients who have established good relations with the school and have experienced a strong impact for their organizations and for the individual participants of the learning measure remain eager to see high cost transparency. Even though the prices are usually divided into different types of services, to allow for comparison with other schools, the programme directors and key account managers are under increasing pressure to report an ever more detailed insight into the actual cost and margins. Thus, for most of the school's clients, the possibility of having an integrated solution–cost approach still seems to be remote.

Summary and outlook

As an organ for executive education and organizational development, the Executive School's custom programme department has engaged in a two-step transformation process (see Figure 9.6). First, it increased the degree of customization. Subsequently, it raised the inclusiveness of the transactions. In 2006, in an effort to move beyond simply delivering standardized training programmes to corporate customers, the Executive School voted for a departure from 'mass customization' to what could be seen as a first move toward tailored, project-oriented executive education or learning initiatives. Success in sales, well-established customer relationships, innovative solutions and a high degree of internationalization made the Executive School a relevant player on the highly fragmented, (mainly) European executive education market. Although the organizations were satisfied with what they got, it seemed that the drive for impact would subsequently become much more relevant.

Figure 9.6 The business model transformation of ES-HSG

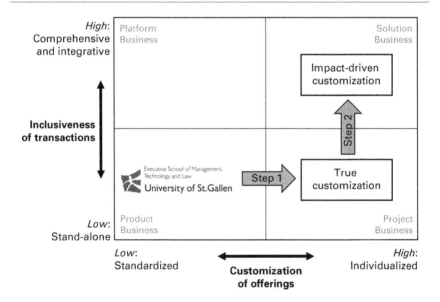

In a subsequent transformational step, the Executive School moved toward 'impact-driven customization'. The training or educational products – as tailored as they could be – no longer formed the focus, which was increasingly on measuring the impact in the short, medium and long term for the individual, the organization or both. This solution-driven approach potentially addressed three different aspects of executive education (or, rather, organizational development): executive training, executive transfer and executive sparring. The measures were to be designed in such a way that all stakeholders involved in the process or initiative would see a direct return in terms of impact.

The clients – whether the L+D function or functional departments – appear to be growing more mature in learning and organizational development issues and demands. Interaction with the organizations' responsible individuals has become increasingly demanding, as there is extensive variation between the needs for customization. While some clients are merely looking for ways to optimize their once-a-year programmes, others are looking to combine the development of the individual competencies of their managers with ramping up their organizational capabilities,[2] or they are setting up a series of executive education measures to improve leadership quality and help their executives successfully manoeuvre a concrete strategic change project. In any case, no matter how different the projects and learning initiatives may be, the customers are always asking for business or industry knowledge, expect proactive innovation in methodology and didactics, and are no longer mere bystanders hoping that the business schools will come up with the right answers.

Whether for business schools or for their clients, as the world continues to change at a faster and faster pace, and reactions to potential disruptions have to be quicker, the way executive education and its adjunct activities are being seen will shift toward greater impact in a shorter amount of time. The Executive School is on a solid path to meet the new demands and has transformed into a more impact- and solution-oriented small organization. Whether the future business environment will give it a chance to prevail or be able to adapt adequately is yet to be seen.

Endnotes

1 It is worth noting that the methodology of the FT ranking is based to a large extent (80 per cent) on client evaluations. This is done in a very candid, strict and open comparison with the performance of the other business schools included in the rankings.

2 Among other impact-driven programmes with Xella and Amcor, see the award-winning EFMD project with Lonza in 2012 and the achievement of winning the German Education Prize for the Porsche Dealer Academy in 2016.

PART FOUR
How to move forward

As we have seen, business model transformation is a challenging endeavour. In this book, we focused on how the configuration of a firm's front end, back end and monetization mechanics must be changed if they are to succeed in a new business model. However, it also became apparent via the cases that, while these configurations are necessary, they are not sufficient to secure transformation success. Further, entrepreneurial leadership is needed to pull off transformation. Entrepreneurial leaders exploit unseen opportunities by creating novel combinations, taking the initiative to pursue them regardless of what it takes, and energize and empower people to act with a revolutionary mission to secure their organization's sustainable, beneficial growth in the interests of all stakeholders.[1]

In Chapter 10, we focus on this specific leadership challenge when guiding a firm along the business model transformation path. We provide additional lessons from our research and case studies regarding the entrepreneurial leadership type, which is geared to effectively changing the business and is centred on a radical shift, which requires renewal of the firm's competence basis while relying on and benefiting from its heritage. We talk also about leadership that creates aspirations for the targeted end-state of the transformation, allows and even creates the organizational slack needed to build the new business model, and fosters an entrepreneurial culture in which change agents spot or create islands of new business model practices that are worth emulating.[2] Such entrepreneurial leadership stands in sharp contrast to the operational day-to-day management, which is geared to efficiently running, securing and sustainably developing an existing business that leverages the firm's existing competences and skills. Entrepreneurial leadership is the framework ingredient of successful transformations; it rallies the troops, drives and orchestrates change across organizational silos and thus builds the transformation foundation to manage and perform the shifts in the front end, back end and monetization mechanics of the firm's business operations. In Chapter 11, we conclude this book with a step-by-step manual that can be used as a hands-on tool to transform your organization's business model.

Endnotes

1 C Linz (2012) Entrepreneurial leadership: Bridging start-up practice and academic research, Paper presented at third Dialogin Conference: Global Leadership Competence, Konstanz, Germany, 29 June.

2 According to Heath and Heath, 'bright spots solve the "Not Invented Here" problem'. See C Heath and D Heath (2010) *How to Change Things When Change Is Hard*, Random House, New York, p 31.

Mastering the transformational leadership challenge

10

The study of business models lies at the intersection of strategy and entrepreneurship.[1] To succeed in a business model transformation it takes a strategy that is contingent on its context (with all the megatrends) and entrepreneurial leadership (which drives the results and implementation of the new business model and motivates the people involved in the change process). In other words, the strategy should be based on a thorough understanding of the competitive dynamics if one is to select the right transformation path and *capture the expected value.* Furthermore, from an entrepreneurial perspective, it takes a leader who guides the people in the organization to *create the value* for stakeholders through the discovery, creation and exploitation of the opportunities associated with the transformation path and the targeted new business model.

Transforming with the mainstream or going your own innovative way

If a company plans business model transformation, the management team must decide how it wants to position the company towards its competitors in the future. One option is to *follow the mainstream*, in the sense that you align your firm's transformation with a prevailing transformation in the industry. An example of such a strategy is Daimler's partial transformation from a product BM to a platform BM. This move came at a time when several automotive manufacturers were beginning to build more inclusive mobility service offerings and platforms, for instance BMW's DriveNow car sharing. Audi's CEO even said that, by 2020, 50 per cent of its sales would be based on apps, software, electronic systems and digital services. The mainstream seems to follow an inevitable development in the industry. If a firm does not follow, it risks being left behind. The same applies for Xerox's transformation from a platform BM to a solutions BM, which followed the market shift in the printing industry from commoditized printing platforms to document management and then process management, hence the outsourcing of complete processes that go well beyond printing.

The alternative strategy is to *go your own way* by deciding to differentiate your transformation from developments in the industry. You see competition as a race, and the winner is the company that challenges its business model first with an innovative next step to create a new competitive edge. That is what Netflix did when using the data from digitization to swing back parts of its platform BM towards a product BM by beginning to produce exclusive content (see Figure 7.4). Netflix built its business on predictive analytics capabilities very early, to take it to the next growth trajectory, which allowed it to develop innovative and even Emmy- and Golden Globe Award-winning offerings. Or take Knorr-Bremse's transformation from a product BM to a solutions BM, a move initiated owing to fierce price competition in the industry, which led many competitors to head even further to the lower left of the product BM box by increasing standardization and focusing on single components. Knorr-Bremse actively decided not to engage in this transformation to becoming a commodity manufacturer, choosing the opposite strategic path instead by substantially driving inclusiveness and customization. You can argue that SAP's transformation into a cloud company is inevitable given the market shift. However, the decisiveness and speed of execution of this combined internal and external growth strategy are striking – especially given the fact that SAP was not the first mover. Ultimately, SAP's HANA in-memory innovation turned the former business application leader additionally into a database and platform company, which since then has fuelled SAP's innovation agenda and driven substantial business growth.

In the case studies in this book, we have seen that both strategies can be successful and that neither is generally superior. Which is the better choice depends on the firm's specific competence base. Interestingly, we see that following the mainstream requires firms to have particularly strong competences that differentiate them from their competitors.

If an entire industry undergoes a business model transformation, there is usually strong consolidation. This is particularly the case for transformations from south to north, since platform BMs and solution BMs typically have strong associated network effects, where the winner tends to take all. Accordingly, there is often little space for profitable number two or three positions in the market. In the automotive industry, for instance, it is highly unlikely that we will see five different mobility service platforms offered by five different OEMs in 10 years. Accordingly, Daimler managers explicitly emphasize that their moovel platform will also be open to its competitors, meaning that it could include BMW's car-sharing service side by side with Daimler's car2go service. In this case and in others, the best platform will win and will become the standard in the market, while the firm that owns and runs the platform will get most of the returns. Thus, clear strategic decisions, stringent execution and swift learning from market feedback are essential. Thus, the potential pay-out of such a follow-the-mainstream strategy is very high, but the risk is substantial.

The strategy of going your own way is better suited if competition along the dominant business model transformation trajectory is fierce, and in particular smaller players in the market face a higher risk of losing the winner-takes-all battle. In these cases, it is often the better choice to transform into a business model in which size doesn't matter as much and in which competitors have little experience. This applies mostly to transformations from west to east, where the most flexible player succeeds. In the braking systems industry of Knorr-Bremse, it is very difficult for large, mainly Asia-based commodity manufacturers to introduce and run customer-individual solutions, since their systems and processes are not easy to change, and it is difficult for them to overcome the entry hurdle of incumbent industry players that have already accumulated in-depth knowledge of customers' business processes. It takes entrepreneurial courage to turn your company against the dominant industry trend, but, if you see that there is a market for this and if you have the innovative capabilities to do this, it can be less risky than following the mainstream.

Focusing on results and implementation

Across all cases, our interview partners emphasized that the right strategic transformation path and configuration only result in transformation success if they are accompanied by entrepreneurial leadership throughout the company. This entrepreneurial leadership must be an ongoing source of transformational energy, because if a new business model proves successful it will be hunted by a crowd of competitors. As we have seen in the case of Netflix, one business model transformation is often not enough to succeed and to stay ahead. We have observed three lessons learned for every transformational leader that should help you to get your teams ready for the transformation effort.

First, it is necessary to *keep valuing the old strengths while building the new ones*. Unlike start-ups, established firms have a heritage. To turn this heritage into a strength, it is important to make it very clear to everyone in the company that a business model transformation does not render the past strengths or the existing employees obsolete overnight. To this end, a leader must support people by finding out how they can individually adjust and contribute to the new business model. At the same time, it is important that people who enter the company with new needed skills and capabilities are not perceived as the outsiders or enemies, but as valuable and much-needed supporters on the transformation journey. Hence, it is best to avoid a strong sense of internal competition, and to foster mutual curiosity, support and trust. As an example, Daimler's new mobility unit moovel is still some kind of artefact that is largely separated from the car production units. When we spoke to a regional sales manager, he emphasized that he does not see such services primarily as competition (even though he might sell fewer cars if competitors are successful) but rather as a great way to get to know customers' mobility needs better and to offer new kinds of vehicles and services in the future.

Second, transformational leaders should *guide their firm with a customer mission*. Companies' mission statements tend to be very broad and to address a large variety of stakeholders. For successful business model transformation, customers must be put at the centre of everything, at least during the change process. Thus, everyone in the company should think about what could be done differently to better address customers' needs or to better solve their problems than previously. For instance, Netflix has followed a very clear and concrete customer mission from the very beginning: 'Give people what they want, when they want it, in the form they want it.' FUNDES is an interesting example of a firm that focused not only on customers but also on the benefit to society during its transformation effort. The case describes the strong tensions leaders experienced owing to distinct and even partly contradictory missions. What really helped was that the societal focus was so deeply rooted in FUNDES's history and people's minds that it continued to guide its customer-focused transformation efforts.

Third, it is important to *build strong and sustainable internal and external relationships* with all relevant stakeholders. Consistent business model transformation can only be achieved through close interactions between functions, departments, partners, suppliers and customers. Thus, vertical silo thinking must be overcome.[2] Driven by the digital revolution that started in the 1990s, we are moving towards a much more horizontal world, a world of networks, where everyone (*internet of people*) and everything (*internet of things*) is able to communicate with each other. Classical boundaries – such as departments, companies and even industries – are losing their relevance. Here, more collaborative capabilities are required of leaders to keep dozens of strategic partners in an ecosystem engaged and committed. They must ensure that there is high transparency across organizational boundaries. During such transformational phases, where many things are in flux, strong networks help to align the various efforts. The LEGIC case is a good example. The firm's successful business model transformation was only made possible by its ability to leverage its heritage ID partner network and combine it with new strategic partnerships with mobile network operators.

To conclude, in Chapter 11 we return to the configuration of a new business model and share a tool that has helped us in many company workshops to structure and support the discussions among business model transformation leaders and their teams.

Endnotes

1 B Demil, X Lecocq, J E Ricard and C Zott (2015) Introduction to the SEJ special issue on business models: Business models within the domain of strategic entrepreneurship, *Strategic Entrepreneurship Journal*, **9**, pp 1–11.

2 According to Boland and Collopy, 'A path-creating design will necessarily involve collaboration among partners who each bring unique expertise and talents to the project. Without collaboration across boundaries of disciplines, organizations and perspectives, a design project has limited possibilities for invention of new solutions.' See R J Boland and F Collopy (2004) Toward a design vocabulary for management, in *Managing as Designing*, ed R J Boland and F Collopy, Stanford University Press, Stanford, CA, pp 265–76.

Navigating with 11 the business model transformation manual

This manual is designed as a step-by-step guide from 1) assessing the status quo, to 2) identifying future business model opportunities, and 3) developing a transformation path, to 4) taking the appropriate actions to follow this path.

Step 1: Where do you stand today to start?

Step 1 is about better understanding the status quo. Based on our business model typology, we have developed a short survey that allows you to *position your business model along the dimensions of inclusiveness and customization*. As noted, it is unlikely you are in one of these extreme positions. Many firms have developed their business models over time to feature some aspects of inclusiveness and/or customization. This makes it critical to understand where exactly it is you now stand – not only overall, but specifically regarding your business model's front end, back end and monetization mechanics.

The first part of this survey refers to your current business model's *front-end* features and domain. To assess the extent of inclusiveness, ask 1) whether the offering integrates multiple components to provide superior end-to-end services, 2) if there is some kind of lock-in of each customer with high resulting transaction frequency, and 3) if customer retention metrics are systematically embedded in most business procedures. The following questions, which concern the extent of customization, ask 4) how many options each customer has to adapt an offering to his or her specific needs, 5) to what extent the firm differentiates itself in the market with its flexibility beyond mass customization, and 6) if sales supports the choice among a complex offering via intense dialogue with each customer.

Figure 11.1 Template step 1

Step 1: Where do you now stand, to begin with?

Please assess the current front end, back end and monetization mechanics of your business model

	Strongly disagree			Strongly agree	
	1	2	3	4	5

Front end:

1. Our offering bundles multiple components. ○ ○ ○ ○ ○
2. Our customers are bound into a series of frequent transactions with us. ○ ○ ○ ○ ○
3. We measure customer retention systematically. ○ ○ ○ ○ ○
4. Customers have broad and flexible choices regarding our offering. ○ ○ ○ ○ ○
5. Our unique selling proposition is our ability to adapt our products or services. ○ ○ ○ ○ ○
6. During sales, we engage in close dialogue with customers. ○ ○ ○ ○ ○

Back end:

7. Our core competence is our shared architecture, which integrates the end-to-end offering. ○ ○ ○ ○ ○
8. Our success heavily relies on a network of contributing and complementing partners. ○ ○ ○ ○ ○
9. Our operations are geared towards flexibility, not scalability. ○ ○ ○ ○ ○
10. Our research and development is driven by specific requirements of single customers. ○ ○ ○ ○ ○

Monetization mechanics:

11. We get long-term revenue streams from our customers. ○ ○ ○ ○ ○
12. Our transaction costs are only covered over time. ○ ○ ○ ○ ○
13. Our prices are based on a mixed calculation that integrates all offering components. ○ ○ ○ ○ ○
14. Our prices are rather driven by customers' willingness to pay, than by our competitors' pricing. ○ ○ ○ ○ ○
15. We have more variable costs than fixed costs. ○ ○ ○ ○ ○

Divide it by 8

Divide it by 7

Inclusiveness score

Customization score

The second part of the survey analyses the *back-end* activities. Regarding the extent of inclusiveness, it inquires 7) if the company has a powerful and shared architecture foundation that supports the integration of multiple components of an end-to-end offering, and 8) how much the firm's success depends on a large network of strong and reliable strategic partner organizations. To assess the extent of customization, it asks 9) if the operational focus is on achieving flexibility and individuality more than on the realization of economies of scale, and 10) how much the research and development activities are really driven by the target customers' needs – market pull rather than technology push. For instance, is co-innovation or co-creation done with customers?

The third part addresses the *monetization mechanics that are applied*. The questions regarding the extent of inclusiveness are 11) whether the business relies on steady long-term recurring revenue streams, 12) whether the transaction costs are covered over the timespan of the whole product life cycle rather than already being covered by the first deal, and 13) whether the pricing is based on a mixed calculation across all offering components.

The questions regarding the extent of customization assess 14) whether the pricing is driven more by customers' willingness to pay for products and services than by competitors' pricing, and 15) whether the firm's variable costs exceed its fixed costs.

Based on the 15 evaluation questions in step 1, the inclusiveness score and the customization score can be calculated as shown in the workshop template in Figure 11.1. The result will tell you what business model type is currently in use, and what the starting point for a transformation path would be. If both scores are below 3, a product BM is currently in use; if both scores are above 3, it is a solutions BM; if the inclusiveness score is above 3 and the customization score is below 3, it suggests a platform BM; if the customization score is above 3 and the inclusiveness score is below 3, it implies a project BM.

Step 2: Where do you want to go?

Once you know which business model type you have now, it is important to find out which business model will make the company successful in the future. Each business model type has strengths, weaknesses, requirements and challenges. It is worth thinking about these and comparing them with the skills and competences in your organization.

We have argued that business model transformation is driven by external megatrends such as digitization and physication as well as servitization and productization. A second short survey will allow you to assess the extent to which your firm and its industry are affected by these trends. It provides a first indication in which direction the business may develop regarding the future extents of inclusiveness and customization. While it is difficult to anticipate what the future will bring, in our experience many entrepreneurial leaders have strong intuitions about how their business will develop and have benefited from the guidance of the transformation approach described here to structure their assessments. In this step, it is important to free yourself from the dominating logic and restrictions of the core business of the past so as to keep an open mind and objectively assess what the best business model for your firm could look like (without thinking too much about how to get there yet). In Figure 11.2, we offer a template that can be used to run this second survey.

A first set of questions refers to the digitization megatrend. To find out to what extent digitization drives inclusiveness, we ask 1) whether digitization will substantially decrease the costs of transferring and sharing the value delivery (offerings), 2) whether digitization allows one to lock customers in more tightly to the company (the lock-in effect), 3) whether customers are willing to engage in long-term collaborations with their products and services providers, and 4) whether digitization helps to differentiate products or services in the competitive arena beyond hardware features (eg via additional features such as communities, etc).

As we suggested, digitization may also drive customization. Thus we ask 5) whether big/smart data and customer analytics may provide deeper customer insights that help to launch offerings that are close to the customers' needs and buying behaviour, 6) whether new technologies increase customer power but also knowledge about customer needs by driving transparency and making it easier for customers to express and share their opinion about products and services actively online in blogs, forums, tweets, chatrooms, etc, and 7) whether digitization can provide new technical opportunities to make the products or services more flexible and more adaptive.

A second set of assessments addresses the servitization and productization megatrends. Questions regarding the effects on the extent of inclusiveness ask 8) to what extent there are new opportunities to come up with additional value-adding services to complement the existing offering, 9) if customers are looking for enduring service contracts and relationships along the product's whole life cycle. Furthermore, customization is fostered 10) if customers are or want to become involved in co-creation and co-innovation processes and on-site implementation services, 11) if customers' main interest is not to own a product, but to have a reliable output at a certain service level, 12) if services that are unique and very authentic increase the involvement of highly qualified service people and customers' willingness to pay for these services, 13) if firms tend to become more dependent on their customers owing to their customer-specific investments, and 14) if scalability can be enabled by

Figure 11.2 Template step 2

Step 2: Where do you want to go?

Please assess how the megatrends drive radical changes in your business or industry

	Strongly disagree				Strongly agree
	1	2	3	4	5

Impact of digitization:

1. Costs of transferring and sharing our products and services become exponentially cheaper via digitization.

2. New technological solutions enable the company to lock customer in more easily than before.

3. Customers are more willing to engage in long-term collaborations with the vendors.

4. There are new possibilities beyond the products to differentiate an offering in the market.

5. Technological progress provides deeper customer insights for better-customized offers.

6. Power shifts to customers because they actively discuss and comment on our offerings in online communities.

7. There are few technical opportunities to standardize our offerings.

Impacts of servitization and productization:

8. There are opportunities to complement our products through value-adding services.

9. Customers are looking for enduring service contracts and relationships.

10. Customers ask for co-creation of the offering and on-site implementation of services.

11. Our customers' main interest is to have a reliable output at a certain service level, not to own a product.

12. In our market segment, scale effects are less relevant, because customers prefer tailored, total solutions.

13. As a vendor, we are becoming more dependent on our customers.

14. The scalability of our services via reusable templates does not really work in our business segment.

Divide it by 6

Divide it by 8

Inclusiveness score

Customization score

increasingly standardizing more services (*productization*), which would allow you to develop repeatable services via the application of reusable templates and thus decrease the optimal degree of customization.

Step 3: Design your transformation path

After you have mapped out your starting point (step 1) and where you want to go (step 2), specify *the transformation path*, which connects the transformation journey's starting point and end point. As the practical examples in this book show, it is very rare for business model transformation to be a linear, one-step process. Even if a firm 'only' needs to cross the meridian or the equator, it might be worth considering a stepwise approach to manage the transformation. While Chapter 6 provides some insights on the benefits and drawbacks of a stepwise approach, it is ultimately a leadership decision how fast, in which sequence and how radical a new business model will be adopted. However, no matter how the transformation path is designed, it is important for the leadership team never to lose sight of their aims.

Figure 11.3 contains a simple tool for discussing the transformation path in a workshop. It provides an example of how to connect the starting point (step 1) and the target position (step 2).

Step 4: Plan your actions

In steps 1 to 3, the strategic choices and conceptual decisions are made. Step 4 requires entrepreneurial leadership to make this happen. The strategic, organizational and managerial *actions to implement the business model transformation* need to be taken. In some domains (eg the front end), the company might already have begun to transform, while other domains (eg the back end) are not at all developed. Thus, it is important to continuously track transformation progress to ensure that, at the end of the transformation journey, all aspects of the front end, back end and monetization mechanics are strategically aligned in order to exploit the new business model's full potential.

Figure 11.4 contains a list of the transformation activities recommended in Chapters 4 and 5, depending on the transformation direction (south–north, north–south, west–east, east–west). We suggest simple *status tracking* that distinguishes between completed actions (green), actions in progress (yellow) and actions that have not yet been initiated or that have failed

Figure 11.3 Template step 3

Step 3: Design your transformation path

Please position your current and future business models on the business model
transformation map and design your transformation path.

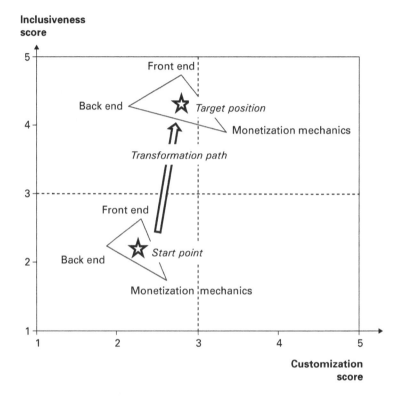

(red). This helps you to control where your company is on its business model
transformation path.

We close our description of a possible transformation journey here. The
intention with this transformation manual is to support you in your work as
a transformational leader, to lend a specific structure and strategic orientation to your work and to help you to master your business model transformation. These are generic templates that must be adjusted to each application
case. We are confident that using the manual in combination with our framework and case studies is much more efficient than starting from scratch. We
trust that your business model transformation will be an exemplary case
study we can all learn from. All the best!

Figure 11.4 Template step 4

Step 4: Plan and control your actions

Please follow the actions for your transformation path(s) and assign a colour to each action (green: completed; yellow: in progress; red: open).

South–north crossing:

Front end

- Develop and provide customer with an integrated end-to-end process or user experiences.
- Orchestrate and integrate holistic offering from own components and third-party complementors.
- Establish a retention-oriented customer engagement approach with a superior experience at every customer touch point.

Back end

- Gain control over a leading platform and shared architectural standard.
- Broaden the firm's competence base (horizontal) and build a performing ecosystem of complementors.
- Establish operations for managing the customer process or user experience (integrated end to end).

Monetization mechanics

- Create revenue streams from recurring fees.
- Build an integrated pricing with subscription-based consumption models.
- Focus on profitable customer life cycles.

North–south crossing:

Front end

- Develop a convincing value proposition for stand-alone offerings.
- Find new business opportunities for the firm's products and services.
- Emphasize new customer acquisition competence for one-off deals.

Back end

- Develop novel competences for a competitive edge in each product or service offering (vertical).
- Establish vertical supplier management with close supplier collaboration.

Monetization mechanics

- Build short-term cash planning and sufficient cash reserves.
- Estimate cost coverage for product or service life cycles.
- Establish simpler and more cost-transparent pricing models.

Please follow the actions for your transformation path(s) and assign a colour to each action (green: completed; yellow: in progress; red: open).

West–east crossing:

Front end

▤ Come up with a broad, flexible service-centred offering.

▤ Improve your abilities to adapt this hybrid offering to customers' individual needs.

▤ Institute direct access to and dialogue with the customers.

Back end

▤ Make production and operations flexible.

▤ Improve capabilities to process and implement customer requirements.

Monetization mechanics

▤ Move to a pricing model in which the price reflects the customers' willingness to pay for customization.

▤ Refocus attention from fixed to variable, engagement-related costs.

East–west crossing:

Front end

▤ Come up with a new and better standard offering.

▤ Implement a low-touch, scalable sales approach.

▤ Develop a broad range of complementary but consistent offline and online sales channels.

Back end

▤ Replace human resources with machines.

▤ Transform services and content into reusable elements.

▤ Develop a knowledge management system and a culture of knowledge sharing.

Monetization mechanics

▤ Identify and set a competitive price.

▤ Actively manage your fixed costs.

INDEX

NB: page numbers in *italic* indicate figures and tables

CPSIA information can be obtained
at www.ICGtesting.com
Printed in the USA
LVOW05s1354300117
522608LV00012B/355/P